Rules versus Relationships

Language and Legal Discourse
A series edited by
William M. O'Barr and John M. Conley

Rules versus Relationships

The Ethnography of Legal Discourse

John M. Conley

and

William M. O'Barr

The University of Chicago Press
Chicago and London

The University of Chicago Press, Chicago 60637
The University of Chicago Press, Ltd., London
© 1990 by The University of Chicago
All rights reserved. Published 1990
Printed in the United States of America
99 98 97 96 95 94 93   5 4 3 2

Library of Congress Cataloging-in-Publication Data

Conley, John M.
  Rules versus relationships : the ethnography of legal discourse /
John M. Conley and William M. O'Barr.
    p.   cm. —(Language and legal discourse)
  Includes bibliographical references.
  ISBN 0-226-11490-2 (cloth). —ISBN 0-226-11491-0 (paper)
  1. Ethnological jurisprudence. 2. Law—Language. 3. Trial
practice—United States. 4. Small claims courts—United States.
I. O'Barr, William M. II. Title. III. Series.
K190.C66   1990
340'.014—dc20   89-20497
                                                    CIP

Contents

Acknowledgments

We would like to emphasize the uniquely joint nature of this work. Many joint projects are the sum of discrete, identifiable parts. This project, however, is something more than and different from the sum of its parts. It is joint property in the strictest legal sense, with each of us having an indivisible interest in the entirety. We are different people with different backgrounds, strengths, and weaknesses. These have been merged in the finished product, however, to the point where we literally cannot remember who had a certain idea or who wrote the first draft of a particular sentence. Thus, we share fully in any credit or blame that may be due.

The research was supported by Grants SES 85–21528 and SES 85–21574 from the Law and Social Science Program of the National Science Foundation and by additional funding through the Law Center Foundation of the University of North Carolina and the National Institute for Dispute Resolution. We acknowledge with appreciation the assistance of the officials of the courts and clerks' offices and the persons whose cases we studied. All are identified throughout by pseudonyms in order to protect their privacy and anonymity. We especially appreciate the contributions of our research assistants, Chris Bashor, Mark Bielawski, Mark Childress, Brian Denton, Sally Perumian, Rebecca Schaller, and Amy Thomas. We also thank colleagues who have read and commented on various papers and presentations based on this project: Max Atkinson, Paul Bohannan, Don Brenneis, Ronald Butters, John Comaroff, Paul Drew, Marc Galanter, Allen Grimshaw, Susan Hirsch, Dell Hymes, Virginia Hymes, Allan Lind, Craig McEwen, Sally Merry, Elizabeth Mertz, Susan Philips, Lawrence Rosen, Gabrielle Spiegel, David Trubek, Neil Vidmar, and Laurens Walker. Finally, we owe special thanks to those who have read and commented on a full draft of this book: Virginia Dominguez, Ernestine Friedl, Rick Lempert, Jean O'Barr, and Tom Tyler.

Permission to adapt from the following earlier reports of our research findings is gratefully acknowledged: John M. Conley and William M. O'Barr, Fundamentals of jurisprudence: An ethnography of judicial decision making in informal courts, *North Carolina Law Review* 66 (1988): 467–507; Hearing the hidden agenda: The ethnographic investigation of procedure, *Law and Contemporary Problems* 51 (1988): 201–218; Rules versus relationships in small claims disputes, in *Conflict Talk,* ed. by Allen D. Grimshaw (New York: Cambridge University Press, 1989). William M. O'Barr and John M. Conley, Litigant satisfaction versus legal adequacy in small claims narratives, *Law & Society Review* 19 (1985): 661–701; Lay expectations of the civil justice system, *Law & Society Review* 22 (1988): 137–161.

Introduction

This is a study of the ways in which ordinary people relate to the American legal system. It deals with such issues as how lay people identify and analyze legal problems, how they decide when and in what form to bring a problem to the legal system, and how they respond to the demands that the system makes of them. The central, recurrent theme in our research findings is the striking divergence between the approaches of lay people and legal professionals to the resolution of everyday problems.

We report evidence showing that lay people tend to analyze their legal problems in two very different ways. Some, whom we describe as *rule oriented*, evaluate their problems in terms of neutral principles whose application transcends differences in personal and social status. In conceiving their cases and presenting them to the court, they emphasize these principles rather than such issues as individual need or social worth. The legal system usually shares this perspective, making it easier for such people to have their cases heard and understood. Other litigants display what we term a *relational orientation*. They come to the legal system seeking redress for a wide range of personal and social wrongs. In talking about their problems, they predicate rights and responsibilities on a broad notion of social interdependence rather than on the application of rules. The courts often fail to understand their cases, regardless of their legal merits, and this frequently results in frustration and alienation.

The objective of this book is to present a model of the interaction between the lay public and the legal system. In undertaking the research on which it is based, we put aside prevailing assumptions about events, attitudes, and behaviors that are significant in the administration of justice. Thus, for example, we had little interest in determining the rates at which particular categories of litigants win their cases, because such an analysis is significant only if one assumes that litigants and the courts define success and failure in the same way. Similarly, we declined to survey lay consumers of justice or conduct focused interviews, because we had an insufficient basis for deciding what to ask. We attempted instead to take an inductive approach that would not bind us to existing theories or analytic structures. This research also differs from much prior social science research on legal topics in that the focus is not on cases, but on individual interactions between litigants and the system.

We chose to conduct the study in informal courts in three different regions of the United States. In these courts (called small claims or magistrates' courts in most jurisdictions), litigants bring cases involving relatively small amounts of money and are usually not assisted in court by lawyers. Accordingly, we believed that informal courts would be an ideal environment to study the beliefs and practices of people who had identified themselves as having legal problems, had reasoned through their problems, and were trying to resolve them through the legal system.

In planning our research, we hoped to discover disputes at their inception and then track them through the system. Our ideal was to capture an early "uncontaminated" account of a dispute—as one neighbor might tell it to another over the back fence, as we often put it—and then observe the evolution of both the dispute itself and the parties' accounts of it. In developing this preliminary design we were influenced by the extensive literature on the transformation of disputes, which argues that disputes tend to move through certain regular phases toward resolution (see, for example, Mather and Yngvesson 1980–81, Felstiner et al. 1980–81).

This design proved unworkable. As a practical matter, it is virtually impossible for a researcher to come upon a dispute in any sort of pristine form. In most cases, by the time the first account is given to a third party, the dispute is likely to have undergone significant changes since the occurrence of the events that gave rise to it.

A related problem was that our initial design presumed that a dispute has some concrete existence independent of the accounts that constitute its expression. On the contrary, early in the study we were drawn to the conclusion that at any particular point in time the dispute *is* the account being given at that time. Each new account that the disputants give—whether in arguing with each other, talking to friends, being interviewed by researchers, or testifying in court—reflects somewhat different understandings, beliefs, and emphases. Thus, any account is both determined by what has gone before and determinative of the present and future shape of the dispute.

We ultimately decided upon a research design that investigated litigants' accounts at three stages of the litigation process. First, we interviewed plaintiffs (persons initiating cases) at the time they filed their complaints with the court. As we explain in chapter 2, we were able to interview significant numbers of plaintiffs in two of our six research sites. However, because defendants are not required to come to court before trial and were generally unwilling to speak with us in their homes, we were not able to conduct substantial numbers of pretrial interviews with defendants in any of the sites.

The core of the data collection effort was the observation and tape recording of trials in the informal courts of six cities. We spent thirty-six days in court. We also obtained recordings from twelve other days when we were not present. We collected a total of 466 cases, including those which we studied at the time of filing but which did not actually go to trial. Finally, we pursued litigants a month or more after their trials in an effort to elicit further accounts, including their versions of what had happened in court. We were able to locate many but not all litigants, and most were willing to talk with us about their cases. These posttrial interviews yielded telling insights and some of the most important clues to the interpretation of earlier phases of disputes. In building our models of lay people interacting with the legal system, we have drawn from what was said in court and in the pre- and posttrial interviews. We have not sought to present all the information we have from the cases we describe but rather to select those portions of trials and interviews that are helpful in building models of the legal process.

In developing our method of analysis, our guiding principle was to treat the language of the litigants as the object of study rather than as a mere instrument. Many other social science research traditions (including ethnography) use language as a window through which other, presumably more important, things may be viewed. Thus, an anthropologist might use an indigenous language as a means of collecting information about the objective reality of local-level politics or a social psychologist might treat language as a transparent means for collecting attitudinal data.

Our premise has been that the window itself is often more interesting than what can be seen through it. As they tell their stories by giving their accounts in varied settings, continually making decisions about structure, content, and forms of expression, litigants leave revealing fingerprints on this linguistic window. In listening to litigants' accounts, we have concentrated on what they say and how they say it rather than trying to impose predetermined structures and categories on the data.

What has emerged is a method we term the *ethnography of discourse*. As the name suggests, it shares with traditional ethnography an emphasis on careful, detailed observation and inductive analysis, but differs in that language is the object rather than merely an instrument of analysis. In practice, this method is deceptively simple. We listen to and record talk as it occurs, and then we meet with research assistants and colleagues to analyze the resulting tapes and transcripts. In sessions lasting about two hours, we repeatedly listen to an account or case while following along on a transcript, make notes for about twenty minutes, and then present our observations in a roundtable discussion. Occasionally, we identify a general topic for analysis (for example, how the litigants deal with questions of responsibility), but most sessions are open-ended, with the analysts attempting to focus on what is important to the litigants. A striking aspect of these sessions has been the consensus among the analysts—even those not previously involved in the research—in identifying and agreeing on issues of interest.

The greatest strength of this method is its intense empiricism. In an important sense, the litigants set the agenda for the research. To some, however, particularly those trained in traditions of quantitative analysis, this same aspect of the method is a source of concern. Critics of our method have tended to focus on two issues.

First, some have objected to what they characterize as the overly interpretive nature of our analysis. Such critics argue that the qualitative interpretation of speech cannot amount to "proof" of the theses we propose. To illustrate the point, they sometimes advance alternative interpretations of particular texts.

In response, we begin with a candid acknowledgment of our reliance on interpretations that have a significant subjective component. But, we ask, how else might we have proceeded? We have taken on a subject—the beliefs that guide lay people in dealing with the law—about which little is known. We might have relied on more conventional techniques, such as controlled experiments or focused interviews, but how could we have identified the variables to manipulate or the questions to ask? To use such techniques, we would have had to make a priori judgments as least as subjective as those on which our method relies.

Moreover, the subjective element in our analysis is patent, and thus subject to the reader's scrutiny. Every research method involves some degree of interpretation. In more structured analyses, it may occur in the identification of issues, the framing of questions, the specification of variables, or the coding of data. Interpretive judgments at these levels may be hidden from the reader of the final research product. In our case, however, the reader is given the resources to question our interpretations. This very openness is, of course, an invitation to criticism that other, less transparent methods may undeservedly escape.

A second, related source of critical concern is the qualitative nature of our analysis. We are sometimes asked why we have not coded our data for statistical analysis. The answer lies in the purpose of our investigation as well as the nature of the phenomena that we have discovered.

As we have already noted, we began this study with no detailed working hypotheses beyond the belief that litigants' talk would yield important clues to the ways that they deal with legal questions. Therefore, we were not in a position to create an elegant deductive research design. Because we did not know what we would find before we started, and did not appreciate what we were seeing until we were well into the analysis of our data, we could not channel our interviews and observations toward the production of readily quantifiable data.

Our situation was much like that of an ethnographer beginning to observe a previously unstudied society. In the ethnographic tradition, we set as our goal the generation of a descriptive model of the range of variation in the litigants' behavior. Those who do quantitative research in well-studied domains sometimes take the existence of such models for granted. But quantitative analyses of the distribution and frequency of particular phenomena are dependent on the often tedious task of identifying and describing the phenomena worthy of analysis.

In addition, the rules–relationships continuum that we have discovered is not readily quantifiable under any circumstances. There are not any particular words or actions that clearly mark an individual litigant as rule-oriented or relational. Rather, each of those terms describes a complex of often subtle tendencies. Moreover, few litigants are strictly one or the other. More often, individuals display elements of both orientations, with one tendency predominating. Some litigants may even shift their orientation depending on the context in which they are giving an account—for example, giving a purely relational account in a pre-trial interview, and then giving a more rule-oriented account at trial in response to cues they receive from the judge. Thus, we worry that any effort at rigid categorization would detract from the credibility of the analysis by creating a misleading aura of precision.

We have attempted to strike a balance between the concerns of quantitative analysts and our own concerns about overstating what is essentially an interpretive case. We provide descriptive quantitative profiles of the occurrence of some of the phenomena we describe. We also offer some tentative thoughts about the distribution and origin of the rule and relational orientations, focusing on their possible association with such variables as gender, class, and race. We have not undertaken a statistical analysis, however, for the reasons just stated.

We view this study as a beginning rather than an end. We have attempted to provide sociolegal scholarship with a new perspective on the fundamental question of the place of the law in the larger cultural context. We do not intend our findings to foreclose further inquiry, but rather to invite it. We present an extraordinary amount of raw data not only to justify our conclusions but also to permit others to test them. Those attracted to our method can make an independent assessment of the theories we have developed. For those more interested in the questions of distribution and frequency that we have only begun to address, we hope that we have identified some issues of interest, described the range of variation, and provided a starting point for further analysis.

1 Discourses and Voices in the Law

American law does not comprise a single discourse. Rather, it is the product of diverse and often discordant voices. Litigants conceive their problems in everyday terms, judges and lawyers transform those problems to conform to the concepts and language of the law, and legal scholars comment on the process using their own modes of expression. On another level, social scientists, legal historians, philosophers of law, and others debate the nature and origins of the law. The various official discourses of law deal primarily with rules whose application transcends, at least in theory, differences in personal and social status. In striking contrast to this focus on legal rules, lay litigants speak often about personal values, social relations, and broad conceptions of fairness and equity in seeking resolution of their difficulties through legal channels.

This book is our effort to record the voices of lay litigants and to comment on the varied discourses of law. As such, it may be read in many ways. Most straightforwardly, the subject of this book is the nature of the law as seen by lay people. It is our report of what we hear them saying and our analysis of the articulation of their voices with the agenda of the law.

But it is also a book about the traditions of the law, especially what its institutions and practitioners consider to be relevant, appropriate, and adequate approaches to solving the problems with which it deals. Read from this perspective, the book is our commentary on the boundaries set by the law in dealing with such matters as evidence, proof, causality, blame, and responsibility.

Finally, this is a book about the conventions of those who study the law, especially the anthropologists of law who are our intellectual forebears. Our perspective is deeply influenced by the anthropological posture of distancing oneself from the assumptions and viewpoints of one's own culture. We have done this both vicariously and literally. We have read and learned from the works of our discipline, and we have made our own efforts to understand legal matters in other cultures. But in this book we come home and seek to combine the lessons of distance and unfamiliarity with the depth of understanding that we cannot expect in any culture other than our own.

THE ANALYSIS OF DISCOURSE

"Discourse" has entered the technical language of most humanistic and social scientific disciplines over the past decade. Neither the object nor the method of analysis is consistent. Discourse is widely used to refer to a stream of scholarly consideration, usually written, of the issues of concern to a particular field of inquiry. For example, the *discourse of philosophy* refers in its broadest sense to all recorded considerations of issues deemed relevant to philosophers from the origins of the discipline to the present. When used in this manner in reference to a particular discipline, discourse analysis means interpretation of the traditions of scholarship in that discipline. It yields understanding of the issues that have entered the purview of the discipline and attempts to explain the exclusion of others.

For those disciplines such as linguistics, anthropology, and sociology that study spoken as well as written language, discourse analysis also refers to the study of connected sequences of speech such as conversations and narratives. The methods used for such studies are highly variable, but all depend on the analysis of the "texts" that result from the recording—whether contemporaneously, with the assistance of mechanical devices, or from memory—of segments of speech.

It is our intention in this book to examine two types of legal discourse: first, the largely written discourse of judges, lawyers, and scholars about law and legal doctrine; and second, what the participants in legal institutions are saying. The records available for the study of these two discourses are very different. The body of judicial opinions, statutes, legislative records, and scholarly commentaries that has accumulated over the centuries is enormous. Together, these sources are the primary materials contained in law libraries. This official discourse of the law is regularly consulted and used as precedent in developing and refining legal doctrine. Even with electronic assistance, access to this official discourse of the law is a formidable undertaking and remains generally confined to professional specialists.

By contrast, the verbal exchanges that constitute the practical, everyday discourse of the law—as, for example, the speech of litigants, witnesses, lawyers, judges, and jurors in courts across the country—are seldom recorded with the intention of preserving them permanently. Sometimes even efforts to listen are proscribed: consider, for example, the strictures that guarantee the privacy of jury deliberations. The talk that is recorded in the official transcripts of trial courts is seldom preserved beyond the appeal process, except for trials that attract great public attention such as Sacco and Vanzetti or the Lindbergh kidnapping. Thus, the voices of the participants in the legal system are rarely heard far beyond the courtroom. In this everyday legal world, there is no parallel to the formal, official discourse of the law, in the sense of a continuous, connected stream of discussion. There are many voices, but the fragments that survive are discontinuous and unconnected.

The consequence of this difference between the official and everyday worlds of law is that some voices are audible while others are effectively silenced. It has been our goal to record some of the largely unheard voices of lay people and legal professionals in the everyday world of the law as they talk about troubles and attempt to effect solutions. By listening to the voices of participants in the legal system and analyzing what they say, we hear everyday discussions that address such issues as fairness, equal treatment, and justice that are also traditional subjects of official legal discourse.

THE DISCOURSE OF LEGAL ANTHROPOLOGY

For more than a hundred years, legal anthropology has focused on two fundamental questions in its examination of other cultures: (1) what are the substantive rules that are the equivalent of law as we define it in our culture? and (2) what are the procedures through which violations of these rules are adjudicated? The history of legal anthropology is generally considered to have begun with the publication of Sir Henry Maine's *Ancient Law* in 1861. His comparative history of law was limited by the scarcity of the data available to him and colored by his evolutionary orientation. Nonetheless, Maine identified a fundamental distinction between societies in which legal rights and responsibilities depend on social status, and those in which they result from contractual arrangements made by individuals.

Bronislaw Malinowski, in *Crime and Custom in Savage Society* (1926), freed legal anthropology from the constraints of nineteenth-century evolutionary thinking and introduced participant observation to the study of comparative law. Following Malinowski, anthropologists have investigated social governance and dispute resolution in traditional societies throughout the world. Leading figures in this tradition include E. Adamson Hoebel, who, with the legal scholar Karl Llewellen (1941), investigated the "law ways" of American Indian cultures, and Max Gluckman (1955) and Paul Bohannan (1957), who studied African legal systems and carried on a spirited debate about the methodology of legal anthropology to which we will return shortly.

Throughout the history of legal anthropology, major differences in approach have developed largely as a result of disagreement over the appropriate analytic framework for the comparative study of the substance and procedure of "law." There have been debates over such issues as whether all societies have law, how the legal systems of stateless societies differ from those associated with states, and whether the concept of private property is universal. But no matter what positions particular theorists have taken on these issues, there has been a common focus on cases as the basic data and unit of analysis. Ethnographies of law usually discuss substance and procedure in terms of illustrative cases from which more abstract principles are generalized. The differences of opinion among legal anthropologists about cross-cultural similarities or dissimilarities have never involved questioning the case as the basic unit of analysis. Even the proponents of extreme faithfulness to local cultural ideas have adopted without comment this unit of analysis which, in the Anglo-American legal tradition, is the basis of the system of precedent and, importantly, the primary mechanism of teaching law. This focus on cases has in turn led to asking legal questions in other societies that are parallel to those asked in the Anglo-American world: questions about winning and losing, the role of precedent, effective strategies, confrontations, and the "facts" at issue.

Not only have legal anthropologists selected cases as the unit of analysis, they have reported them in an Anglo-American legal format which delineates the "facts," the respective positions of the parties, and the decision and reasoning of the tribunal. All reports of cases—whether in appellate opinions, media reports, or accounts given by one person to another—are necessarily interpretations of what is at issue. These accounts are never verbatim, but rather highlight the details that the reporter considers essential for the particular circumstances of the report. By following essentially similar reporting conventions, the Anglo-American judge writing an opinion for the case books and the anthropologist writing a summary of a dispute in a distant society impart a similar bias to their respective reports. Because it gives voice to some concerns, while excluding others, this bias shackles the reader of the report with the decisions of the reporter, however unwittingly made.

Against this background, it is useful to examine some of the conventions employed in the study of comparative law. To do this, we turn to one of the classics of the field, Paul Bohannan's *Justice and Judgement Among the Tiv* (1957). Bohannan's ethnography focuses on the procedures for dispute settlement in both the imposed colonial courts and the indigenous moots of the Tiv. In his investigation of law in this Nigerian society, he uses the case method to uncover the substantive issues that disrupt social life and occasion legal accusations. He takes great care "to report accurately the ideas and institutions of the people" (1957, p. 4). Consequently, he makes considerable use of native terms that are not easily rendered in simple English but which he explains richly and discursively. Some anthropologists, most notably Max Gluckman (1969), considered Bohannan's emphasis on native terms overly cautious and an impediment to comparative analysis. But Bohannan has been persistent and, within the discourse of legal anthropology, stands for the effort to present the culture from the point of view of its participants.[1] In describing the legal system of the Tiv, it was his goal to describe both the substantive issues and the procedures for adjudicating them as understood by and described by the Tiv themselves. Thus, one might assess Bohannan's role in the tradition of legal anthropology as emphasizing the need to give voice to the indigenous perspective on these matters.

It is now more than three decades since *Justice and Judgment* was published and nearly four since Bohannan conducted the field research on which it is based.[2] The discipline of anthropology itself has taken a reflexive turn which has occasioned scrutiny of its received wisdom and its traditions of approach and understanding. There has been a pause in the discourse and an unprecedented focus on the processes of knowing and the means of presenting and representing findings about societies and cultures. Questions that were seldom asked are being raised, and the classics are being given new critical readings.

Accordingly, we reexamine how Bohannan, champion of the natives' perspective, recorded and represented their voices in his ethnography. We gain some important background information from Bohannan's explanation of his method for recording materials in the field:

> Our method of working was that [my assistants] took their notes and then did reconstructions in narrative form. Both the notes and the reconstructions were worked over, and I usually but not always made translations. In the *jir* itself, I took down as much direct quotation as the effort of following the cases allowed me to do. I took this part of my notes entirely in Tiv. The 'continuity' I wrote in English, usually in shorthand (1957, p. vi).

But what form does this information take in the reports of cases that constitute a substantial part of *Justice and Judgment?* We have excerpted

Text 1.1 from one of Bohannan's case summaries (which he is careful to call a *jir* rather than a *case*). This is his report of the witness's testimony, given in quotations and thus presented as an English rendition of the words she actually spoke. Text 1.1 contains all of the testimony that Bohannan quotes in his summary of this case.

Text 1.1

'My co-wife, Ierun, and I often go to Tarkighir's compound. It is near our farms, and we go there to rest. We sit in the reception hut and talk. On this day, Tarkighir asked Ierun to go into his hut with him. I was shocked and surprised that
5   Ierun did so.' . . . 'I sat in the reception hut. Tarkighir was in his sleeping hut with Ierun. After they had been there a long time, I became uneasy and went and rapped on the door.'
Chenge interrupted to ask, "Was the door shut?"
. . . [S]he replied, 'Yes, the door had been pushed to. I rapped on the door and told my co-wife to come out and
10   that we should go. Ierun came out, and we went to our farms. That is all I know' (Bohannan 1957, p. 45).

As it turns out, this is one of two cases that Bohannan analyzes for more than one purpose in *Justice and Judgment*. In a second summary of the same case within the context of his consideration of marriage and divorce, he reports the woman's testimony in an entirely different way. Text 1.2 contains the excerpt from the second case summary that pertains to her testimony.

Text 1.2

She stated that she and Ierun often went to Tarkighir's compound to rest while working on their farms, which were nearby. On this particular day he had asked Ierun to go into his hut, and she did. After some time, she (Girgi) had rapped
5   at the door and told Ierun to come out, so that they could go back to their farms (Bohannan 1957, p. 85).

Examining these alternative reports in the light of the skepticism and concerns of contemporary anthropology as well as in the light of Bohannan's explanation of how he took notes, how are we to understand his choice to paraphrase and thus interpret Girgi's testimony in Text 1.2? Why are her words so clear in one report and not the other? Is this difference merely accidental, or does it convey some deeper sense of the anthropologist's own entanglement in the interpretive process?

We get some clues from yet another version of the testimony quoted in Texts 1.1 and 1.2. In Text 1.3, Bohannan's purportedly verbatim report of Girgi's testimony is presented along with his commentary—perhaps the "continuity" to which he referred in the passage quoted on page 5—about the manner in which she spoke.

Text 1.3

'My co-wife, Ierun, and I often go to Tarkighir's compound. It is near our farms, and we go there to rest. We sit in the reception hut and talk. On this day, Tarkighir asked Ierun to go into his hut with him. I was shocked and surprised that
5   Ierun did so.' *She looked about her and back at the ground, as if she were ashamed of what she was saying.* 'I sat in the reception hut. Tarkighir was in his sleeping hut with Ierun. After they had been there a long time, I became uneasy and went and rapped on the door.'
10   Chenge interrupted to ask, "Was the door shut?"
With a look that indicated that she disliked him greatly both for having made her swear (and thus to tell the truth) and for asking this particular question, she replied, 'Yes, the door had been pushed to. I rapped on the door and told my co-wife to come
15   out and that we should go. Ierun came out, and we went to our farms. That is all I know' (Bohannan 1957, p. 45; italics added).

When the ethnographer's report of Girgi's testimony is read in progressive stages as we present it here, his practices of reporting, of representing the native's viewpoint, and of giving voice take on a new significance. We are given what purports to be an English version of the actual Tiv words as spoken in the hearing, enabling us to interpret their meaning for ourselves. However, we cannot but be influenced by the ethnographer's evaluative comments on the witness's style and the import of what she says. We are led in turn to question what limits are placed on our understanding of Girgi's voice by the way Bohannan permits us to hear it.[3]

The representation of the speech of others, whether orally or in writing, is an ancient practice. Students of Latin, for example, cannot read Caesar's

Commentaries on the Gallic Wars without learning the different grammatical conventions for representing discourse directly and indirectly. Similar grammatical markings in other languages have attracted the attention of many twentieth-century linguists (e.g., Bloomfield 1927, Coulmas 1986). However, only recently have sociolinguists and anthropologists begun to ask about the significance of variations in reporting the speech of others.

Various hypotheses have been advanced. These include: (1) using direct quotations displaces responsibility because the authority of reported speech resides with the attributed source;[4] (2) direct quotations, especially when performed,[5] are more dramatic and engaging;[6] (3) using direct quotations demonstrates that the reporter was present at the reported event;[7] and (4) direct quotations identify those aspects of an account that the reporter seeks to present as more reliable.[8]

These suggestions are provocative ones and are helpful in considering what reported speech may mean in the various contexts where it has been investigated. In the present context, we ask related questions: What does it mean to quote some people and paraphrase others? How does the reader respond to such differences? What are the consequences of the ethnographer's choices?

Similar questions may no doubt be asked about our reports of voices in this book. We, too, have had to make choices among the many speakers competing to be heard. But we believe that we should allow the speakers we have chosen to speak in their own voices, quoting them whenever possible. Our wide use of excerpts from trials and interviews reflects our attempt to let the authority of the speech we report reside with those who uttered the words. We also believe that the account of what we have learned is more engaging when presented in this manner.[9]

Lest we be misunderstood, we do not shirk the responsibility that comes with reporting what others say. We have made choices about what to include, and we interpret heavily. Many choices have been conscious and intentional. We do not doubt that we have made others which are beyond our awareness and which likely will be interpreted by those who succeed us. Like Bohannan, we have tried to be open in the exposition of our methods. But the methods are different in that we seek a more extensive verbatim record of the events we have studied. Additionally, as we shall explain, we have chosen as our primary unit of analysis not the case but the encounter of the litigant with the legal system. In one sense, the encounter is less than the case because it consists of the interaction of a single litigant with the legal system. In another sense it is more, because a litigant's encounter with the system may include interactions that occur outside the actual trial of the case. Most importantly, this alternative focus directs attention to different issues: away from winning and losing and "facts," and toward expectations, accounts, and perceptions. We could not, and would not, have developed these methods without the lessons we have learned from both the strengths and the shortcomings of the classics.

THE DISCOURSE OF THE LAW

The ongoing professional debates about the nature of law in general and about the application of relevant portions of the law to specific cases constitute the official discourses of the law. The debate about the nature of law is the preserve of jurisprudential scholars and is rarely noticed by the great majority of judges and practicing lawyers. The other sort of official legal discourse—statutes, collected decisions of appellate courts, and scholarly commentary—is, of course, routinely used by lawyers in presenting cases, and in turn consulted by judges in making their decisions. Laypersons may encounter this discourse directly when they testify in court or serve as jurors, or through the mediation of lawyers when they seek professional help in drawing up or interpreting a legal document.

Official legal discourse of the latter type is far removed from the language of ordinary people. It tends to transform or simply to ignore the discourse of the disputants whose problems are the law's very reason for being. Moreover, despite the fact that the law exists to solve human problems and regulate human conduct, its professional discourse has been predominantly about purportedly neutral principles whose application is believed to transcend human variation.

The nature of this discourse can be illustrated with reference to *Pennoyer v. Neff,* a case decided by the United States Supreme Court in 1877. It is a canonical case that is widely used in instructing first-year law students. The legal issue in the case is the circumstances under which a state court may compel a resident of another state to come and defend a lawsuit.

On another level, it is a case about ordinary people and their encounters with the many discourses of the law. A man named Neff made an agreement with an Oregon lawyer named Mitchell to have some legal work done. Mitchell did the work and asked to be paid for it. Neff did not pay. Mitchell sued Neff in an Oregon court. Since Neff had left Oregon, Mitchell could not notify him about the suit in any direct fashion. Instead, Mitchell followed an Oregon law that allowed him to publish notice in an Oregon newspaper. Neff never came to court, and Mitchell obtained a judgment for the amount of his bill. But since Mitchell could not find Neff, he was not able to ask for his money. However, Mitchell had brought it to the court's attention that Neff had some property in Oregon. At Mitchell's behest, the local sheriff auctioned the property and gave Mitchell enough of the proceeds to cover his bill. Pennoyer was the unlucky buyer. Eventually, Neff returned to Oregon and told Pennoyer to get off his property. Pennoyer refused, relying on the deed he had obtained at the sheriff's auction. Neff took the position that the whole proceeding that led to the auction was illegal. The Supreme Court agreed with Neff and he got his property back.

Every significant event in the case revolves around talk. Mitchell and Neff talked about Neff's legal problems. Mitchell demanded payment. Through the appropriate legal formalities, Mitchell told Neff about his suit. Mitchell told the sheriff to sell the property. The sheriff conducted an auction. Pennoyer bought a deed, a written statement about ownership. Neff came back to Oregon, and he and Pennoyer disputed the ownership of the property. Moreover, all of this must have been repeatedly reported, transformed, summarized, and excerpted by witnesses, lawyers, and judges as the case made its way through two Oregon courts and onto the docket of the Supreme Court.

In a decision rendered eleven years after Mitchell initially sued Neff, the Supreme Court reduced this discourse to the case summary contained in Text 1.4.

Text 1.4

This is an action to recover the possession of a tract of land, of the alleged value of $15,000, situated in the State of Oregon. The plaintiff asserts title to the premises by a patent of the United States issued to him in 1866 under the Act of
5   Congress of September 27th, 1850, 9 Stat. at L., 496, usually known as the Donation Law of Oregon. The defendant claims to have acquired the premises under a sheriff's deed, made upon a sale of the property on execution issued upon a judgment recovered against the plaintiff in one of the cir-
10   cuit courts of the State. The case turns upon the validity of this judgment.

It appears from the report that the judgment was rendered in February, 1866, in favor of J. H. Mitchell, for less than $300, including costs, in an action brought by him upon a
15   demand for services as an attorney; that, at the time the action was commenced and the judgment rendered, the de-

> fendant therein, the plaintiff here, was a non-resident of the
> State; that he was not personally served with process, and
> did not appear therein; and that the judgment was entered
> 20   upon his default in not answering the complaint, upon a
> constructive service of summons by publication.

The Supreme Court's statement of the case is full of references to discourse. Note, for example, the following words and phrases: alleged, asserts, claims, appears from the record, judgment was rendered, upon a demand, judgment was entered, summons by publication. Each describes a significant occurrence that was primarily linguistic in nature.[10] The specific content of each of these occurrences has been lost, however. In an effort to facilitate the application of the decisive legal principles, the Court has reduced all that was said and written to two terse paragraphs. The discourse which is the raw material of the case is treated as transparent, transformed into a window through which the law views the set of constructed meanings it calls "facts." This is what appellate courts routinely do; a lawyer would ask, What else could they do? What is remarkable is that the process is taken entirely for granted by lawyers and has elicited virtually no scholarly commentary.[11]

Similar processes can be seen in the professional discourse about the nature of law. Traditional legal theory has focused on rules, rights, and responsibilities rather than the idiosyncracies of litigants. Most law school teaching is still premised on the formalist belief that law is a set of discoverable principles and its corollary assumption that judges find facts, and then identify and apply the relevant legal principles.[12] Traditional legal theory has long been, and is increasingly, interested in discourse, but it is the discourse of law makers, not of the law's constituents. Ronald Dworkin (1986, p. 410), the leading contemporary exponent of liberal jurisprudence, argues that law is an interpretive concept, implying that discourse therefore plays a central role in the legal process. But who is to do the interpreting, and whose discourse are they to interpret? The answer to both questions is "judges," who, in Dworkin's view, "should decide what the law is by interpreting the practice of other judges deciding what the law is" (p. 410).

Much recent jurisprudence, in particular the critical legal studies movement, attacks the traditional focus on purportedly neutral rules, and argues instead that such factors as class, race, and gender influence the making of law (e.g., Unger 1975, Kennedy 1976, West 1988). Critical legal theorists condemn the separation and alienation that allegedly result from the rule-centered approach, and assert the primacy of such social values as caring, community, attachment, and connection (West 1988, p. 9).

This jurisprudence has emphasized language in two important ways. First, it has questioned whether statements of legal principles can be "determinate," in the sense of having meaning that transcends particular contexts (Boyle 1985). Second, it claims that the traditional professional discourse of the law has given voice only to the powerful. Critical legal theorists usually state this argument in class terms. Feminist jurisprudence asserts that legal discourse has been distinctly male. Radical feminists go beyond this general observation and see subtle evidence of male dominance even in the current rhetoric about equality through community. They condemn it as another effort to deny separate identities to women (West 1988). In a particularly persuasive elaboration of this theme, Fineman (1988, p. 727) describes "how the rhetoric used by social workers and mediators has been successful in appropriating the business of child custody decisionmaking," and analyzes how this change has affected mothers.

These jurisprudential debates are, of course, a discourse about the professional discourses of law. Despite its condemnation of the discourse of the appellate courts and more traditional scholars of law for failing to give voice to women and other powerless groups, critical jurisprudence has not found a way to discover what these unvoiced voices are saying. For the most part, this work simply assumes what these voices must sound like.[13] In this respect, it does not differ fundamentally from traditional legal discourse. Thus, while legal scholarship may have at last identified the voiceless, it is still in the process of determining how their voices should be represented.

THE STUDY OF ORDINARY DISCOURSE IN LEGAL CONTEXTS

Our goal in undertaking the research on which this book is based was to find a means to hear the voices of those who are the consumers of the law and the nonprofessional participants in its institutions. As we began this effort, we were not writing on a blank slate. Our previous work on the speech styles of witnesses had made us aware of some of the frustrations that lay people experience in their encounters with formal legal discourse.

In that earlier research project, we examined witnesses'[14] speech styles in courts where accounts are typically given in response to questions posed by lawyers (O'Barr 1982, Conley et al. 1978). We collected over one hun-

dred hours of tapes and transcripts of criminal proceedings in a North Carolina trial court. Although it was not a focus of major attention in the earlier project, we were repeatedly told by witnesses that the process of
testifying under the constraints imposed by the court environment had
been one of the most frustrating aspects of their experience with the legal
system.

We began the present study by reviewing our previously collected data,
paying particular attention to the structure of witnesses' accounts.[15] We
recognized, of course, that the law of evidence places substantial restrictions on courtroom testimony, and that accounts given in court would necessarily differ from those given in other contexts. We suspected, however,
that by examining instances in which evidentiary constraints were placed
on witnesses' accounts, we would be able to make useful inferences about
how witnesses would structure their accounts in the absence of such restraints. We therefore focused on those aspects of accounts that engendered
evidentiary objections which seemed to cause witnesses difficulty, following Llewellen and Hoebel's (1941) dictum that situations in which a system
breaks down often yield the most interesting information about the nature
of the system.

Our analysis of our earlier data repeatedly confirmed the intuition that
lay witnesses come to court with a repertoire of narrative conventions that
are often frustrated, directly or indirectly, by the operation of the law of
evidence. Consider, for example, the following constraints that are imposed
on witnesses in most American courts:

1. A witness may not ordinarily repeat what other persons have said
about the events being reported;

2. A witness may not speculate about how the situations or events being
reported may have appeared to other people or from other perspectives;

3. A witness may not ordinarily comment on his or her reactions to, or
feelings and beliefs about, events being reported;

4. In responding to a question, a witness ordinarily may not digress from
the subject of the question to introduce information that he or she believes
critical as a preface or qualification;

5. A witness may not normally incorporate into his or her account any
suppositions about the state of mind of the persons involved in the events
being reported;

6. Value judgments and opinions by lay witnesses are generally disfa-
vored;

7. Emphasis through repetition of information is restricted;

8. Substantive information should not be conveyed through gestures alone; and

9. A witness is generally forbidden to make observations about the question asked or to comment on the process of testifying itself.

These restrictions and prohibitions are supported by the statutory or common law of evidence or by unwritten custom widely followed by the courts. Yet reflection on how we ordinarily speak suggests that each forbidden practice is common in everyday narration.

Frustration and dissatisfaction are inevitable results of such constraints. One federal trial judge has commented on the fact that litigants frequently feel dissatisfied because the trial process does not afford them a fair chance to tell their stories (Weinstein 1977). He reports that greater satisfaction for litigants in small claims courts appears to be related to the absence of formal rules of evidence. On the basis of his experience, Weinstein believes that

> allowing litigants to introduce evidence relatively freely and to rely on hearsay, provided the opponent can call the declarant and otherwise attack him with a minimum of barriers, tends to tranquilize them. This truism is demonstrated repeatedly in magistrates' courts where a complaining witness pours out his heart to an attentive judge and then, having had his day in court, withdraws the complaint (1977, p. 521).

Carlin (1976) reports that the experience of litigants and witnesses in Britain has been similar. The rules governing courtroom procedure, Carlen notes, place defendants in positions where they must plead their cases or give supporting testimony in a manner that is "quite divorced from the conventions of everyday life outside the courtroom" (1976, p. 24) and where the logic of the legal process is opposed to "commonsense interpretations" (1976, p. 85).

These observation were confirmed by conversations we had with courtroom witnesses. Witnesses—both parties to the dispute and others—complained about their inability to convey their versions of the facts at issue. Some even went so far as to assert afterwards that they would never have taken their cases to court or agreed to testify if they had realized ahead of time how little opportunity they would have to tell their stories.

The source of this frustration is obvious from segments of testimony we collected in which a witness's narrative efforts engender objections. In each instance, the agendas of the witness and the court conflict. Although the witness attempts to tell the story on his or her own terms, the court will hear the evidence only when it is structured in ways alien to the day-to-day lives of most of those who testify.

Texts 1.5–1.9 illustrate several difficulties that witnesses encounter. Texts 1.5 and 1.6 are drawn from a vehicular homicide case in which an allegedly drunk driver was charged with running a red light and colliding with an ambulance. As a result, a heart attack victim on her way to the hospital was thrown out into the street and died. In Texts 1.5 and 1.6, the witness is an ambulance attendant who was riding in the back of the vehicle with the patient. In the testimony quoted, the prosecution is attempting to establish that the patient was alive before the collision and died as a result of it. This witness has already run into difficulty several times for attempting to report what others said.

The account given in Text 1.5 differs in important ways from the type of account that one would expect in ordinary discourse, where a speaker has greater control over the organization of the story and where reports of conversations are common.

Text 1.5

WITNESS: Well, I went, uh, Mr. N told me to go outside.

LAWYER: Object.

WITNESS: Well, I—

JUDGE: Just describe the physical act of what was done. Not
5   what was said, but what actually transpired.

WITNESS: Well, I wasn't really doing anything in relation to
    the patient. Mr. N was doing all that.

LAWYER: Did you go, did you go back, did you return to the
    emergency vehicle?
10   WITNESS: I returned to the emergency vehicle.

The objection sequence in Text 1.5 occurs precisely at the point where the witness attempts to do what he would ordinarily do. The problem (and hence the objection) occurs as a result of the witness's attempt to use everyday discourse rules in the courtroom. When he violates the rule that reporting a conversation (hearsay, from the perspective of the law) is not ordinarily allowed, an objection occurs. As in this instance, evidence conventions (read: *the rules of courtroom discourse*) are seldom explained in any detail to those who must conform to them. At most, witnesses receive some instruction from attorneys in the course of pretrial preparation.

In Text 1.6, the same witness attempts to state the basis of his knowledge, and finds that, because he heard it from someone else, it is disallowed. He comes up against two related rules. The first limits non-expert witnesses to their firsthand knowledge. The second, the hearsay rule, holds that even firsthand knowledge of what another has said (as opposed to done) is not a permissible basis for testimony offered to prove the truth of what the other person has said: in the example, the color of the victim's lips.[16]

Text 1.6

LAWYER: Were her lips blue at the time?
WITNESS: Uh, I don't remember. I think that, uh, the patient's
    family said they were blue.
LAWYER: Object to what the family said.
5   JUDGE: Sustained.

Text 1.7 presents a somewhat different hearsay problem. The text is taken from an armed robbery trial. The convenience store clerk who was held up is attempting to describe the car in which the robber fled. In her initial answer, the witness acknowledges the hearsay source of the information, and the judge excludes it. When she later reports the same information as firsthand knowledge, her account is allowed to stand. This text shows a good deal about the curious workings of the court. The witness first states that she knows the year of manufacture of the car because someone told her. Originally disallowed because she includes the basis for her knowledge, the witness's testimony about the year of manufacture is allowed to stand when she presents it as firsthand knowledge.

Text 1.7

LAWYER: Now could you describe the year or approximate
    year?
WITNESS: Uh, seventy-, I was told seventy-three.
LAWYER: Object, your honor, to what she was told.
5   JUDGE: Sustained as to what she was told. Disabuse your
    minds of that, members of the jury. It is not competent.
LAWYER: Could you describe whether it looked like a new or
    an old car?
WITNESS: Well, it was seventy-three then. It was a seventy-
10   three Pontiac.

Texts 1.5–1.7 are typical of instances of reported conversations that the courts treat as hearsay. These texts suggest that witnesses often attempt to tell their stories in court as they might tell them in everyday situations, and are frustrated in the attempt. If witnesses did not tend to report conversations in their testimony, the hearsay rule would not be needed; in any event, there would not be such frequent objections resulting from attempts to keep reported speech out of testimonial accounts.

Evidentiary rules regarding the expression of opinions, conclusions, and generalizations in the course of testimony also cause frequent problems. Except in the case of expert witnesses, the law of evidence expresses a strong preference for concrete descriptive testimony. Lay opinions, conclusions, and generalizations are not necessarily impermissible but they are frequently restricted on the grounds that they are incompetent and/or not relevant to the issues at hand. Judges have considerable discretion here.[17]

Text 1.8 illustrates the problem that many witnesses have in adapting to this preference for concrete testimony. The witness is a woman who has filed a criminal complaint against her father, alleging that when drunk he threatened her mother with a gun. In this excerpt, she is attempting to describe his behavior on a particular occasion. Rather than describing the behavior in concrete terms, however, she summarizes it in a conclusory fashion ("he gets uglier and uglier"). Moreover, she does not limit her account to events she observed on the occasion in question but appears to generalize from observations she made on other occasions when he was drunk ("After he gets a certain amount of drink in him"). Although such generalization may be common in everyday conversation, it is often unacceptable in court, since the law does not usually permit a witness to prove what happened on one occasion by reference to other, similar occasions. In this objection sequence, the basis for the objection is not explained to the witness. Nor does this witness show any understanding of the objection sequence; rather, she ignores it and proceeds with her account.[18]

Text 1.8

	WITNESS: After he gets a certain amount of drink in him, he gets uglier and uglier and he does become very violent.
	LAWYER: Objection, if your honor please.
	JUDGE: Objection sustained.
5	WITNESS: Anyhow, I was afraid—about the gun. That's what petrified me.

Text 1.9 contains a similar objection sequence, but this time the judge comments on the reason for his ruling on the objection. In this excerpt, which is taken from an appeal of a speeding ticket, the police officer who stopped the defendant is attempting to account for the events in question by referring to what often happens in similar situations. As in Text 1.8, the generalization is disallowed. Note that the judge's remarks are directed to the jury and not to the witness who has made the "mistake." As in most such instances, no instruction is given to the witness about the legal problem he has encountered in testifying. As a consequence, witnesses do not understand such "errors" and our transcripts show witnesses making them repeatedly.[19]

Text 1.9

LAWYER: After you entered the fifty-five zone, what happened
next?
WITNESS: Um, our cars have the electronic siren and I tapped
it a few times hoping he would pull over because, uh,
5   sometimes when people decide to run they wait till they
get to open road and so I was trying to get him to stop—
LAWYER: Objection. Motion to strike.
JUDGE: Sustained as to what people sometimes do. Disabuse
your minds of that, members of the jury. It is not compe-
10   tent. Motion to strike is allowed.

The law of evidence is in one sense epistemological: it imposes on witnesses' accounts the law's views on what constitutes a fact and what sources of information are reliable. Texts 1.5 through 1.9 demonstrate that witnesses come to court with their own epistemological assumptions, and that these assumptions are often in conflict with the ones embodied in the law of evidence. Witnesses' reactions to objection sequences suggest that they have little understanding of the nature of this conflict and that the explanations offered by the courts do little to enlighten them about why the law deems their accounts unacceptable. Difficulties of this sort may contribute to the frequently reported dissatisfaction of witnesses with the formal judicial process.

These observations of problems encountered when testifying under the rules of evidence suggested several specific questions for further study. For example, are there "folk" approaches to narration that are being frustrated by court procedures? Are there any consistencies in the way that lay litigants would structure legal accounts in the absence of evidentiary constraints? Would their unconstrained accounts tell us anything about how they conceive their legal problems, and how they define their objectives? We saw in the operation of the law of evidence a striking illustration of how the official discourse of the law manages the voices of ordinary people, and we were strengthened in our determination to hear what these people were saying. In the next two chapters, we describe our methods for finding these people and listening to their voices.

2   The Courts of First Resort

In Search of Informal Justice

You live in a medium-sized city. You bought a new car four months ago. It has 4,500 miles on the odomoter. It will not start on rainy days. You go back to the dealer, brandishing your 3-year/50,000 mile bumper-to-bumper warranty. The dealer refuses to fix it under the warranty, claiming that the car needs "ordinary road adjustments." This will cost an estimated $75–$100.

You have had enough. You have seen Judge Wapner on television's "The People's Court," and you know that there is a court where ordinary people can bring suits without lawyers, technical legal knowledge, or great expense and delay. In your state, this institution is called a small claims court. You decide to sue the dealer for failure to live up to the terms of the warranty.

You take an hour off from your job to go by the courthouse to do the necessary paperwork. The third office you go to is that of the small claims clerk. She hands you a "complaint form" to fill out in triplicate. Under the "Defendant" heading, you are asked to indicate whether the business you are suing is a sole proprietorship, a partnership, or a corporation. You do not know, and ask the clerk for advice. She responds that she is not allowed to give legal advice, and walks away. Guessing, you check the "corporation" box. Under the heading "Basis of Claim," you write two sentences explaining why you are suing: "My new car is still under the warranty. It won't start on rainy days, and they want to charge me $150 to fix it."

You return to the clerk's desk and hand her the completed form. She collects $19 from you. She assigns you a trial date three weeks hence, returns two copies of the complaint form, and says, "Keep one of these for yourself and have the other one served." You respond, "What does that mean?" The clerk says, "You have to serve the complaint on the defendant. You can have it done by any disinterested person over eighteen, or the sheriff's office will do it for $12. Fourth floor, third door on the left off the elevator."

Being unfamiliar with the niceties of service of process, you take the elevator to the fourth floor. You give the papers to the sheriff's deputy at the desk. She looks at them and says, "Who's the registered agent of this corporation that we should serve?" You stare at her incredulously, and finally say, "How about if you give the papers to the service manager?" The deputy collects $12 from you.

The trial date arrives. Your case is scheduled for 9:30 in the morning, so you have arranged to take your last half-day of personal leave time. However, your case is very simple, and you are optimistic that you will get back to work by mid-morning. You arrive at the courthouse at 9:15 and find the small claims hearing room. It is very small, more like an office than any courtroom you have ever seen on television. About two dozen people are crowded into the room. All the seats are taken, so you stand at the back. Behind the last row of chairs there is a horizontal dark smudge along the wall where generations of litigant heads have reclined.

The judge enters the room at 9:40. She is a middle-aged woman in a business suit. She places a name plate in front of her saying that she is a judge. You are struck by the absence of a robe. She begins by calling the names of all the plaintiffs and defendants whose cases are scheduled for this morning's session. Answering for the car dealer is a young man in a coat and tie. He identifies himself as the financial controller for the dealership.

Your case is fifth on the list. Two of the preceding cases are long and hotly contested. The judge is courteous but firm, and the judgments she announces in the earlier cases seem fair to you. She calls your case at 11:20. With a mixture of confidence and trepidation, you walk up and stand at one of two small tables in front of the judge's desk. She is absorbed in reading papers and does not acknowledge you.

After what seems like several minutes, the judge stops reading and looks directly at you. "May I see the warranty, the bill of sale, the installment sales contract, and the service records for the car?" Dumbfounded, you stare back at the judge with your mouth slightly open. You finally regain your composure and mutter that you have the warranty, but not the other documents. In fact, you are not really sure what the judge means. The judge says, "Well, this is a contract case, after all, and I can't try it without all the relevant contract documents." You respond, "But I thought this was supposed to be informal." She says, "It is, but it's still a court, and we have to do things according to the law." Ultimately, the judge writes you out a list of the necessary documents and explains what she has in mind. She reschedules the case for a week later. The dealer's representative has not said a word.

A week later, you return to court at 9:30. Things move a little bit more quickly, and your case is called at 10:40. You have brought all the documents the judge requested. You hand them to her and remain standing, eager to tell your story. However, after reading through the documents the judge turns to the man from the dealership and says, "What do you have to say about this?" He responds, "Well, Your Honor, I hate to bring this up now, but dealers don't give warranties, manufacturers do. This suit should've been brought against the manufacturer. You have to dismiss the case against us." As you look on anxiously, the judge stares down at her desk and shakes her head. Finally she looks up at the dealer's representative and says, "Technically, you might have a point, but you should've said something last week. I'm not gonna let you bring this plaintiff in here twice and then raise a technical defense. We'll try it. If you don't like the result you can appeal and tell them about it in district court." You are relieved that you have apparently survived this initial skirmish.

Before you can say a word, the defendant hands the judge a written report from the dealer's service manager. It says that your car has simply gotten out of tune. It concludes, "There is no defect covered by the warranty. The car needs timing and tuning, which is normal maintenance that the customer is required to pay for." The judge turns back to you and says, "Do you have a report from a mechanic, or did you bring a mechanic to testify on your behalf?"

You are getting angry and struggle to control yourself. You say, "Look, Judge, this is ridiculous. I paid $12,000 for this car four months ago and it won't go in the rain. I'm not a mechanic and I don't need one. Common sense tells you that there's something wrong with the car, and the only fair thing is to make them fix it." You sit down.

The judge stares at her desk for another several seconds. Finally she looks up at you. "You have a tough case here without any expert evidence to contradict theirs." Then she looks at the defendant. "But it seems to me that it would be in everyone's interest to get this problem resolved without any further aggravation or bad blood. If I refrain from entering a judgment against your company, would you be willing to try to fix this problem voluntarily?" The dealer's representative responds, "Well, we don't see that we're responsible here, Your Honor, but if that's what you want, we won't go against you."

The judge turns back to you. "I'm going to continue this case for two weeks so you can make an appointment with the dealer and let them try to fix it. If they don't, come back two weeks from today and we'll talk about a judgment. If I don't see you, I'll assume everything is okay and dismiss the case." You start to say something about your filing fees and the value of all the time you put in. The judge cuts you off, saying "I don't want to hear about that now. If you're not happy in two weeks, come back."

A week later, the dealer repairs the car, albeit grudgingly. Finally, after investing $31 and substantial parts of three working days, you have gotten what you were certain you were entitled to in the first place.

This is not a real story, but it is based in reality. It is a composite drawn from the experiences of the hundreds of litigants whose cases we studied. The overall tone of the story, as well as some of the individual details, would have a ring of truth for almost all of these litigants. As in so many of the cases we studied, two litigants attempt to relate to the court in fundamentally different ways. From the plaintiff's perspective, what matters is that the car should start but will not, and the dealer is violating an unambiguous obligation to fix it. That obligation may have its roots in a legal document, but it depends just as much on considerations of fairness and common sense and the conventions of ordinary social behavior. From the dealer's perspective, the contract and the technical rules of conduct that it creates supersede all other considerations.

This book is about such efforts to relate to the legal system. We chose courts like this as our research setting because they offer a unique opportunity to study people who have defined and analyzed a legal problem, but may not have had any contact with lawyers or other legal professionals. We thought that these courts would provide us with a window on how lay people conceive of the law and interpret legal rights and obligations, and what expectations they have of the legal system. In this chapter we review the history and theory of informal justice in America, describe the practices and procedures in the specific courts we studied, and explain our data collection techniques.

INFORMAL JUSTICE: HISTORY AND THEORY

The term "informal justice" refers to a wide range of judicial and quasi-judicial procedures whose common purpose is to achieve the simple and economical resolution of disputes involving limited sums of money (Ruhnka and Weller 1978; Steele 1981). In most states, the principal component of informal justice is a court which offers litigants simplified procedures, reduced cost and delay, limitations on the right of appeal, and, above all, the chance to appear in court without a lawyer. Nonetheless, it is a real court in the sense that it issues binding legal judgments. Depending on the state, this court may be called a small claims court, a magistrate's court, a justice of the peace court, or a *pro se* court. We refer to them collectively as "informal courts." The degree of legal training required of informal court judges also varies by state. We use the term "formal courts" to refer to those courts which observe procedural and evidentiary formalities, and in which lawyers customarily represent litigants.[1]

In some states, the system of informal justice includes such alternative dispute resolution mechanisms as court-supervised or community-based mediation or arbitration. "Mediation" generally refers to discussions among the litigants and a neutral third party (not a judge) conducted in an effort to reach a consensual resolution of the dispute. "Arbitration" usually describes a similarly informal process which leads to a decision by the third party. The parties to mediation or arbitration typically agree in advance that the result reached may be enforced by a court; state or federal law provides for judicial enforcement in some kinds of cases.[2]

Informal courts were first created in the United States in the early years of the twentieth century (Ruhnka and Weller 1978, pp. 1–5). They were established in response to the recognition that formal courts, with their substantial filing costs and attendant legal fees, had priced themselves out of the reach of consumers and small business people. As originally conceived, informal courts were to be true "people's courts." Toward this end, most relax the technical rules of procedure and evidence that apply in formal courts. Trials are intended to be informal, with many of the specific procedures employed left to the discretion of the judge. Early in the history of informal justice, some jurisdictions did not even require judges to decide cases according to the law, as long as their judgments comported with a commonsense notion of justice. Litigants need not be represented by lawyers. Some courts do not permit lawyers to appear, requiring those who wish to have a lawyer represent them in court to transfer the case to a higher court.[3]

Since the 1960s, researchers have identified a number of areas in which informal justice has failed to live up to its earlier promise (Ruhnka and Weller 1978; Yngvesson and Hennessey 1974–75; Abel 1982; Nader 1979). This research has shown that informal court dockets are dominated by suits brought by business plaintiffs against individual debtors and tenants. Moreover, these plaintiffs win the vast majority of their cases, often by default or admission. This is not surprising, since the business plaintiff's claim typically involves simple proof of unpaid rent or an unpaid debt, whereas defendants often must rely on complex housing or consumer protection laws. Even when individuals and small businesses win, they often are unable to collect their money. An important side effect of crowded dockets is that judges must hurry through their cases. This puts a premium on concise presentations, which in turn confers an advantage on those with courtroom experience.

Such findings confounded the original hope that informal courts would be a panacea for aggrieved consumers, abused tenants, and "mom and pop" merchants. Instead, in the words of one critic, these courts "are primarily a mechanism for enforcing the rights of business" (Abel 1982, p. 296). In response, a number of partial remedies have been tried (Ruhnka and Weller 1978, pp. 3–5). A few states bar corporations from their informal courts, and others specifically exclude collection agencies. Some states limit the number of cases that a single plaintiff can file within a specified time period. Another device is to require a party filing in small claims court to forgo its right of appeal, in order to prevent businesses from waging wars of attrition against defendants.

There is general agreement that such measures are stopgap at best. Statistically speaking, it is still fair to characterize informal courts as state-sponsored collection agencies (Abel 1982, pp. 295–96). Nonetheless, each day thousands of unrepresented litigants go to informal courts throughout the country seeking redress for grievances of every imaginable sort. Such cases have attracted the attention of researchers interested in a range of theoretical issues, and the process of informal justice has become the source of a substantial literature dealing with the nature of disputes.[4]

Perhaps the most important contribution to emerge from this literature is an enhanced understanding of the origin and evolution of disputes. For example, Miller and Sarat (1980–81) have identified the origins of disputes in grievances and claims. Others have analyzed the processes through which grievances are transformed into disputes and ultimately resolved. In this vein, Coates and Penrod (1980–81) have considered the social psychological factors at work in the transformation process. Felstiner et al. (1980–81, p. 631) have observed that "disputes are not things: they are social constructs," and have put in social perspective the transformation from perception of an injury ("naming") through statement of a grievance ("blaming") to initiation of a dispute ("claiming"). Mather and Yngvesson (1980–81, pp. 777–81) have noted that disputes undergo rephrasing, or "some kind of formulation into a public discourse," early in the disputing process, and that thereafter the disputants endeavor to frame the dispute in recognized, coherent paradigms of argument.

Other researchers have noted the influence of speaking opportunities on disputants' attitudes toward the process of informal justice. Yngvesson and Hennessey (1974–75, p. 260) have argued that the opportunity for self-expression seems to contribute to disputants' willingness to compromise. Abel (1982, p. 284) has made the related point that informal courts "allow grievants to let off steam, performing an expressive rather that an instrumental function," and thereby help to neutralize social conflict.[5] Such observations raise larger questions about the possible role of informal justice as a mechanism of social and political control, an issue to which we return in chapter 9.

The Selection of Research Sites

We were attracted to informal courts because of the opportunity they present to study people managing legal controversies with minimal intervention by legal professionals. We shared a general interest with other researchers in these courts and the degree to which they are providing low-cost legal assistance to the public. But these courts were important to us for another reason—we suspected that they might provide a means to study lay views about law. In choosing specific research sites, we were influenced by a number of logistical factors, as well as by structural variations.

In a preliminary national telephone survey of informal court administrators, we found that most jurisdictions were willing, even eager to serve as research sites, subject to agreement on measures to protect the rights and privacy of litigants. Because the research method required tape recording of trials, courts that routinely taped proceedings were particularly attractive, allowing us to avoid the introduction of a new and potentially disruptive element into the courtroom. The critical logistical concern was the volume of cases that actually went to trial. In some jurisdictions we considered, the number of cases filed was too small to justify the time and expense of data collection, whereas in others the filing rate was high, but almost all cases were dropped or settled before trial.[6]

From a structural standpoint, the vast majority of informal courts share a number of common features, including low jurisdictional limits,[7] reduced filing fees, prompt trial settings, the elimination of procedural and evidentiary technicalities, and the custom of litigants trying their cases without lawyers. There are two critical structural differences, however, that were of particular interest to us.

First, the qualifications and duties of informal court judges vary considerably. In some states, the judges need not be lawyers. Within such states, it may be customary for the judges in the largest cities to be law school graduates, whereas elsewhere they are more likely to be non-lawyers who have previously worked in court administration. In most states, however, informal court judges must be members of the bar. In many smaller communities, presiding over the informal court is not a full-time job, and the judges' duties may also include setting bail for persons who have been arrested, issuing search and arrest warrants, and hearing traffic cases. Another variant is represented by states in which judges from the lowest level of the formal court system rotate periodically through the informal courts.

The legal background of judges is of interest because a trial is a collaborative effort between the judge and the litigants. In informal courts, where cases are rarely screened and organized by lawyers before trial, judges face a manifold task. In many cases, as they hear the evidence they must select the appropriate legal category (for example, contract violation, negligence, or fraud), recall the standards of proof for that category, decide which portions of the evidence are credible, and then determine whether the evidence has satisfied the applicable standards of proof. We suspected that the extent of a judge's legal training and experience would influence his or her ability to perform these tasks, and, ultimately, the form and outcome of trials.

A second structural variable is the amount of pretrial assistance provided to informal court litigants. In most states, litigants are left entirely to their own devices in bringing and defending a suit. Although a few litigants consult lawyers (primarily corporate litigants), most do not. When asked about anything other than paperwork and scheduling, court clerks routinely respond that they are prohibited from giving legal advice. In some cities, local court officials have taken the initiative in developing litigant assistance programs. In one such program, informal court litigants have access to a clinic staffed by law students. Litigants can obtain advice about whether they have sufficient grounds for a case and what evidence they will need to prove it. In another city, plaintiffs are interviewed by members of the clerk's staff before they are allowed to file a complaint. The interviewer listens to the plaintiff's story, makes sure that the plaintiff has all necessary documents, and types out a summary of the complaint which, along with the documents, is sent to the judge in advance of the trial date.

We suspected that the extent of pretrial assistance that litigants received would influence the way in which they interacted with judges. We expected that a litigant whose case had been organized into a coherent legal framework might derive some practical benefit from having simplified the judge's task. Even the routine matter of having all the relevant documents in court could affect a judge's reaction both to the case and the litigant.

Motivated by these considerations, as well as the inevitable concerns about time and money, we chose to conduct the study in six cities located in three different geographic regions.[8] These cities include two major metropolitan areas, three cities with populations of 100,000–200,000, and a city of about 10,000. Both urban and rural areas fall under the jurisdiction of these courts, and the populations they serve are economically, ethnically, and linguistically diverse.

The six jurisdictions we chose also differed in terms of the structural variables just discussed. In five of the cities, the jurisdictional limit is either $1,000 or $1,500. In the sixth, where the limit is $5,000, we expected to find more cases involving corporate litigants and more appearances by lawyers.[9] In the five cities with the lower jurisdictional limits, the filing process is similar. The plaintiff fills out a complaint form that contains a brief statement of the basis for the suit, and a deputy sheriff delivers to the defendant a copy of this form and a summons with the assigned time and place of trial.[10] These courts do not provide either party with any pretrial assistance. In the sixth city, plaintiffs filing complaints are required to participate in intake interviews conducted by members of the clerk's staff. The interviewer types a one-page summary of the claim for the plaintiff's signature. This summary is sent along with copies of relevant documents to the judge in advance of the trial date. In all six cities the courts need not follow the formal rules of evidence and procedure and almost never do so. One of the six cities prohibits lawyers from appearing; in the other five litigants may be represented by lawyers but this rarely happens.

The six courts vary widely with respect to the qualifications of judges. In two of the cities, the judges are required by law to be lawyers. In another, they are customarily lawyers, but there is no requirement that they be. In the other three cities, none of the judges is a lawyer. In five of the cities, the judges are appointed by the clerks or judges of the local formal court; in the sixth, they are elected formal court judges who preside over the informal court on a rotating basis. We studied all of the judges on duty in all six cities, a total of fourteen.

THE UNIT OF ANALYSIS

As we noted in chapter 1, both legal scholars and social scientists have traditionally focused on the case as the unit of analysis. Thus, law students learn the law by analyzing cases and judges look to previously decided cases as guiding precedent. Social scientists studying the fairness and efficiency of our legal system have tended to measure rates of occurrence of various phenomena in terms of cases (e.g., Vidmar 1984). And legal anthropologists have imported this perspective into their investigations of non-Western legal systems.

This selection of the case as the unit of analysis is appropriate if one's focus is on the outcome of disputes. Accordingly, a legal anthropologist seeking to discern substantive principles of dispute resolution in another society or a sociologist interested in the rates at which certain types of litigants prevail will necessarily examine cases. Although we too have devoted considerable attention to cases and their outcomes, we have a different focus, which led us to select a different unit of analysis. We are concerned not so much with the substantive issues that litigants take to court or with rates of occurrence of different types of cases, but with the relationship of lay litigants to the legal system. Thus, our unit of analysis is the encounter of the litigant with the legal system. The primary element of our data is the litigant's account[11] of the problem that has brought him or her into the legal system. At trial, a litigant's account is influenced by interactions with the judge and the other party. As we describe in the next section, we have also studied litigants' accounts given in interviews before and after trial. These accounts are necessarily different from those given at trial because of the phase of the legal process in which they occur and the fact that they are given under different circumstances.

Given our interests, the case is not only an inadequate unit of analysis, it is a misleading one. Since we are investigating the nature of the legal process, we are particularly interested in those events which consume the time and attention of the courts. We observed 466 cases and transcribed and studied 156 of them. (These numbers are explained in the succeeding section.) One might infer that each of these cases is equally significant. However, most cases take very little time. To illustrate this point, we examined the seventy-four cases that were heard during three typical sessions in three different cities. Only twenty of these cases took more than five minutes to complete. In one typical session at one of the sites, the court handled forty-nine cases. The record of the day's events occupies ninety double-spaced pages of transcript. However, only two cases account for forty-three of these pages. Thus, it is fair to say that many cases provide little evidence of the interactive aspect of the legal process. Conversely, much of an individual judge's daily "interaction time" is devoted to a very few litigants.[12]

Data Collection

We studied litigants' accounts at three stages in the litigation process: at the time the plaintiff filed the complaint, at trial, and several weeks after trial. We adopted this three-stage process because we were interested in both the nature of accounts at different phases of the legal process and the perceptions, attitudes, and assumptions they reflected. We were also interested in determining how interaction with the court and the opposing party might influence or change the accounts given by litigants.

In one of the cities, there is a steady flow of litigants into the small claims clerk's office, so we were able to interview plaintiffs immediately after they filed their complaints. In another, we interviewed plaintiffs as they emerged from their intake interviews with the clerical staff. We were also able to tape record some of the intake interviews.[13] Because of the lower volume in the four other courts we studied, it was not practical to wait for litigants at the courthouse, so we took litigants' names from the public files at the clerk's office and telephoned them to arrange interviews at their homes or businesses. We recorded interviews with a total of 101 plaintiffs at the time they filed their cases.

We did not use any formal selection procedures in interviewing these 101 plaintiffs. In the two cities where we interviewed litigants at the courthouse, we selected interviewing days to suit our schedule and then attempted to interview every plaintiff who filed a complaint while we were present. Every plaintiff whom we approached agreed to speak to us, but we undoubtedly missed some people who filed while we were speaking to others. In other cities, we copied the names off all the cases filed over several days (the number of days in each city was dependent on volume) and attempted to call or visit every litigant. Thus, although our sample of plaintiffs is not random, we have no reason to believe that it reflects any systematic biases.

Our original intention was to conduct pretrial interviews of defendants as well, but this did not prove feasible. Informal court defendants are not required to appear at the courthouse or file any papers prior to trial. When we tried to speak to defendants on the telephone or in person, we met with uniform resistance. Some suspected we were law officers or somehow connected with the plaintiff, whereas others were simply angry or unhappy about being sued and unwilling to talk about it.

We used an open-ended interview technique designed to encourage litigants to talk about their cases as they saw fit. With as little prompting as possible and a great deal of active listening, we and our research assistants spoke with plaintiffs for periods ranging from two or three minutes to half an hour. The question at the heart of each interview was: "What is your case about?" We had a loose agenda of topics covering the facts of the case and the litigants' plans and expectations that we raised in the interviews if the litigants did not bring them up first. The litigants talked about the details of their cases, often providing successive and elaborated versions of "what happened" as the interviews developed. In addition, they often raised such topics as their general views of the legal system, what they would have to prove in court, and what they would use as evidence. We tape recorded all of these interviews.

In the second stage of the research, we observed and tape recorded informal court trials.[14] The hearing rooms vary from small offices to large courtrooms with elevated benches. In all of the jurisdictions cases are scheduled at short intervals (although not every day in the smaller cities), and the courtrooms are thus usually crowded with people awaiting trial. At least one of us was present during all the cases, observing and making interpretive notes. There were fourteen judges conducting trials in the six cities we studied. We spent approximately equal time observing each judge's courtroom. During breaks in the trial calendar, we had many opportunities to ask questions of the judges and engage in informal discussions. These opportunities varied from day to day and from judge to judge. We also conducted a formal interview with each judge which lasted from thirty minutes to over an hour.

In each of the six cities, the research was authorized by the judge with supervisory responsibility for the informal court. In accord with the agreements we had reached with the courts concerning informed consent of litigants and protection of their identities, the informal court judges informed the litigants at the start of each court session that we were observers conducting an academic study. We believe that we largely ignored by most litigants, who tended to be more concerned with their cases than with us as observers.

We spent all or part of thirty-six days in court[15] and collected tape recordings of 466 cases. As in the pretrial interviews, we followed no formal selection procedure. We picked sessions[16] to attend on the basis of personal scheduling considerations, confirmed with the clerk's office that a representative number of cases was scheduled, and then attended and recorded the entire session.

We transcribed 156 of these cases for further study. In this instance we did employ selection criteria. We made transcription decisions on a session-by-session basis. Since the original objective of the research was to study litigant accounts, we selected for transcription those sessions that seemed especially rich in dialogue. In practice, this meant that we excluded many sessions dominated by landlords, collection agencies, and other corporate plaintiffs filing large numbers of cases against defendants who usually failed to appear. The sample is thus heavily biased in favor of cases in which the defendant presents an active defense. Because our interest is in litigant speech rather than in rates, results, or other judicial statistics, we believe that this selection process is appropriate and the resulting bias tolerable. Moreover, as explained in the preceding section, the 156 cases we transcribed are the kinds of cases that consume most of the courts' time.

Posttrial data collection proved the most difficult. Our intent was to locate and interview as many litigants as possible. However, we were unable to locate many litigants, presumably because they had moved. Others, particularly those who had been unsuccessful, were unwilling to talk. Nonetheless, we were able to interview twenty-nine litigants, both plaintiffs and defendants, whose trials we had observed. The selection of these twenty-nine was not based on any conscious choice on our part, but simply their availability. This group of twenty-nine is somewhat unrepresentative in that it excludes litigants who had no permanent address or who changed addresses shortly after trial. We used the same open-ended technique as in the pretrial interviews, but this time our agenda of topics included the litigants' overall reaction to the informal justice system, the extent to which their experiences had met their expectations, and their satisfaction with both the process and the result. Because of the litigants' interest in talking about their cases, these interviews tended to be longer than the pretrial ones, sometimes lasting more than an hour.

We regard the interview data as supplementary to the trial tapes and the transcripts based on them, which are our primary data source. For the practical reasons just described, conducting interviews before and after trial proved to be extremely difficult. As a result, we obtained three-stage data for only 19 cases. The full three-stage sample is thus both meager and potentially biased.

From a theoretical standpoint, we do not believe that an answer to an interview question about something that happened during a trial is definitive evidence of the respondent's state of mind during the event in question. Rather, the interview response is one of many clues to the interpretation of the primary text. Moreover, it is a clue which comes in the form of a text which is itself subject to interpretation. Thus, while we would have preferred to have more complete interview data, we are not persuaded that such data would have materially affected our conclusions. As we present our findings in chapters 4, 5, 6, and 7, we introduce relevant interview texts whenever they are available.

We emerged from the data collection phase of our research with several hundred hours of interview and trial tapes. In the next chapter we discuss our methods for transcribing the tapes and analyzing what they contained.

3   Learning to Listen

A principal reason that the voices of lay people go unheard in the formal legal process is that the conventions for talking about troubles in legal institutions differ from those that apply in noninstitutional contexts. Lawyers and judges learn the law's conventions through the formal education they receive in law school and the informal modeling of their courtroom behavior on their observations of other legal professionals. Most litigants lack training in the conventions of official legal discourse. In instances where they are represented by legal counsel, as is usually the case in formal courts, litigants rely on their lawyers' skills for formulating and presenting their cases.

In the informal courts that have been the locale for our research, litigants typically represent themselves and thus must draw on their everyday skills and expectations. Thus, these courts are a unique environment for examining the modes of expression and the legal thinking of unassisted litigants. In this book, we document the discrepancies we have found between the institutional requirements for talking about troubles and the everyday conventions employed by lay litigants. In this chapter, we discuss the method we have used to investigate these discrepancies.

Our approach owes a significant debt to the analysts of conversation working in the enthnomethodological tradition and to the ethnographers of conversation. From the former, we have learned the value of scrutinizing even small and seemingly irrelevant details of verbal interaction. We have gained from them an appreciation of the possibilities of explaining macrosocial organization by examining the myriad encounters that constitute social institutions. From the latter, we have learned the value of viewing language not as a transparent means for reaching the objects of our analytic concerns, but as an end in itself, a fundamental part of social life. Our method draws on these bases, yet is distinct from them. Its premise is that the act of listening carefully to how lay litigants talk about their problems can illuminate their concepts of law and the legal process. In this chapter we take up the basic methodological issue of how to listen, and we demonstrate what can be heard.

THE ETHNOGRAPHY OF DISCOURSE

Stated most simply, our method, which we call the ethnography of discourse, consists of examining what litigants actually say in and out of court. The basic assumption underlying this method is that careful, qualitative study of legal discourse provides evidence of the goals, strategies, and thought processes of the speakers. In contrast to our own work a decade ago which dealt with speech styles and that of the conversation analysts who have studied both institutional and noninstitutional uses of language,[1] our current approach focuses on relatively large segments of speech. In particular, we have examined the full accounts that litigants give in court and in out-of-court interviews and have listened to how their accounts differ from what the court and other parties to the dispute require or expect.

Using the collection of audiotape recordings from the six cities, we prepared transcripts for each of the trials and interviews. The transcripts contain the data needed for the discourse-level analysis we conduct. We believe, following Ochs (1979), that the act of transcribing is a theoretical statement about what parts of the data are significant and deserving of analysis. Because we are focusing on the sociolegal issues involved and not on the interaction patterns per se, we consider it appropriate to use a set of straightforward, easily accessible transcribing conventions that do not introduce issues that we do not intend to discuss. Moreover, as anyone who has worked with transcripts knows, no transcript is ever truly complete. Thus, we have not attempted to indicate such details as phonology, pauses, and intonation except as we believe them to be relevant to the particular issue being discussed.

Analysis of the trials consisted of detailed scrutiny of both tapes and transcripts. In most instances, we were joined in data analysis sessions by other researchers. A typical data analysis session focused on a single witness's account in a trial or interview or on a portion of a trial such as the rendering of the judgment. The session, usually lasting about two hours, consisted of repeated playings of the tape until all present were satisfied that they had heard it enough. (Sometimes this would require five or six playings.) Then, each participant wrote detailed notes about the aspects of the account or interaction that were most interesting to him or her. (This usually took twenty minutes or so.) The remainder of the session was devoted to a roundtable discussion of each participant's observations. The striking thing about such sessions was the high degree of overlap in the observations of the different participants.

We had identified our general interest in such matters as blame, responsibility, proof, causality, and evidence from the beginning of this investigation. However, the specific issues we discuss in this book were not identified a priori, but rather emerged as significant after repeatedly attracting the attention of the analysts. Since the speech of the litigants and judges is our only data, it is important to note that every issue we discuss was drawn to our attention by the court participants themselves in the course of litigating or discussing cases. In the remainder of this chapter, we demonstrate this method by exploring what may be learned from such an approach to courtroom discourse. In subsequent chapters, we focus more intensively on particular issues that have emerged from our investigation.

LEGAL ACCOUNTS WITHOUT EVIDENTIARY CONSTRAINTS

The informal courts we observed provide litigants an opportunity to tell their stories without evidentiary constraints.[2] Litigants' accounts in these courts are indeed more like everyday speech than the accounts we heard in formal trial courts. Informal court accounts include reported conversations and expressions of opinions as well as such other features as comments by witnesses on the process of testifying and various organizational devices related to the longer and more flexible accounts that these courts permit. These accounts also embody the jurisprudential theories of the litigants and witnesses who gave them.

Our tapes are replete with evidence that informal court litigants realize that the opportunity to tell a relatively uninterrupted story to a legal decision maker is a rare one. In one case, the plaintiff sought to recover some personal property that his former wife had retained after their divorce. After a long trial marked by several emotional exchanges among husband, wife, and two sons, the judge ruled against him. His closing remarks indicated that he understood the ruling and felt that the trial itself had been a useful, even therapeutic, exercise. In another case, the defendant in an eviction action, who happened to be a law school graduate, had fallen on hard times and was behind in his rent. He recognized that he had no legal defense to the eviction. Nonetheless, he took several minutes to relate all his troubles to the judge, finally commenting that it had been worth the effort to come to court and that it had at least made him "feel better."

Other expressions of such sentiments could be cited. The most telling bit of evidence, however, may be the simple fact that *every* litigant we observed responded to the judge's invitation to speak by giving a narrative description of the situation. The invitation to speak was typically in the form of a question such as "Why are you here?" or "Why have you brought this matter to the court?" Litigants, however, invariably responded by not answering the question narrowly but by commencing a sequential account of the dispute as they perceived it. The scope of these accounts often went far beyond the facts that the court was empowered to adjudicate.

All of this suggests that, from the litigant's perspective, the opportunity for unconstrained narrative is an important component of informal court procedure. Litigants uniformly take advantage of the opportunity, apparently viewing narration as an appropriate trial strategy. And, as we have seen, some offer unsolicited favorable comments about this aspect of the procedure. These findings are supportive of Abel's (1982, p. 284) view that these courts neutralize conflict by allowing grievants "to let off steam."

Text 3.1 illustrates a typical account given in an informal court. (Appendix II contains summaries of the cases from which the texts that appear throughout the book have been taken.) Here the plaintiff presents his case against a dry cleaning establishment. The plaintiff is a highly paid skilled industrial worker. He alleged that a suit he bought from a store was damaged when he got it back after its first dry cleaning. He sued both the store and the cleaner, asking the court to decide whether the damage resulted from defective material or negligent cleaning and to award damages against the appropriate defendant. The judge severed the cases against the two defendants, first hearing evidence against the cleaner. The cleaner had sent the suit for analysis by the International Fabricare Institute, which reported in writing that the material was defective. The judge accepted this report as conclusive. The owner of the cleaning establishment then testified for the plaintiff in his case against the clothing store. The court accepted the argument of the store manager that the manufacturer was at fault and ordered the case continued while the store attempted to gain a refund from the manufacturer. The plaintiff's lengthy account contains reports of conversations and expressions of opinions, some of which would be disallowed in a formal court. The reported conversations constitute, from the plaintiff's perspective, relevant parts of his account, as do his own opinions and those which he attributes to others.

Text 3.1

JUDGE: Okay, Mr. Norris, if you want to state to the court the reason you are bringing this action against NDE Company.

NORRIS: Uh, the reason I am bringing this action against NDE

5   Company, I got a suit, bought a suit from Feldman's
        around the last of May, I wore the suit one time, and I
        sent it to the laundry to have it, have it cleaned, and I,
        they send the suit back to me, the suit, well I can show it
        to Your Honor.
10   JUDGE: Okay, show it to Mr. Cashwell also. ·
        NORRIS: The suit come back to me like this here [*pointing to
        spot on suit*], like it had maybe, I thought maybe, it wasn't
        enough heat on it.
        JUDGE: Uh, huh.
15   NORRIS: Mr. Rogers at the laundry, he told me that it was a
        defect in the material that was in the suit. He—I, I, I
        brought the suit home and I wore it and I seen this here
        [*indicating spot*] that it was on there so I took the suit off
        and I told my wife, "Well, we goin' send it back to the
20   laundry the next day." This is the laundry ticket [*indicating
        ticket*] where they redone the suit. See, they didn't put this
        tag here on there till the second time I got the suit, okay.
        This first time I got it—the suit—they just had it in the
        plastic. I thought it was okay until I seen it, so I sent it
25   back to the laundry and I was talking to a Mr. Rogers and
        he said that, uh, that the suit was—it was a defect in the
        material—he say, "What about waiting two weeks?" So I
        spent time out of work going back and forth talking to Mr.
        Rogers, and he put this on, on [*pointing to paper attached
30   to suit in the plastic bag*], on the suit about the second time
        I picked it up. He said, "Well,"—you can see that [*indicat-
        ing paper*]—he said, "Well, it's probably a defect in the
        material." He said, "What I'll do, I'll send it off and I'll
        have it analyzed and when it come back," he said, "if
35   we're in the fault," he said, "we'll send—we'll, uh, refund
        your money." So I was waiting at the time two weeks, I'm
        hoping that maybe they'd find the fault and pay me my
        money, but he said that—"I can't pay you no money."
        He's given me, when the suit come back, he gave me this
40   information here [*holding up several pages*].

The plaintiff provides three types of evidence in his account. First, he
produces documents which support his story. Second, he "calls witnesses"
by performing their parts. Third, he introduces physical evidence, the suit
itself. In an everyday account, some of these might not have been included.

Their inclusion in this account hints at the plaintiff's conception of the law and its standards. These features of his account suggest that he believes that written records are more powerful pieces of evidence than his recollections; that the words of others speak for themselves more forcefully than his own paraphrases or interpretations; and that physical evidence is perhaps the best type of all since it can "speak" for itself. Analyzed in this manner, relatively unconstrained narratives offered as evidence reveal the models that laypersons have of accounts that are appropriate and sufficient to prove the contentions they assert.

Other interesting features of his account include the perspective from which it is told, the performance of the story, and its structural features. The story is told from a frequently shifting perspective, sometimes from the vantage of the narrator's home and other times from the vantage of the cleaner's. Deictic markers[3] give clues to the perspective throughout the story. Abelson (1975) argues that a story told from a single vantage point[4] is easier to comprehend, but accounts given in informal courts suggest that most litigants are unlikely to maintain a consistent vantage point. In fact, the shifting of vantages in an account is common in both informal and formal courts. In the latter, however, the shift away from the vantage from which the speaker has the authority to speak as a result of his own actions and observations may occasion an objection that the witness is engaging in speculation or reporting hearsay.

One may well ask what significance the shifting of perspective has if, following Abelson, we understand accounts containing multiple points of view to be more difficult for the listener to comprehend. Having looked through a large number of accounts without discovering any pattern, we have two hypotheses about what may be occurring.

First, the multiple vantages may reflect the natural tendency of the speaker to triangulate on the events being described. Narrators ordinarily tell stories from many perspectives. As listeners, we are taken from scene to scene, we hear the relevant parties "speak," and we may even get privileged information about the motives and thoughts of various parties to the action. Abelson's study of consistency in perspective was a laboratory study. There is no reason to suggest that his findings about consistency of perspective and corresponding ease of comprehension are incorrect, but there is also no reason to assume that the artificial situation studied in the laboratory actually replicates the way people tell stories in natural settings.

Second, as Wolfson (1982) found in her study of the conversational historical present tense in English, it may be that the shift of perspective is

more important than the actual perspective that is assumed. Following
Wolfson, we suggest that the shifting of perspective serves to highlight
points in the story and hold the listener's attention. (The reader is invited
to test Wolfson's theory by reformulating Text 3.1 so that it is told from a
single perspective.)

Another interesting aspect of Text 3.1 is the fact that the plaintiff performs the story rather than merely relating it in some more distant or indirect manner. Students of folklore know from the writings of Hymes (1981),
Bauman (1977), and others that the "breakthrough into performance" is
considered in many cultures to be an important feature of persuasive narratives.[5] Although acceptable stories may be told without performance, it is
generally true across cultures that those who perform stories in telling
them are perceived as giving better accounts. If this is in fact true, then one
of the consequences of the evidentiary constraints that proscribe performance by eliminating what other persons say is to reduce the rhetorical force
of the account. It may well be that those who are accustomed to performing
stories and who are not allowed to do so may have their accounts reduced
in such significant dimensions as interest or even credibility.

Tannen (1981) suggests that major differences exist between stories told
in oral and literate cultures. One such difference she reports is the tendency
for accounts to be performed in oral cultures and in literate cultures to be
related according to the rules of written discourse, which place a higher
value on consistency of vantage point. Accordingly, we suspect that some
persons within a pluralistic culture such as our own may tend toward the
oral mode of narration whereas others may be more familiar with the literate mode. Informal courts, which have relaxed rules of evidence, allow
and tolerate either mode, whereas formal courts, based as they are on the
literate tradition and its record-keeping requirements, follow the conventions of the literate tradition.[6] Under these circumstances, it is easy to
understand why many people may feel constrained and inhibited by the
formalities of courts of record and why they may prefer the less rigid environment of informal courts.

Another feature of the account in Text 3.1 is its sequential organization.[7]
Although attention to the sequential order of events might be expected as
an organizational device for legal accounts, there are situations in which
sequential ordering of an account does not occur. Perhaps the most common occurrence of nonsequential accounts is in cross-examination. Trial
practice manuals advise lawyers to break sequence in order to unsettle witnesses. By contrast, most direct examinations tend to be sequentially or-

dered. From a legal standpoint, it is sometimes necessary to proceed sequentially in order to demonstrate that the witness has the requisite firsthand knowledge of the evidence to be introduced—what lawyers call "laying a proper foundation." Equally important, however, is the fact that sequence is related to our cultural understanding of causality (i.e., only events that occur prior in time can cause subsequent events).

In informal courts, most narratives are organized sequentially. For most witnesses the difficult decision is where to begin and end one's account. The form of the invitation to testify does not seem to provide much assistance with respect to where to begin. In Text 3.1, for example, the judge invites the witness to state his reason for bringing the action. In Text 3.2, a fuller invitation is issued. Yet there is no appreciable difference between the accounts that these different types of invitations elicit. It is also the case that witnesses sometimes embark on long sequential narratives in response to highly specific factual questions.[8]

Text 3.2

JUDGE: Now likewise as a witness for the plaintiff, you've heard everything that has been said and you're closely related to all of this, and I believe you understand that, uh, your mother is, uh, alleging right to recover for the ex-
5   penses that she's incurred over this long history and also she, it's her opinion that in the process she's been harassed and annoyed and all of that and she's seeking recovery for that as well. Now you're as familiar with this perhaps as anyone. From you, what is there that I can learn that will
10   help me decide this case?

THOMAS: Uh, as you can see from the pictures of the trees that there were several trees on the Barrett's property, that a particular tree grows underground and up on to other people's property. Uh, under the fence line and all the way
15   up against the foundation of the house, these sumac trees have grown and spread out and, if I can point out something here [*pointing to photograph*] uh, this is the particular tree—

JUDGE: In such a way that the defendant can see it as well.

20   THOMAS: These have grown up from their property onto our side of the house, okay, and they were removed by me. These, this is where the hedge line was, but now it is grown up with the same sumac trees that came out of

their backyard and off of their property, and these are the
25   trees that my mom was talking about having to cut after
the hedge was actually dead and gone. There have been,
um, a couple of instances where I, days where I went out
and cut down the trees that had grown under the fence
and it started to grow all over our yard and against the
30   foundation, and poisoned those trees. They grew up
through a bush that we had there and, uh, so there are
several instances where I've had to go out and cut those
trees and dig out and poison them, uh, to get them to stop
growing on our property and then they grew up in the
35   hedge area and then the hedge was removed and taken
out. Um, it was a very poor choice of shrubs—something
that spreads all over the, you know, area. Uh, the, uh,
trees have dropped, you know, there's one [*indicating picture*] like that already. There's another picture with the
40   trees growing up on the property and that's after they've
already been cut several times. Um, and the big trees—
you can see there—keep dropping things and the bushes
keep growing through the fence which is onto our property, on to my mom's property.

Notice that after his narrative begins, the witness receives few clues
about when to continue and when to quit. Atkinson (personal communication) has suggested that judges in British small claims courts give cues
about continuing through response tokens such as "yes" and "I see." In the
informal courts that we studied, such tokens are infrequent and witnesses
are left more to their own devices with regard to how long to continue. In
these circumstances, witnesses employ turn preservation techniques which
allow them to continue speaking, usually until the witness decides that the
story is complete. Look, for example, at the use of the connective "and" in
the narrative in Text 3.3, which is taken from a negligence case arising out
of a collision between a car and a moped. Several times, the witness, the
driver of the car, reaches a point where the listener might reasonably conclude that the story is over. The witness pauses, but then preserves his
speaking turn with an "and," which is followed by another segment of the
narrative. In addition, at several points in his narrative the witness employs
rising intonation in an apparent request for acknowledgment and understanding. Because the judge gives no verbal response on any of these occasions, the witness is required to continue without the response he has re-

quested. In formal court proceedings, the witness need not be concerned about where to begin and end, since the interrogating lawyer manages the allocation of speaking turns.

Text 3.3⁹

JUDGE: You tell your, please tell your story. She tells her story, then we decide. Okay?

FISHER: Alright. Uh, there's a, there's a four-way intersection here in town up close by the Oyster Bar, and we was mak-
5   ing a left-hand turn—

FERRY: Mmhmm.

FISHER: —and, um, was pulling into, as we turned in—it's a short, very short distance, fifty foot, seventy-five foot, something like that where there's a parking area ↑ (1.0)
10   to be parked at. We, she turned on the left turn, uh, the right turn signal to make a right-hand turn into the park-ing lot ↑ (1.0), and we started, the front, the front end of the car was into the, um, little uprise to get onto the park-ing lot area ↑ (1.0), and when we did, first thing I know
15   of something hit me behind, the arm, pushed my arm up into the mirror, my arm come back into the car, (1.5) and then maybe I looked back to see what was going on and here's this lady on a moped all over us (2.0). And we had stopped right there in the road, and, um, she was on the
20   ground, and Nancy [Ferry] went ahead and put the car into the parking lot to get us out of the middle of the road, and we got out to see what we could do to help the woman. And (1.0) about twenty minutes later, I guess, the cop—police—finally come up, (1.0) and they, we
25   went after they wrote out the summons for both of us to come to court and then—me and Nancy and Miss Devlin here to come to court—and we did. And we thought it was to get the money to fix the repairs for the car which, what we found out was the only thing that done there was
30   charged with a traffic violation. (1.5) And we was told— we asked the, uh, not the arresting officer, the man that was there—

FERRY: Carl.

FISHER: —and he said we could, um, bring it to civil court or
35   whatever ↑ (1.5), to get, to get, um, to get the payments for the damages. (2.0) And that's—we, come down here and we was told where to go to talk to the lady, and she

told us what to do and she's apparently set up a date to
come here ↑ (1.5). And that's all we was told. We didn't
40   [*inaudible*] anything else about the car . . .
JUDGE: Anything else? You want to add to that?
FERRY: No.

INFORMAL COURT ACCOUNTS AND LAY JURISPRUDENCE

The most significant practical question faced by informal court litigants is whether their accounts will satisfy the court. The strategies that
they employ in their efforts to meet this burden reflect their varied understandings of the law. For example, from a commonsense perspective, the
plaintiff in Text 3.1 appears to give an adequate account of why one of the
two defendants should be held responsible for the damage to his suit. It is
evident from an examination of the suit that it has been damaged. Each of
three parties in court is a possible responsible agent: the man himself, the
cleaner, and the store. By describing his own behavior, the man excludes
himself, at least by implication. When he concludes, he apparently believes
that he has given the court an adequate basis for finding against either or
both of the defendants.

Despite the commonsense appeal of his story, the man got no immediate
compensation for his damaged suit. The cleaner presented an exonerating
report from a purported expert, and the judge accepted it without question.
The cleaner's representative then testified for the plaintiff, stating that the
material in the suit was defective. This testimony shifted the burden to the
store, whose representative quickly persuaded the judge that the fault must
lie with the manufacturer, which had not been sued. The man was told to
come back later, after the store had tried to work things out with the manufacturer.

It is difficult to see in what respect the man's case fell short. From a legal
standpoint, he acted properly in joining the two defendants and asserting
that one must be held responsible. Even if one accepts the cleaner's "expert" report at face value, as the judge did, the man would seem to have a
valid defective merchandise claim against the store, to which the ultimate
responsibility of the manufacturer should be no defense. The shortcoming
appears to be not in the legal theory adopted, but in the structure of the
account itself.

It may be significant that in his account, the man proceeds as if the facts
will speak for themselves. In particular, he never deals explicitly with the
issues of blame, responsibility, and agency. The assessment of responsibility

for the damage he has suffered is accomplished only to the extent that the listener can draw inferences from the very filing of the c se and from the facts recounted. In this respect, his approach might reasonably be characterized as inductive. He does not lay out a theory of the case for testing. Rather, he presents the facts he considers relevant and expects them to lead the court to a conclusion.

Compare the man's account with the case as a lawyer might have presented it. The lawyer would not have added any facts; on the contrary, some information, such as the reported conversation with his wife, might have been deleted. What the lawyer would have done would be to begin the presentation with an opening statement that posited a hypothesis about who was responsible. The evidence would have been organized around testing that hypothesis, and the case would have concluded with an argument that emphasized the ways in which the evidence demonstrated the validity of the hypothesis. In contrast to the man's inductive approach, a lawyer would have organized the case as a deductive experiment in which the issue of responsibility was addressed directly.

Both defendants dealt explicitly with the allocation of responsibility. The cleaner had his expert's report while the store manager laid blame directly on the absent manufacturer. The significant point for our analysis is not whether either defendant's theory is right or wrong, but the mere fact that each defendant articulated a theory of responsibility in the deductive form familiar to lawyers and legal decision makers. The plaintiff may have been at a serious disadvantage because he failed to appreciate the conventions of legal discourse and to structure his account accordingly.

The point is further illustrated by Text 3.4, taken from a case brought by a woman against a garage owner. The woman claims that she—or, rather, a "friend" of hers—bought a rebuilt car engine from the defendant, that the engine never worked properly, and that as a result she spent hundreds of dollars on oil, her transmission was damaged, and she lost her job when she was unable to get to work. She testified later in the case that her life had ultimately deteriorated to the point where she had been evicted from her apartment for nonpayment of rent and was sleeping in the disabled car.

A lawyer would probably characterize this as a breach of contract or breach of warranty case in which the plaintiff sought two kinds of damages: direct (the money paid for the engine) and consequential (the money paid for oil and compensation for the loss of job and eviction). The judge accepted the defendant's argument that the language on the bill of sale limited his liability, and ordered him to refund the price of the engine—something that he had apparently been willing to do all along.

Text 3.4

JUDGE: Okay. At this time, Miss Harrell, if you want to state
to the court the reason you're bringing this action against
the defendant.

HARRELL: Well, on January the third, a friend of mine paid,
5   uh, him $312 for a motor for my car. It was installed the
seventh of January, and for a week—first week after that
it was leaking oil all—everywhere around the lifters and
all around the motor on the other side and there was a
big puddle of oil in my yard. Every time the car was
10   stopped it was leaking oil. I went back on the following
Friday and told him about it, he—one of his mechanics
told me to try some gaskets. So I went down and got the
gaskets, came back, he reimbursed me for the bill for that,
and the gaskets were installed. Um, two hours later, I de-
15   cided to drive it up the street to see how it was doing, and
it started knocking and making all kinds of noises, and
since then, well, I have been back and forth over there.
One of his mechanics even checked it out, it was smoking
and everything else. And since then I have put over two
20   hundred thirty-some dollars worth of oil in the car. It has
damaged my transmission, uh, I've had it checked by a
number of mechanics that said the motor was bad and
it—uh, it was—the vacuum lines were intact, they, um,
everything was checked on that and it has caused the
25   transmission to—quite a bit of damage to that, and, um,
so it's, um, it's been one thing after another. I called him,
and, um, about the middle of March, I was calling him
every day just about. Or two or three times a week anyway, and had to call him to remind him to find me a mo-
30   tor, and always—he, um, I offered to take my old motor
back if they had, had been able to do anything with it,
work on that, do anything with it, he didn't want to do
that. This motor has, he said, has 62,000 miles on it,
which is 162,000, and all the mechanics that I have con-
35   tacted, you know, they've checked it out, the transmission, everything, said that the motor was bad and there
was not enough vacuum coming from the motor to cause
the transmission to change. I've had to put no transmission fluid in there, uh, it's, um, it's, um, it's just not, it's
40   not changing, and it's, it's really played, uh, a havoc with
my, um, livelihood.

A particularly striking feature of this case, and one that it shares with a number of others we studied, is that the two parties talked past each other. Neither contradicted what the other says. Rather, each took a different approach to recounting a problem whose essential facts did not seem to be in dispute. Their respective approaches reflect radically different visions of the law and divergent expectations about the legal process.

Note first the highly personal quality of the woman's account. Listening to her story, one hears in detail how the malfunctioning engine has intruded on her life. However, the facts that she relates include little information about the contractual arrangement between the garage owner and herself. All we learn about her business dealings with the garage is that an unidentified friend paid for a motor for her car. She fails to say explicitly why the garage owner should bear responsibility for her troubles. On the contrary, to the extent that she describes the owner's behavior, one might conclude that he behaved well: he apparently talked to her several times, he paid for new gaskets, he had his mechanic install them, and he had the mechanic check out the car on a subsequent occasion. His major shortcoming is his failure to respond to further telephone calls.

The combination of what she includes in her account and what she leaves out suggests that her theory of legal responsibility derives from a broad notion of social justice rather than a set of more precise rules and principles. She appears to base her claim against the garage owner on her dependent social status. Irrespective of the details of the business transaction, her account implies, people in helpless positions are entitled to assistance from those in positions of social and economic dominance. The fact that she brings the suit and then presents the case in this way further suggests that she believes that the court shares her vision of social justice.

The focus of the garage owner's account was very different. He did not respond to the woman's recounting of her troubles. Instead, he talked about his limited contractual duty to the woman, as evidenced by the written form contract that he produced. He asserted that he had met that limited duty, making specific reference to actions he had taken and offers he had made. He assessed his own conduct not in terms of a broad social duty to take responsibility for the sufferings of the powerless, but in terms of contractual principles which, in his view, transcend such personal concerns. He expected, correctly, that the court would share this theory of justice.

The two litigants also differ markedly in the way that they organized their accounts. On a general level, the woman's account is inductive, whereas the garage owner's was deductive. She describes her troubles in great detail, but leaves it to the court to dig her theory of the case out of the avalanche of facts.[10] The garage owner imposed a structure on his version of the facts. He explained the contract, gave his interpretation of the obligations that it created, and then attempted to demonstrate by reference to selected facts that he had not violated any of those obligations. Such a deductive structure is characteristic of legal argument, and the judge accepted it. From a legal standpoint, this may well be the appropriate structure for this case; in any event, since it was the more familiar of the two approaches offered to the court, the defendant seems to have gained a substantial advantage by proposing it.[11]

A specific manifestation of the woman's generally inductive approach is her treatment of the issue of agency. Like other litigants we have observed, she tells about the problems that have brought her to court, but fails to identify the defendant as the blameworthy human agent of her distress. On the contrary, if her account has an agent that the woman explicitly blames for her troubles, it is the engine itself.

This tendency to talk about the action and the person acted upon without identifying any responsible human agent is common among informal court litigants. Other examples include such statements as:

> "The rent started falling behind."
> "The tools got stolen."
> "I got injured."

The legal system has difficulty dealing with such assertions, since the law generally requires a plaintiff to show an injurious *action,* the defendant as *agent,* and the plaintiff as the *acted upon,* as well as a causal link between the action of the agent and the harm the plaintiff has suffered. Even though the establishment of agency is critical for the legal process, informal court plaintiffs often avoid dealing with it. This finding is understandable when we compare narratives given in informal courts to how people talk about troubles in everyday conversations.

The analysis of everyday conversations shows that people concerned with blame and responsibility tend to talk about these issues and to assess responsibility in interactive sequences rather than to attribute blame directly and unambiguously. In her study of blaming, Pomerantz (1978)[12] shows how people talk about troubles in everyday conversational contexts. She finds that when trouble-tellers fail to deal with the issue of agency, those they are conversing with seek further clarifying information. For example, a speaker reporting that his car blew up is asked what he did to it. In another of Pomerantz's examples a woman complaining that her face hurts is asked what another person did to cause her face to hurt. These instances show the recurrent pattern of an interactive search for responsibility or blame when problems are described without the specification of a responsible agent. Often missing in informal courts is this interactive search for responsibility, which is typical of everyday trouble-tellings. By contrast, in formal courts where rules of evidence apply and attorneys structure the telling of troubles by litigants, it is part of the lawyer's role to state a theory of responsibility.[13]

In the form and substance of their accounts, the woman and the garage owner display different conceptions of the law and the legal process. The woman interprets events in terms of her place in the social network. The organization of her account suggests a belief that the assessment of responsibility will follow automatically from an understanding of the social context. Given this belief, an explicit search for a human agent is gratuitous. The garage owner, by contrast, interprets the same events from the perspective of purportedly neutral contract principles. He understands that he will be held responsible for the woman's troubles only in the limited circumstances specified by these principles.

The Role of Judges in Shaping Accounts

Judges also play important roles in the production of witnesses' accounts. In Texts 3.1 through 3.4, witnesses present accounts of their problems without the intervention of the judge. In each instance, the judge issues an invitation to speak, and the witness responds with a lengthy and largely uninterrupted account. In other cases we studied, the judge plays a far more active role in eliciting and directing testimony, with the resulting account of the events in question emerging as a complex product of the dialogue between judge and witness. As the texts that follow illustrate, the effect of the judges' participation is often to provide the theory of responsibility and explicit assessment of agency that is lacking in many unassisted lay accounts.

Texts 3.5 and 3.6 are drawn from a case brought by the owner of a brass bed against a moving company that allegedly damaged the bed. Factually, the case is strikingly similar to the one described in Text 3.1. The plaintiff claims that the movers scratched the bed while moving it, and then damaged the finish by treating the scratch with a chemical. This all happened about six months before the trial; during the interim, the moving company sent the bed to a furniture repair shop, and it remained there while the parties tried repeatedly but unsuccessfully to settle their differences. At the trial, the judge heard the two witnesses, examined the bedstead, which had been brought into court, and awarded the plaintiff partial compensation for the damage, although he denied a claim for the replacement cost of the bed.

In Texts 3.5 and 3.6, the plaintiff's case is presented in two different ways. In the early part of the case (Text 3.5), the judge asks the plaintiff a series of highly specific questions. It is clear from this dialogue that the judge, himself a lawyer, has already constructed a legal theory of the case, which he is proceeding to test. He views the case as a bailment, which involves entrusting one's property to another, such as a mover, mechanic, or parking garage, for a fee. If the property is not returned in its original condition, the bailee, or recipient, is liable for any loss in value, or for the replacement cost of the property if it has been destroyed.

Text 3.5

JUDGE: When did this move take place?

ALLEN: It took place at the end of April, sir. April 1987.

JUDGE: '87? And it's obvious this must or was this, uh, commercial property from a, uh, retail store or otherwise? Or

5   was it personal—

ALLEN: It was personal, uh, property from my, uh, former, prior, uh, the prior place of residence to my new place.

JUDGE: And, did the defendant, was the defendant hired to move you?

10   ALLEN: Yes sir.

JUDGE: And in that process, according to the complaint, and by reason of some of the preliminaries in this case are more or less admitted that the move was accomplished and yes there was some damage and when did you turn

15   the headboard back to the defendant for examination or repairs?

ALLEN: Approximately a week after, uh, I moved.

JUDGE: Alright sir.

ALLEN: Right around that time.

20   JUDGE: Did they pick it up or did, uh, you deliver it to them.

ALLEN: Well, Harry, uh, attempted to repair it, it at home with the, uh, a kind of chemical. I don't exactly know what the name is but the chemical, uh, removed, the, uh, finish,

	the lacquer finish. Therefore, it was decided to take it out
25	to, uh, a place where it could be refinished.

After the completion of this dialogue, the judge invited the mover's representative "to respond and to further develop your defense or your answer," and he replied with a lengthy narrative. The representative did not refute any of the facts alleged by the plaintiff. Instead, he began by talking about how he and his boss had acted in good faith by trying to help the plaintiff even though he had failed to complain within the time specified by the contract. He talked about his friendly relationship with the plaintiff, and concluded by deflecting responsibility for the damage toward the furniture repair shop. Following this portion of the trial, in Text 3.6, the plaintiff responds to the judge's request for "anything additional by way of conclusion."

Text 3.6

	JUDGE: Back to you, Mr. Allen, as the plaintiff. Anything additional by way of conclusion?
	ALLEN: Your Honor, only that, that, I, I find some discrepancy
	in the position of the firm. When I spoke to Mr. Jefferson
5	three weeks ago, uh, and at that time, I, I asked the rea-
	son, I, I called them was look, um, I, I've been dealing
	pretty well, uh, with Harry, you know, with his employee.
	I had no, no problem. I think the most unpleasant expe-
	rience was with Custom Antique Finishing. Uh, but we've
10	been able to talk with each other. And, and I said, there
	are some, some salient facts which he should be aware of.
	Uh, that I had gotten delivery without the proper as-
	sembly, that the buffing marks were there, that folks ad-
	mitted, uh, that it had taken many months and I wanted
15	to know if, if, uh, I said, "Can we resolve it?" and he said,
	"Yeah," I think, "you know we'll try to resolve it." In fact
	he was suggesting that I get ahold of some other firm that
	might rebuff it and he says, "We can work something out."
	I attempted to do so and, and I, I called several firms in,
20	uh, here in town and, and it's, it's a complicated, uh, pro-
	cess, I guess. They, the, to rebuff it they would have to do
	the thing over again and I called him back and I gave him
	the, the prices on that. I also gave him the price of what
	a, the new headboard costs. He called me back to say that

25 he felt that it was worth no more than $65 and that he
would be willing to settle at that point, keep the, uh,
headboard, and give $65, which I thought was an absurd-
ity, especially if you, uh, price the, uh, this particular
headboard. So I find some discrepancy in saying things
30 are okay but willing to pay $65 and then, and then keep
my headboard and probably sell it for a higher amount.
I'm not saying that Harry, uh, you know, said that. I got
that directly from Mr. Jefferson. I think many months
have passed on this thing. I sure waited a long time for
35 that, uh, silly headboard. I'm beginning to have some
feelings about it myself and the reason I'm fighting so
hard is that if I don't get something back there at home,
my wife was gonna, you know, really take care of me. So,
uh, that's, that's practically [*inaudible*] to her, and it's so
40 [*inaudible*] but I think you know, Your Honor, that, uh,
uh, I have been very patient in it. That, uh, we take care
of our things. We have no children. We take care of our
things and make sure that they're in good shape and uh,
that's, that's the way we like to keep them, and, that's why
45 we called and that's why we're unhappy with the shape
that's in and we feel that, uh, once they accepted responsibility for it, then they should see that responsibility
through, and if they felt strongly that, uh, we had no case
in the matter that they shouldn't have accepted responsi-
50 bility and simply said, "Allen, you're going to have to live
with your scratch." I guess that's my case, Your Honor.

In content, this account is reminiscent of the plaintiff's account in Text
3.4. In form, it resembles the accounts given by the plaintiffs in both the
case involving the leaking engine (Text 3.4) and the case of the damaged
suit (Text 3.1). With respect to content, the plaintiff in Text 3.6 develops a
complex theory of responsibility that bears little resemblance to the theory
of bailment pursued by the judge in Text 3.5. Whereas the judge implies
that responsibility for the damage to the bed is a yes-or-no proposition determined by legal rules, the plaintiff appears to see responsibility as deriv-
ing from social relationships. At the end of his account, he acquiesces in
the defendant's view that the mover assumed responsibility for the damage
only by making a gratuitous offer of help. He seems to agree with the proposition that the mover could have avoided responsibility simply by ignoring
his complaint (Text 3.6, lines 46–51). Note particularly the reference to the

mover's settlement offer, which the plaintiff characterizes as "an absurdity" (line 25). The implication is that the mover's offer of help created a relationship, and that each party then assumed a duty of socially responsible behavior toward the other. As long as this duty was met, the plaintiff felt that he had no grievance. When the mover breached the duty by making the "absurd" offer, the plaintiff, prodded by his wife, concluded that it was time to press his case.[14] He construes the defendant's cooperative actions as an admission of responsibility.[15]

With respect to form, this plaintiff, like the plaintiffs in the two earlier cases, presents an inductive account. His theory of responsibility is stated nowhere explicitly, but is embedded in the account. He appears to believe that the facts will speak for themselves.

The critical difference between this case and the ones involving the damaged suit and the leaking engine is the approach taken by the judge. Unlike the owner of the damaged suit or the woman with the malfunctioning engine, this plaintiff does not have to rely solely on his own unaided account. The judge in this case proves willing and able to develop his own legally sufficient theory of responsibility, frame the case in deductive terms, and then, through his questions, test his theory against the evidence.

Text 3.7 presents a final situation where the judge and the litigants pursue different agendas. As the text suggests, the case was brought against the parents of a teenaged driver who borrowed a friend's car and then collided with the plaintiff's car. The judge, who has already heard from the plaintiff, is now attempting to impose a legal structure on the parents' position. In his questions, he breaks the problem down into three components: (1) the boy's legal liability for causing the collision; (2) the parents' legal liability for the actions of their minor child; and (3) the extent of the damages for which they might be liable. The judge's questions suggest that he assumes that point (1) will not be contested because the boy is not in court and the parents were not eyewitnesses to the accident, and that point (2) is beyond dispute as an established rule of law. His apparent belief is that the parents have come to court solely to contest the amount of the damages sought by the plaintiff.

Text 3.7

> JUDGE: Have you any questions as to the liability of parents
> for minors under ordinary circumstances?
> MR. FLOYD: Uh, in some cases because, uh, what chance do
> we have when he doesn't mind us, you know?

5   JUDGE: Well sir, that's, that's nothing that I can decide here
       today. There's a case has been filed. It appears that a case
       has been filed against two parents for the operation of a
       motor vehicle owned by the parents and in the possession
       of the minor, uh, son of the party. An accident arose and
10   there was damage.
       MR. FLOYD: Well . . .
       JUDGE: Now we're back to this again. Were either one of you
       there at this time?
       MR. FLOYD: No.
15   JUDGE: So you have no knowledge as to how it happened?
       MR. FLOYD: No.
       JUDGE: Basically the question is this, and I understand your
       concerns that the driver should pay but that's, he's not a
       party to this and cannot be a party, uh, because of his age.
20   He may have obligations to you. That's not before the
       court today. But are you concerned only with the dollar
       amount of what this is going to conclude to us.
       MRS. FLOYD: No. We're concerned with that also, but we don't
       feel that we're responsible. We feel that he should have to
25   be responsible for it.
       JUDGE: Alright, well you're bypassing the question now. Are
       you saying that it, the accident was not the fault of your
       son?
       MRS. FLOYD: No, we're not saying that. We don't know whose
30   fault it was.
       JUDGE: Alright. We don't know. Then maybe that answers the
       next question, which is how this all got started. Uh, do
       you deny that it was your son's fault?
       MR. FLOYD: Could be. His friend loaned him the car.
35   JUDGE: Well, at the accident when this thing happened, are
       you admitting, let's phrase it that way, are you admitting
       that it was your son's fault?
       MR. FLOYD: Yeah, I admit that.

       [testimony from plaintiff]

40

       JUDGE: Back to the defendants. Anything additional?
       MR. FLOYD: Well, you know, I can see paying for the rental car
       and everything else. That was $157.27. But this, uh, this
       Holt, you know, uh, I think he just typed up something
45   since it was a friend of Sally's and everything else. You

know, this is a kind of large amount for, you know, a short
time. Three thousand miles. That's a thousand miles, you
know, a month, but it's, I really don't know. I'd just like
to see Carl pay for and, you know, get it off my back. We
50   don't have much control over it. We don't—
JUDGE: What restraints were there placed on Carl as to the
use of the vehicle?
MR. FLOYD: I didn't even know his friend loaned him the car,
gave him the keys, you know, where he was going or
55   nothing else.
MRS. FLOYD: We don't let him drive our car.
JUDGE: Logical question from the opposition with attorneys
present would be why. We won't get into that. That will
conclude the testimony. . . .

It can be inferred from the parents' answers that they have come to court
with a different view of the significance of the issues in the case. They are
less concerned with the specific legal rules that interest the judge than with
the problems arising out of their relationship with their son. In particular,
they are prepared to discuss the issue of whether they, as parents, should
be "responsible" (lines 23–25) (contrast the judge's use of "fault" and "liability" on lines 1, 27, and 33) for the actions of a child "when he doesn't
mind us" (line 4). After a series of specific questions from the judge, the
parents admit the legal "fault" of the son (line 38), but it is unclear whether
even then they appreciate the divergence between their agenda and that of
the court.

Texts 3.5, 3.6, and 3.7 are illustrative of a number of cases we observed
in which the judge intervened to take an active role in developing the testimony of one or both of the parties. Two important points emerge from
these cases. First, the timing and substance of the judges' remarks and
questions indicate that they have found many of the witnesses' accounts to
be inadequate in the sense of not containing the information necessary to
support a legal judgment, or at least not containing that information in a
form they find useful. In Text 3.7, the problem is primarily one of content:
the defendants are insistent on introducing a problem that the judge believes is not appropriate for him to solve. In Texts 3.5 and 3.6, by contrast,
the differences between the unaided narrative and the elicited account relate as much to the way in which information is presented as to the information itself.

Second, these cases highlight the critical role of the judge. They suggest that most of the problems encountered by lay litigants, whether substantive or stylistic, can be resolved by a judge who has the time, inclination, and ability to intervene.

SOME ETHNOGRAPHIC CONCLUSIONS ABOUT ACCOUNTS IN INFORMAL COURTS

We have presented several texts drawn from cases we observed and taped to illustrate the sorts of things that can be understood by listening to and analyzing the accounts that witnesses give in informal courts. Several points that these texts have in common are particularly significant. First, each speaker employs certain linguistic devices that have been reported to recur in noninstitutional, everyday narrative contexts. Speakers thus appear to bring to the court the same narrative strategies and conventions for talking about troubles that they use in ordinary social interaction. Second, many of the more common features of these accounts would violate the rules of evidence in force in formal courts. Third, the narrative freedom that these speakers enjoy may be a mixed blessing, as many cases seem to turn on the conflicting discourse conventions of the litigants and the courts.

In particular, informal court litigants often display a lack of understanding that the law imposes highly specific requirements on both the form and substance of their accounts. In presenting accounts in court, witnesses rely on the conventions of everyday narratives about trouble and their informal cultural assumptions about justice. From the law's perspective, such accounts often have disabling shortcomings. For example, it is common to find accounts which fail to link an agent with an action that caused harm to the plaintiff. Because the court functions to test hypotheses about relations among agents, actions, and recipients of the actions, it is unable to respond affirmatively to what it considers incomplete propositions. Failure to generate a complete hypothesis for testing against the facts being presented may result in losing the case.

The frequent complaint of witnesses who have testified in formal courts that they did not get an adequate opportunity to tell their story takes a different turn in the informal court context where evidentiary rules are relaxed. These courts do allow accounts to be given in a relatively unconstrained manner. As a result, people generally do feel that these courts allow them the opportunity to speak in their own voices. However, new and potentially more serious problems emerge when litigants fail to deal adequately with issues of blame, responsibility, and agency; when they fail to employ a deductive framework which enables the court to test a theory of the case against the evidence presented; or when the agendas of the litigants are at variance with those of the judges who hear their cases. A critical further question is whether certain categories of litigants are more prone to present their cases in ways that articulate less well with the agenda of the law. It is to such specific issues that we turn in subsequent chapters.

4　Rules versus Relationships

In this chapter we begin the process of listening to the voices of lay litigants by examining the accounts of their problems that they give in and out of court. Lay litigants exhibit two contrasting ways of looking at the world and their places in it. These divergent outlooks are reflected in two distinct sets of expectations about the rights and responsibilities that they have toward others and that others have toward them. These sets of expectations are the end points of what we term the rules-relationships continuum. As we demonstrate, this continuum is a powerful tool for interpreting the discourse of lay litigants, for explaining the different approaches to disputes that are evident among them, and for understanding their views of the place of the legal system in the larger American culture.

In conceptualizing a dispute, interpreting rights, and allocating responsibility for events, *relational* litigants focus heavily on status and social relationships. They believe that the law is empowered to assign rewards and punishments according to broad notions of social need and entitlement. This belief appears to be associated with a general social experience in which the individual lacks autonomy and is instead a passive victim or beneficiary of decisions that he or she is powerless to influence.

In court, such litigants strive to introduce into the trial the details of their social lives. Their accounts of their troubles emphasize the social networks in which they are situated, often to the exclusion of the contractual, financial, and property issues that are typically of greater interest to the court. Even an event such as an automobile accident involving strangers may be described in terms of the social history of the parties. Whereas the law demands specific proof of responsibility, litigants giving relational accounts are more likely to assert that certain things "just happen" to certain kinds of people. Predictably, the courts tend to treat such accounts as filled with irrelevancies and inappropriate information, and relational litigants are frequently evaluated as imprecise, rambling, and straying from the central issues.

By contrast, *rule-oriented* litigants interpret disputes in terms of rules and principles that apply irrespective of social status. They see the law as a system of precise rules for assessing responsibility, and reject as irrelevant everything not circumscribed within these rules. This view of the law seems to be rooted in the belief, undoubtedly shaped by social experience, that society is a network not of relationships, but of contractual opportunities that each individual has the power to accept or reject on a case-by-case basis.

In describing the phenomena reported here, we have sought terminology that is both simple and descriptive, and we believe that the terms "relational" and "rule-oriented" accomplish these goals. It should be remembered, however, that both types of accounts are in fact oriented to rules, although the kinds of rules vary. A relational account is oriented with respect to *social* rules, whereas a rule-oriented account addresses specific *legal* rules.[1]

In presenting their cases in court, rule-oriented litigants structure their accounts as a deductive search for blame. Every injury is presumed to have a human agent as its cause. Alternative theories of responsibility are mooted and disposed of until the litigant is finally able to point to the opposing party as the only person on whom responsibility for the events complained of can be plausibly fixed. Rule-oriented accounts thus mesh better than relational ones with the logic of the law and the agenda of the courts. They contain few "extraneous" facts, but instead concentrate on the issues that the court is likely to deem relevant to the case. For example, in a dispute involving a contract, a rule-oriented account would contain a statement about the existence of a valid contract, interpret the meaning of the contract, and present facts that bear on whether the parties have met their obligations under the contract. It would not emphasize motivations, feelings, or reasons why the contract should have never existed, nor would it beg for understanding of contract violations on the basis of social considerations that supersede the duty to perform contracts.

Rule-oriented and relational accounts are models based on our observation of more than 1,000 litigants. Many litigants rather closely approximate one or the other of these models. Others may exhibit aspects of each type in their accounts, or their relative emphasis on rules or relationships may vary with the circumstances of the telling (e.g., in an out-of-court interview as opposed to in the trial itself). After describing each of the orientations, we turn to a consideration of the distribution of these types among litigants.

LITIGANT ORIENTATIONS

The law, of course, is rule-oriented, in theory if not always in practice. Law students are taught a thought process that involves finding the so-called facts, selecting the proper legal rules, and then applying these rules to the facts to produce a legally correct result. The principal method for teaching this approach to problem solving is the discussion of written judicial decisions, which suggests to students that this apparently straight-forward process is the actual means whereby specific cases are decided. Although there has been more than fifty years of debate within American jurisprudence over the role of politics, economics, and personal and social values in judicial decision making, it is fair to say that the dominant view in both the teaching and practice of law continues to be that most cases are decided by a value-neutral process of rule selection and application.

Lawyers and judges are well aware that their dedication to rules is not shared by all consumers of the law. They report continual frustration with clients and litigants who cannot or will not understand the law's narrow focus. Such people expect the law to be interested in the whole range of their personal and social problems. In the lawyer's office and in court, they insist on talking, often at great length, about issues that are not pertinent to the legal analysis of their situations. At trial, they frequently violate rules of evidence that are designed to keep the testimony within the boundaries defined by the controlling legal rules. Judges often excoriate such people for "wasting the court's time," and their own lawyers sometimes label them "illogical," "stupid," or even "crazy."

Not unexpectedly, informal courts are full of people to whom the law's orientation toward a specific set of rules is foreign. Since they are not con-strained by the evidentiary rules that apply in formal courts, these litigants have abundant opportunity to display their concerns and to reveal the ways in which they analyze their situations and allocate rights and responsibili-ties. Contrary to legal folklore, they are not illogical in the sense of reacting to problems in an unstructured or random fashion. Their reasoning is in-deed systematic, but their logic is so different from the law's as to be largely imperceptible to those in whom the tradition of formal legal analysis is deeply ingrained.

The Relational Litigant

The relational form of account is illustrated by the testimony of an unsuccessful plaintiff (Rawls) who has sued her next-door neighbor (Ben-nett) for removing a hedge on her side of the property line, failing to con-trol the growth of his shrubbery onto her property, and generally harassing her. In the excerpt of her testimony contained in Text 4.1, she responds to the judge's questions about how the hedge was removed. Previously, he has asked her a series of specific questions about the location of the property line, but she has been unable to provide specific information about that issue.

Rawls's testimony typifies the tendency of relational account-givers to analyze and describe legal problems in terms of social relations rather than the kinds of rules that constitute legal doctrine. She rarely responds specifically to the issues raised in the judge's questions. Instead, his questions evoke lengthy digressions about the history of her relationship with Bennett. These digressions meander through time and place, drawing her audience ever deeper into her social world, but providing little information about the specific issues that are of interest to the court. Her account contains frequent references to personal status (e.g., line 37: "I'm getting crippled up"; line 66: "I only got one [trash] can"), items which are significant to her social situation but are irrelevant to the court's more limited and rule-centered agenda. Additionally, the account assumes that the listener shares her knowledge of background events and places. Although the assumption of shared knowledge is common and appropriate in familiar conversation, it creates difficulties for a stranger who is trying to extract a set of facts and to apply strict legal rules to them.

Text 4.1

JUDGE: You're alleging that these trees and, and the shrubs and apparently the hedge included were removed. When did this happen?

RAWLS: Oh, well now that happened this year. At uh—

5 JUDGE: And how did it happen?

RAWLS: Well I can, well, well I have to jump back because, uh, for three years when Mr. Bennett moved back—because he was there once before and then he moved and then he come back into that house—and all the time be-

10 fore—I have to say this though Judge—because all the time before everybody took care of that hedge and they wouldn't let me take care of it. They trimmed it and I even went to Mr. Bennett when he was there before—

JUDGE: Wait a moment. Now the question that I asked you—

15 and I would like to have you answer it—and that is how did the hedge get removed?

RAWLS: Well, um, Mr. Bennett said he told me when he moved back in, uh, because I was taking care of my trees coming up through the hedge, I was cutting them off and

20 he told me not to do that. He said, "Don't do it," he said,
"I'm going to have, the church is going to pay to take
them out of there, because my wife wants to put a fence
and plant roses on the other side." He said, "Is that alright
with you?" I said, "I don't care what you do with it," you
25 know, and I said, "If you need, uh, money for tools,
maybe I can rent a tool and help in that respect because I
can't dig," you know. And I said, "If you need uh, a tool
to help you remove the hedge," I said, "uh, I will," well it
wasn't the hedge then it was all the stumps underneath
30 because he wanted that removed because he, his wife
wanted the fence and she wanted roses on it. And so then
three years went by and they let these trees grow up like
you see the picture there. I think you've got it. And
they're so big and then when he told me to stop taking
35 them out because he was gonna take out that hedge, uh,
the stumps, why uh, in the meantime I called a man and
I had them, because I'm getting crippled up and I can't
bend down sir, and here I was still taking out those trees
and he wasn't coming to help me like he said he was. So
40 then I had a man come—here Jim give him this—and I
paid $45. There's the bill there and he cut it right off down
level with the ground. Well, I knew that wouldn't take it
but at least it would keep me for a little bit trying to get
them tree things out of that shrubbery there. Well, um,
45 Mr. Bennett, when he finally come out he said, "You
know, that isn't going to do it," and that's when he told
me, "My wife wants to put a fence," and he said, "You
know that isn't going to do it. Those stumps are going to
have to be taken out." And that's when I told him, and he
50 said he would do it, "I and the church would take them
out," and I, that's when I told him, "If you need, uh,
money for a tool or something to help you. I'll pay for the
tool or whatever." And he told, didn't do it, and so then I
just had a, the Milehigh, uh, Tree Service come uh, uh,
55 and um, a, and Mr., I had his name here—Mr., uh, Cook
come and he come in the house and sat down with me
and he looked at that and he said well he surely should
help in the shrubbery in the back because there's shrubbery in the back that was over on my line that I've got to
60 take out and I've got pictures of that too, sir. And he said
he didn't know what the man or what the man was because the tree was dead why didn't he take it out? Well

all he wants to do is harass me so he leaves it there so I
have to keep taking the stuff out and bending over and
65   using my trashcan, you know. This is something else. I
only got one can. Why don't he pick up his own trash?
And so I went ahead and paid it. He told me he would
come if I need. He says, "I'll cut it when you need me."
Yet I could never get this man. I tried to have him subpoe-
70   naed, yet I could never get him because I think Bennett
got to him first. But, anyway I got the Milehigh Tree Service here for 275, and I got his mess in the backyard—if
you want the pictures here—that's what I took them for.
Did you give him the ones with the trees?

The Rule-Oriented Litigant

Text 4.2 illustrates the alternative rule-oriented method of presenting a case. This witness (Hogan) is a sales executive who is appearing in
court on behalf of her company, the defendant in the case. The plaintiff
(Webb), a former sales representative of the company, is suing over the
company's refusal to pay him a bonus commission on the sale of an expensive scientific instrument. In the excerpt of the case contained in Text 4.2,
Hogan presents the company's defense to Webb's claim. She deals directly
with the issues that the judge must resolve to decide the case. She treats the
dispute as a contractual problem between two parties and does not discuss
personalities or social relationships. Her account is highly factual: names,
dates, and the contents of conversations and documents are reported precisely. Unlike the relational account of Rawls in Text 4.1, this account presumes no prior knowledge of people, places, or events on the part of the
listener. It is given in chronological sequence and without the constant in-
terjections of background information that typify relational accounts. The
litigant presents the court with information relevant to the narrow principles of contract law on which the outcome depends in an efficient manner and with a minimum of extraneous matter.

Text 4.2

JUDGE: We'll come back to you in just a moment. Let's turn
over to you ma'am. We do need your name, business address, and connection with the uh, Instrument Supply
Company.
5   HOGAN: My name is Lynn Hogan. Uh, my address, do you
want my business address or—

JUDGE: Business address is fine.

HOGAN: 1200 Cavanaugh Street. I am the scientific sales manager for Instrument Supply, Denver.

10   JUDGE: As such of course you've heard everything that's been stated so far. We have several exhibits. I believe in this case you're probably familiar with all of them.

HOGAN: Yes sir, I am.

JUDGE: But if not, you're certainly free to look them all over

15   and your opportunity to react to what you've heard and to further develop whatever answer or defense you may have.

HOGAN: Okay, thank you. Um, as uh Dan [the plaintiff] stated, uh, Instrument Supply is a scientific distributor.

20   Uh, we represent over 1500 manufacturers and we sell over 60,000 products. Um, we are continuously being exposed to gimmicks from our manufacturers to boost the sale of their products. Uh, the only control that management has, um, over these prod-, over these promotions, is

25   to pick and choose the ones that uh, best support our local selling programs, where we want the local emphasis to be. Um, then it is my responsibility, as well as the district manager, to assist the sales reps in focusing on these sanctioned programs. Uh, in order to keep track of what we

30   have sanctioned, we have a calculation sheet that specifically shows the sales representative what we are sanctioning. This is one for the first half. I have highlighted that that particular promotion for spectrometers was on the first half, from March until August of 1984, giving the

35   particular payouts, and as you'll see there is a $200 payout there for 1001 Spectrometer. In the, we, uh, usually will change some of the programs on the second half uh, PIP program. Um, we also as sales managers, provide to the representatives, um, some sort of indication that we

40   are bombarded, our plate is full. So I put out to them in September of 1986, a list of the sanctioned promotions. You will see on there that the Diller and Macy double payout is not on there. Uh, I was unaware that this, um, letter had gone out from D and M. Approximately October of

45   1986 they did send this out to the sales representative. Uh, I received notification that it was out amongst the reps late October, early November, upon returning from vacation. My management told me of his conversation with Mr.

Harper and the agreement was made between John Tay-
50   lor, uh the dis-, the then district manager and Mr. Harper,
that there had been a, uh, an advance notification put out
on an unsanctioned program through Diller and Macy,
not sanctioned by Instrument Supply. And uh, that Mr.
Harper was more than uh, uh, uh, he was more than open
55   to go ahead and pay his $200, but that we would not pay
the matching $200.
JUDGE: What is his basis for that? Which seems to be contrary
to the flier that he put out.
HOGAN: Um, Mr. Harper in a, in a letter that Mr., I asked for
60   Mr. Harper to write, which I believe you already have a
copy but here is another copy. In there it states the events.
It does say that he um, prematurely put the promotion out
to the sales force without talking to local management.
Um, in early, either late October, early November, I asked
65   him, he told me at that point about um, what was going
on with Mr. Webb and I asked him at that time, I said,
"Would you please call Mr. Webb and tell him that you
have prematurely put a promotion out that's not sanctioned and that you will honor your $200 and that Instru-
70   ment Supply will not." He told me that he had. Uh, it is
true that I was semi-aware of this 1001 from um, uh, the
sale at Lakeview. Mr. Webb did a quotation to Lakeview
on November 15th of 1986, uh, stating on there that this
particular quote was good until December 15th, 1986 to
75   the customer. Um, it is my job to encourage the sales representatives to close sales. At that time I was not aware of
the fact that Dan did not know it was not 400 but only
200 through Diller and Macy. Upon his resignation, um,
when he came into the office the end of December, he did
80   at that time state the $400 and I did at that time tell him
that it was $200 from Diller and Macy and not a matching
$200 from Instrument Supply. Um, at that point, um, Dan
continued to pursue it and um, you know we, you see the
answers that we have have uh put out. So we have paid,
85   we did pay $200 out for Diller and Macy. Diller and Macy
is reimbursing us for that $200 through the PIP program.
And um, excuse me, if I could just present one other
thing.
JUDGE: Go right ahead.
90   HOGAN: For the second half, and this goes with that one other

thing that I gave you, this is the second half PIP calculation sheet, and you will see on there is no Diller and Macy
payout for the second half.

JUDGE: Anything else before we hear again from Mr. Webb?

95   HOGAN: No sir.

Rules versus Relationships

A comparison of the testimony of these two litigants reveals how a rule-oriented account articulates better with the agenda of the law. Despite the fact that small claims courts allow considerable leeway to litigants as to both the scope of the evidence and the manner in which it can be presented, judges must nonetheless adjudicate disputes within the bounds of the law. And although they often listen to a much broader range of issues than likely would be allowed in formal courts, informal court judges are not empowered to solve every problem arising out of the social relations of disgruntled people.

It is evident from even the brief excerpt of Rawls's testimony presented in Text 4.1 that she and Bennett have had a series of disagreements prior to the dispute that has brought them to court. The particulars of this case represent only some of their difficulties in getting along. Such a "story behind the story" is by no means unique to this case; nearly every case we have studied has a broader context than the specific issues which eventually make their way to court. The fact is, however, that some litigants limit their accounts in court to issues that fit well within the framework of the law while others do not choose or manage to do so. One might wonder whether Rawls is less concerned about the dispute over the hedge than finding a means of getting back at Bennett for the many injustices she feels he has done to her over the years.

By contrast, the testimony of Hogan in Text 4.2 is devoid of the details of her relationship with Webb, their respective relationships with the company, what Scientific Intruments is like as an employer, etc. She has limited her testimony to a specific issue—whether Scientific Instruments had a contractual obligation to pay a certain commission to Webb—and the details she introduces into her testimony are for the most part directed specifically to this issue. It is understandable why most lawyers and judges prefer witnesses like Hogan to those like Rawls. Hogan has presented a case that is relatively easy to examine within the limits of contract law, while Rawls has made a claim about expenses incurred in removing a hedge that is almost lost in a complex set of complaints against Bennett as a neighbor.

With some effort, the court might sift through Rawls's account for the legal issues that may be involved. But what can it do about "neighborliness" and social relations gone sour? The structure of an informal court may indeed allow Mrs. Rawls to "tell it to the judge," but what can he do about the larger issues that lie behind her specific claim?

It is also interesting to compare the two accounts at the level of speech style. In a previous program of research, we examined the speech styles of witnesses in formal court trials (O'Barr 1982; Conley et al. 1978). We distinguished between powerful and powerless speakers, and demonstrated that jurors found the latter group to be significantly less authoritative and credible than the former. Powerless speech is characterized by the frequent use of words and expressions that convey a lack of forcefulness in speaking. Among the specific features of this style are the abundant use of hedges (prefatory remarks such as "I think" and "It seems like"; appended remarks such as "you know"; and modifiers such as "kinda" and "sort of"); hesitation forms (words and sounds that carry no substantive meaning but only fill possible pauses in speech, such as "um" and "well"); polite forms (for example, the use of "sir," "ma'am," and "please"); question intonation (making a declarative statement with rising intonation so as to convey uncertainty); and intensifiers (for example, "very," "definitely," and "surely")—words that, although they normally increase the force of an assertion, may be so overused that they suggest that the speaker is not to be taken seriously in their absence. We also observed frequent instances of powerless speakers trying to use direct quotations in reporting the speech of others, although such efforts were usually frustrated by the invocation of the hearsay rule.

In her account in Text 4.1, Rawls—taking advantage of the absence of evidentiary restrictions in informal court—almost always uses the direct quotation form for reporting prior speech, whereas in Text 4.2, Hogan introduces only one direct quote into an account of similar length, otherwise paraphrasing prior speech. Also, Rawls peppers her account with the filler "well," whereas Hogan's account marches along briskly with few unnecessary words.

Observations such as these suggest that the rules-relationships continuum may be a discourse-level manifestation of the power-powerless continuum that we identified at the stylistic level. The discovery of this apparent connection raises the obvious and highly significant question of how the two phenomena are distributed. We return to this question in the conclusion of this chapter.

Conflicting Modes of Presenting Information: A Case Study

We next examine a single case, a landlord-tenant dispute, to illustrate what can happen in a confrontation between litigants from opposite ends of the rules-relationships continuum. The plaintiff (Broom) is a commercial landlord who owns a number of rental buildings; the defendant (Grumman) is a handyman and former tenant in one of the plaintiff's buildings. During the spring of 1986, Broom bought an industrial building in which Grumman had been renting a large room that he used as both a shop and his living quarters. In May 1986, the two signed a one-year lease. By May 1987, Grumman was behind in his rent and Broom evicted him. In this case, Broom is suing for back rent, late charges, cleaning costs, and the expenses associated with replacing a heating system that Grumman installed during his tenancy (it is unclear whether Grumman installed it before or after Broom bought the building). Grumman's position is that he does not owe the allegedly overdue rent, that he and Broom had an implicit agreement to give him credit for the value of the heating system he had installed, and that the space was in poor condition when he first occupied it.

Text 4.3 is an excerpt from Broom's testimony near the beginning of the trial. Prior to this point, the judge has summarized Broom's written complaint and Grumman's response to the complaint and has begun to ask Broom a series of specific questions about his case. In Text 4.3, Broom responds to the judge's questions concerning the calculation of damages and offers an explanation of his reasons for removing the furnace that Grumman had installed.

Text 4.3

JUDGE: Alright. Now several other questions can be answered
   this way, what are the arithmetic parts of your 487? How
   did you get there and why?
BROOM: May I submit this as a—
5 JUDGE: Come right ahead. Mark this likewise for the plaintiff.
   This being a letter of June 29, '87 addressed to the defendant and uh, citing certain statutes and uh, rental for May
   '87 at the 375 plus the 50 late charge. Is, does the lease
   contain a provision for a late charge in that amount?
10 BROOM: Yes sir, your, your attention is directed to a—
   JUDGE: A written-in portion about a third of the way down?
   BROOM: Yes, sir. I said, "Postmarked after the fifth, add $50."

JUDGE: Then you're looking for recouping those first four days of June—

15   BROOM: Yes sir.

JUDGE: —at the rate of 12.50 and, without going through the arithmetic process, is that based on a 30-day month into 375?

BROOM: Yes it is.

20   JUDGE: The next is to clean up, and that turns into a $185 amount, including a dumpster for 125, broken glass, debris, and uh, the labor.

BROOM: 35 for dog feces on the floor, sir.

JUDGE: Alright sir. So that added in brings you to 310.

25   BROOM: Yes.

JUDGE: Then we're just going over the arithmetic. We're gonna back up to the 185 item just a moment. And labor to remove unauthorized gas service you had installed, labor, materials that he installed[2] comes to 182. And then

30   deducting the deposit brings you to a 487 figure. Then let's back up to, where's the furnace at this date?

BROOM: It's, it's discarded, was put in the dumpster, sir. I had to remove the furnace because, uh, this is a, uh, I went over to the city of Parkwood and uh, did some further uh,

35   leg work on this. I have found this is a garage, it has a garage door. This is a, a garage repair type of facility, and when Mr., uh, Grumman moved in we had just installed prior, three months, ninety days prior to his taking uh, commune of that area, a new overhead hanging furnace

40   which is about oh, six feet above the floor and this was a 90,000 BTU furnace which is adequate to heat this thousand square feet. Now he removed that furnace and threw it in the back and I subsequently installed it in another area of the same building. It's working fine today. He had

45   a used house-type furnace that he put into this area and he uh, cut some ducts and ran some ducts down through the ceiling of this, of the leased area and put this furnace back in the back area. Could I, could I show you some

50   pictures perhaps?

[explanation of pictures]

BROOM: You see, uh, Your Honor, that type of furnace injects combustion air off the floor and—

JUDGE: The one that was installed by the defendant?

55   BROOM: Mr. Grumman.
       JUDGE: Alright.
       BROOM: And if, if he had called me and said, you know "Uh,
           Mr. Broom, can I take out your furnace and, your heating
           unit and put this in, that I obviously got left over from a
60   job?", I would have said, "No, because I don't want that
           kind of a heating unit in my building because if you have
           gasoline or volatile fumes or anything of that nature in
           these areas, those fumes can lie on the floor and be sucked
           into this furnace." Now it might be one chance in a thou-
65   sand, but I would rather have that furnace up in the air
           and it's my building and I certainly could decide what
           kind of heating I wanted. But instead without my permis-
           sion, he took my heater out and installed this, this house-
           type of furnace. Now I understand, I know that he's gonna
70   say, "You know, I incurred a lot of expense and time and
           labor and such as that to put this in." But my rebuttal is,
           "I didn't want that furnace and I don't think that uh. . . ."
           It cost me money then to, I had to go buy another heater.
           I hired some people to install the furnace. I had to first
75   take his furnace out, all the ducting and all the grills and
           everything, I got rid of that and then I had to install this
           overhead furnace at my expense.

Like Hogan in Text 4.2, this witness is oriented to the legal rules that he
believes are at issue. Both Broom and Hogan treat written contracts as
binding and minimize personal and social factors that might be claimed to
mitigate the effects of the contract. Although Broom represents himself, as
do most informal court litigants, the court can readily extract from the details he recounts a case that can be examined in the light of landlord-tenant
laws.

In Text 4.4, Grumman, the defendant, is given an opportunity to respond
to the case presented by the plaintiff. His approach is markedly different.
Instead of being oriented to the specifics of his written lease with the plaintiff, he presents a case that focuses on his own personal problems and the
consequent reasons why he did not pay the rent that the plaintiff alleges is
owed. The details of the lease are of relatively less concern to Grumman
than are the details of his relations with Broom and how these relations
bear on the manner in which he behaved in this dispute.

Text 4.4

JUDGE: Now as the defendant, of course, you have heard all
the statements so far. We have two exhibits which I believe you're familiar with. The copy of the lease and then
the copy of the June 29 letter and plaintiff had other ex-
5   hibits which the court and you have both had the benefit
of looking at, the photos that uh, were taken. Now of
course this is your opportunity to tell me what you think
I should know about this, and included in that, your reactions to what you've heard and then what is there about
10   this settlement that you rely upon. Why do you believe
that everything has been taken care of?[3]

GRUMMAN: Well, to start with, I didn't rent the building, lease
the building on the date that he stated. American Builders
uh, American Wood Products had the building leased and
15   I don't know where he was at, at the time I was looking
for a building. I leased the building from the other man at
a cheaper rate and a cheaper deposit. Because the roof
was leaking it had a dirt floor in the back and it had inadequate heat. It had a broken window and another one
20   cracked and the stool was leaking out the back of it and it
had two big piles of trash in the back of the building. After
I got it all cleaned up and everything—I'd just got it
cleaned up, and spent about two weeks moving—he
comes back, raises the rent, raises the deposit, and "You
25   can either take it or leave it."

JUDGE: Who did you have a lease with at that time?

GRUMMAN: His pre-, uh previous tenant, which was suppose
to have had a lease on it.

JUDGE: Did that previous tenant assign it over to you or how
30   did—

GRUMMAN: Yes he did.

JUDGE: Do you have a copy of that with you?

GRUMMAN: I don't, I can't find a copy, but I had one.

JUDGE: How long did that lease run?

35   GRUMMAN: For about—

JUDGE: American Wood Products lease?

GRUMMAN: I don't know when his lease run out.

JUDGE: Do you remember the date that you took over?

GRUMMAN: But uh, according to Mr Elrod, the man, that was
40   there with American Wood Products, he was suppose to

have had authority from Mr. Broom to lease the building
at what, at the same rate as what he had it for such and
he rented it for 200, uh $200 a month, more than what
he had been paying.

45   JUDGE: Then, first of May rolled around, of '86, and we have
before us what appears to be a business lease form, which
purports to have your signature on it. Did you then at that
time lease from the, uh, plaintiff in this case, Mr. Broom?

GRUMMAN: Yes, I did. Uh, I really had, I'd already moved into
50   it and didn't really have too much choice. I'd spent two
weeks plus fixing the roof.

[Judge examines letter from Broom to Grumman]

JUDGE: Well, it appears that whatever prior situation existed,
that it all terminated by a new agreement signed up on
55   May 1, '86 between yourself and the landlord and that
would put the rest whatever happened in the past.

GRUMMAN: Right.

JUDGE: Alright sir. Then carry forward from there, you uh, do
you disagree about moving out on the fourth of June?

60   GRUMMAN: I'm not through yet sir.

JUDGE: Well I, I realize that but uh, did you move out on the
fourth of June?

GRUMMAN: Yes I did.

JUDGE: And did you pay rent for the uh, month of May '87?

65   GRUMMAN: May, uh, no I did not. I used the deposit.

JUDGE: Alright, now you paid that at the time you signed the
lease?

GRUMMAN: That's correct.

JUDGE: Now then what else is there that I should know as to
70   why you don't believe you're obligated?

GRUMMAN: Okay here's a, here's another deal from Mr.
Broom, stating that, I took the hanging heater down and
set it in the back and had it setting back there so that
when I got ready to, to move I could rehang it 'cause the
75   only thing I moved was a piece of gas line. He was gonna
sue me if I took that furnace out of there and he took
pictures of it and everything. If I took it out of there he
was gonna to sue me. So then he finally decided to give
me credit for it.

80   BROOM: Could I see that?

JUDGE: You certainly can. Uh, go right ahead uh, Mr., uh, Grumman, we're still with you.

GRUMMAN: Okay I, that, I have another slip signed here from Mr. Elrod.

85 JUDGE: And what does this one, what does it do, say?

GRUMMAN: Well, what it conc-, that the windows were broken when I went into the building and the window was cracked, the stool was leaking and I also fixed the stool on the other side and ran a copper line to the other side,

90 which I never charged nobody for. I fixed the roof on the building, I fixed the roof on the shed back behind and I hauled all the trash off that was back behind the building.

JUDGE: Anything further sir?

GRUMMAN: Also my, at the time, he, when he served the three

95 day notice, I went to my attorney because I couldn't be out of there in three days and my attorney contacted his attorney and asked his attorney for me to stay the additional four days right there.

JUDGE: What was that deal?

100 GRUMMAN: That everything would be fine and use the deposit because he was doing nothing, he wasn't standing by and had men standing by. Brown's right next door was empty and he wasn't doing anything with that building either.

JUDGE: Was this deal uh, reduced to writing?

105 GRUMMAN: Beg your pardon?

JUDGE: Was this reduced to writing, the deal to stay until the fourth of June? Did the lawyers put anything down on paper?

GRUMMAN: No, they, I don't think they did. They had an

110 agreement between them. It cost me actually where I paid my attorney $200 for taking care of the matter, before this popped up.

JUDGE: Anything else you want me to know? Do you understand the nature of the claim, the plaintiff is seeking rent

115 for uh, the month of May, and uh, for the removal, installation, removal of your furnace, the installation of the, a replacement and then the uh, clean up cost of 185 and the late charge.

GRUMMAN: I understand it. But I mean when he, when he

120 offered to give me credit for that furnace and he took the other furnace that I took down, that I planned on reinstalling, at the time that I left.

JUDGE: What happened after this memo, which states, "I will
give you credit for the heater that you've installed as a
125   fixture"? What happened after that? Did anything get put
down in writing, other than that lease?

GRUMMAN: I've got another, sir, I've got another letter that I
cannot find where he was gonna sue me if I took the
heater out of the building.

130   GRUMMAN: Well this says, "As soon as possible. Let me hear
from you since time is getting short." This sounds as
though this memo was awaiting getting signed up on a
lease. Is that correct?

GRUMMAN: I don't recall at this point.

In Text 4.5, Broom responds to Grumman's testimony and the concerns
expressed in it. He draws the court's attention to his interpretation of the
dispute in terms of the lease and makes his case for the legal irrelevance of
Grumman's understandings, motives, and explanations.

Text 4.5

JUDGE: Come back to you in just a moment. Return at this
time to you uh sir, Mr. Broom. You've heard those statements and the production of the letter from American
Heating and Cooling, uh Herb Elrod that the defendant
5   has talked about, that states that uh, yes we did rent it
and this is always referred to as the cold room. Then sec-
ondly the memorandum that says that there will be a
credit for the heater and I've inquired as to where it went
from there and how much of a dollar amount was to be
10   extended as credit and all of that. What else should I learn
from you?

BROOM: Well sir, that was, was predicated on us for throwing
out the lease. And, and as he installed the heater, I wasn't
interested in it at that time. He didn't get back to me. Uh,
15   everytime I call him he doesn't return my calls. I would
like to just draw your attention sir to, uh I, I put this in
the lease because this has come up before in this business
and I'm sure you've heard this about 400 times but uh, I
said, "The 375 security deposit, not to be used as rent."
20   And I try to point that out to people when they sign these
leases. I say, "Now this security deposit is an apple and
rent is a banana and they, and you just, they don't mix."

And then I put a disclaimer in this also, this same lease
that Mr. Grumman signed. I said this is an old building. It
was built in 1947. I want to, I just want to get it so we're
talking. This is an old building, no representations as to
security, heating, cooling, etc., other than what is here
and now as of 1 May 1986. I put that in the lease, when
they signed that then that, I assume that they know the, I
said, I tell these people, "Read your lease, read that thing."
In other words I, I , what you see is what you get. This is
a, and then later on when they discover that it's cold or
it's uh, it uh, you know, it isn't exactly what they want,
then they can't come back and say, "Well, gee whiz, you
know, I thought it was this and that." Well I want to emphasize that what you bought, it was a cheap lease at, at
375, it's a $4.50 a square foot. It's 280,000 square feet of
stuff available in Lakewood you could have leased any
place and I would just say, "Did I use any coercion of any
type when I, when I asked you to sign the lease on 1 May,
1986? You, you read it and signed it, I, I certainly didn't
force it on you." And there's one other item that said that
in the same Bradford Lease, which is a standard business
lease that, "Uh, the uh, the tenant would not not make
any alterations or change in, upon or about such premises
without first obtaining the written consent of the landlord," and I found out that's very helpful to put because
many times a tenant will cut a hole in the wall and put in
a door and I've never seen a tenant yet that didn't put in
the most expensive mill work, $200 and $300 door and
he always put in Tiffany glass and they always, they do
these things, then after a couple of months it becomes an
obligation that they do, that the landlord should reward
them for doing all these great things that they've done to
the lease space and I, it's a communications problem I, I
recognize this, and I suppose the basis of this thing is that
I inherited this gentlemen because I was out of the country when he moved in and Herb Elrod had leased the
whole building. Herb had no right, in the same Bradford
Lease it said you can't sublease without permission of the
landlord. Then I came back and discovered that I had inherited this gentleman and I said, "Well, let Herb Elrod,"
and I, points in his letter said you don't have a legal right
to this property because Mr. Elrod did not have the right
to lease this thing to you. But really that's not germane to

what we're, we're discussing right now. We did have a
valid business lease and it was a period of one year. I did
not get the, the rent for May. Uh, I tried to follow the laws
as much as I posted my three-day, I received this letter
70   from Howard saying that he was going to leave on the
thirty-first, which he didn't quite make and he said he
wasn't gonna pay his rent. And I've heard that before,
you're gonna use security for a rent, and they can't do
that. That's an apple and the rent is a banana. . . . [*long*
75   *pause*] Uh, I don't which I need to amplify it's my building.
I should be able to decide what kind of rent, what kind of
heating system I want in it and I want the kind I feel is
the safest for my, for my uh investment and here is the
uniform build-, building code for Lakewood, which I
80   have, if I could show you that this is the reason that I don't
want that kind of heater in my building.

At the conclusion of Broom's rebuttal, the judge gave Grumman a brief
opportunity to conclude and then ruled in favor of the plaintiff, Broom,
adopting his argument in its entirety.

Texts 4.3–4.5 reveal several points of comparison between the relational
and rule-oriented modes of presenting cases. An important distinction is
the rule-oriented litigant's greater responsiveness to the judge's specific
questions. In Text 4.3, Broom's precision with reference to the amount of
damages suggests that he has anticipated such questions. He is able to itemize the damages and has brought pictures that he believes support his
claim. He has also prepared a detailed explanation of why he removed the
furnace the defendant had installed. His entire testimony has an aura of
precision and authority: it contains many quantitative references (lines
38–41: "ninety days, "six feet, "90,000 BTUs"); it suggests that careful
research preceded his coming to court (lines 33–35: "I went over to the city
of Parkwood and uh, did some further uh, leg work on this"); and it contains numerous legal- and technical-sounding words and phrases (lines
34–36: "city of Parkwood," "garage repair type of facility"; line 48: "leased
area"; line 62: "volatile fumes or anything of that nature"; line 72: "rebuttal").

In Text 4.4, by contrast, Grumman seldom provides direct or precise responses to the judge's questions. In response to an initial question about
why he believes the matter has been settled, he relates a lengthy account of
his relations with the prior landlord and the condition of the premises

when he moved in. When the judge pursues the issue of the prior landlord, the defendant is unable to say when the lease expired; when asked the date he moved in, he talks instead about the amount of rent he was charged. Later, when the judge asks him to summarize the contents of the note from Mr. Elrod, he begins to do so, but quickly digresses into a lengthy description of the work he performed. Note also that he lacks written evidence of either of the agreements on which he relies, the lease with the prior landlord (line 33: "I can't find a copy but I had one") and the "deal" arranged by his lawyer (lines 104–109: "Was this deal uh, reduced to writing?"; "Beg your pardon? . . . No. . . .").

These differences in the parties' ability to anticipate and respond to the judge's questions appear to reflect fundamental differences in the way that each has conceived of the dispute. Broom sees the problem in purely commercial and contractual terms. He contends that the relationship between Grumman and himself is governed entirely by a commercial document, the 1986 lease. As he argues in Text 4.5, many lay persons try to invoke everyday rules of social relations in such situations, but from a legal perspective the document renders such considerations irrelevant (lines 65–67: "But really that's not germane to what we're, we're discussing right now. We did have a valid business lease. . . .").

Grumman sees the dispute as a problem in social relations. At the start of the second segment of Text 4.4, he appears to accept Broom's analysis of the dispute (lines 54–57: ". . . it all terminated by a new agreement signed up on May 1, '86 between yourself and the landlord and that would put the rest whatever happened in the past." "Right."). Throughout Text 4.4., however, his primary emphasis is on the work he did in cleaning up the premises, the inherent unfairness of Broom coming in and raising the rent when he had nowhere else to go, and the fact that he paid a lawyer $200 to straighten out the situation. His position seems to be that the court cannot take the side of the landlord against a person who not only is in a dependent status but has gone out of his way to behave responsibly. To him, perhaps, such an argument is coherent and adequate; he seems unaware that the law's conception of the dispute might render his own conception irrelevant.

Throughout his presentation, Broom strives to impress his conception of the case on the judge. For example, at the beginning of Text 4.3, he directs the court's attention to specific provisions of the lease. When the judge asks narrow, businesslike questions about damages, he reinforces the court's approach by giving precise, businesslike answers. Finally, in Text 4.5, he makes an explicit comparison between the competing outlooks on the case, and denigrates the defendant's approach. By contrast, Grumman is unable to respond to Broom's imposition of a structure on the facts of the case. When the judge seeks to engage Grumman in the sort of focused dialogue that Broom has initiated, he fails to furnish appropriate answers. Then, when given open-ended opportunities to speak, he is unable to suggest an alternative structure of his own.

The law would have permitted the judge to evaluate the case in terms other than those suggested by Broom. For example, he could have considered whether Broom was unjustly enriched by Grumman's uncompensated work on the building, or whether an agreement to credit Grumman for some of the value he added to the premises could be inferred from the parties' conduct. Once Broom provides a familiar framework, however, the judge works entirely within it. Grumman's plea to probe the underlying social relations evokes no response. Thus, Broom seems to benefit from approaching the court as a limited-purpose institution which deals most readily with issues that are presented in a rule-oriented format. Conversely, Grumman seems disadvantaged by his implicit assumption that the court has the willingness and ability to impose solutions on broader social problems.

What is particularly interesting is that the way that each party deals with the dispute in court appears to mirror the way that he dealt with it as it occurred. Grumman ignored such technicalities as leases, he did what he thought was socially appropriate, and he expected others to do the same. Broom, by contrast, ignored Grumman's social expectations, and instead took care to define all the terms of their relationship in writing. The radically different accounts given at trial epitomize these equally different approaches to life.

The Social Distribution of Rule and Relational Orientations

By analyzing a single case that contains both relational and rule-oriented accounts, we emphasize that the distribution of the two approaches is not merely a function of the facts at issue but rather of the capabilities and proclivities of individual litigants. Because these approaches articulate so differently with the issues of concern to the courts, the question of their distribution in society is important.

We have observed many litigants who are strictly rule-oriented or relational in their approach, but we have also found many others who cannot be categorized easily. Many litigants may exhibit tendencies toward both approaches in a single account, or their approach may vary with the context in which the account is given. As a result of this variability, we characterize the rules-relationships distinction as a continuum rather than a dichotomy.

As we explain in more detail in Appendix I: A Note on Quantification, we have chosen not to attempt to describe the rules-relationships continuum quantitatively. Because of the nature of the phenomenon, the complexity of its distribution, and the difficulty of defining operational measures, we question whether quantification would be meaningful. We believe that it is more important at this point to concentrate on the development of the model. Nonetheless, we have given considerable thought to the question of distribution, and we believe that our observations support a number of inferences. In particular, we believe that the distribution of rule and relational orientations may be related to such factors as gender, class, and race.

With respect to gender, the parallels between our observations and the work of Gilligan (1982) are significant. Gilligan argues that as part of the childhood socialization process, girls learn to resolve moral dilemmas on the basis of feelings, relationships, and contextual factors, while boys emphasize impersonal principles. The male and female moral reasoning patterns that Gilligan describes are similar to the rule-oriented and relational approaches to disputes that we have observed.

We suspect a greater tendency among women to emphasize social relations over legal rules and a countervailing tendency among men to be oriented toward rules in preference to social considerations in their arguments to the court. However, our data also suggest that gender alone does not account for the distribution of the continuum. To underscore this, we chose Rawls and Hogan, both women, to illustrate the two approaches. We also chose Grumman and Broom, both men, to illustrate the consequences of a trial in which the opposing parties present their cases in the two different modes.

The complexity of the distribution can be explained in terms of social roles. The gender component of the rules-relationships distribution may be the result of differences in the socialization of males and females. Following Gilligan, we suspect that greater sensitivity to social concerns emerges from the primary socialization of females in our culture to be attentive to the web of social relations that is the fabric of domestic and everyday life. By contrast, male socialization commonly focuses on preparation for roles in public and business life where attention to rules predominates. Although these differences are typically inculcated early in life, women who assume roles that have traditionally been assigned to males (like Hogan, for example) can and do approach business matters from a rule-oriented perspective. Thus, the pattern we observe appears to derive initially from primary socialization but can be altered in response to later role experiences.

These differences are also a manifestation of class distinctions. Rule-orientation is typical of those who operate in the public and business spheres. It is clear that only some people are socialized into the segment of contemporary culture where contractual relations are the essence of daily activities. Hence, the greater tendency of business people, landlords, and professionals to approach the court with rule-orientation comes as no great surprise.

The social and political significance of the class factor can best be appreciated from the perspective of the critical legal studies movement. Critical legal scholars argue that law is the domain of a political and economic elite who manipulate indeterminate legal postulates in furtherance of their economic and ideological objectives. Under this view, rule-orientation could be characterized as an acquired skill which is the property of the literate and educated business and legal class. The mastery of rule-orientation is an instrument of class hegemony: the dominant class maintains its authority over those below it by seeing to it that legal and business affairs follow a system of logic that members of the subject classes have little opportunity to acquire. This system of control is both subtle and particularly effective because rule-oriented decision making has an appearance of strict neutrality. Thus, those whose relational orientation denies them access to legal and economic power derive false comfort from the illusion of a system that treats all people equally.

The factor of race may operate in a similar manner because it is still the case that disproportionate numbers of blacks in America are poor, under-educated, and relegated to occupations on the peripheries of economic and political power.

The distribution of the rule and relational orientations appears to parallel the distribution of powerful and powerless speech styles that we described in a previous program of research (O'Barr 1982, Conley et al. 1978). Our experimental research on speech style and its effects on legal decisionmakers demonstrated that powerless speakers are believed significantly less often than their powerful counterparts. We find a convergence of the tendencies toward the powerless speech style and the relational orientation, and a complementary convergence of rule-orientation and the absence of powerless stylistic features. Thus, it may be that the burden of stylistic pow-erlessness, which falls most heavily on women, minorities, the poor, and the uneducated, is compounded on the discourse level by the tendency among the same groups to organize their legal arguments around concerns that the courts are likely to treat as irrelevant.

5 The Jurisprudence of Informal Court Judges

The litigant voices that we analyzed in chapter 4 do not speak in a vacuum. Rather, each litigant's voice is juxtaposed with those of the opposing party and the judge. The Litigant's actions are in part a result of the cues, responses, and evaluations provided by the other parties to the interaction. In formal courts, where the dominant interaction is between lawyer and witness, the judge rarely speaks and generally does so only to resolve disputed points of law. By contrast, in informal courts, where litigants seldom bring lawyers or even consult them before coming to court, the judge must be simultaneously master of ceremonies, inquisitor, and referee. Accordingly, the vast majority of the discourse in informal court trials consists of interaction between the judge and the litigants and their witnesses.

In this chapter we examine courtroom discourse from the perspective of the informal court judge. The variability we have discovered even among the fourteen judges whose courts we studied is perhaps our most unexpected finding. It stands in marked contrast to the prevailing popular and legal views of the law as neutral, invariant, and consistently oriented around a set of legal principles. Indeed, our analysis of judges shows them to be even more diverse than the litigants. By paying detailed attention to the interactions of judges with litigants, we have identified five contrasting approaches to the judicial role. These approaches are distinguished by different conceptions of the legal process, beliefs about the mandate of judges within that process, and decision-making styles. The *strict adherent to the law* sees the judge as a passive conduit for the application of unyielding legal principles. The *lawmaker* considers the judge to be empowered to do whatever is necessary to reach fair results, even to the point of bending or inventing rules of law. The *authoritative judge* renders definitive judgments readily, but often presents them as based on the judge's personal opinion rather than the dictates of the law. The *mediator* attempts to avoid pronouncing judgment and instead uses the adjudicative process as a means for effecting compromise. The *proceduralist* purports to be concerned with simplifying procedure, but this concern often leads to an obsessive focus on procedural details that can distract litigants from the substance of a case.

The distinctions we identify among judges are based on the ethnographic study of what they say in court as they hear cases and announce their decisions to litigants. Since these remarks are made during interactions with litigants, the judges have far less opportunity to rationalize their decisions or disguise their methods of deciding cases than do formal court judges delivering written opinions after cases have ended. Thus, the questions, comments, and pronouncements of informal court judges constitute a nearly contemporaneous record of judicial reasoning and offer a rare and unique window on the underlying thought processes.[1]

SOME OBSERVATIONS ABOUT THE LINGUISTIC STRUCTURE OF JUDGMENTS

The portion of the trial that often gives the most succinct evidence about a judge's orientation is the rendering of judgment. This is not surprising, since in every practical sense it is the most important moment in the case. Informal court judges almost invariably render judgment as soon as the parties have finished presenting their evidence, with no delay for research or contemplation.[2] In contrast to the variability in general orientation among the judges, we find considerable regularity in the linguistic structure of their judgments.

Text 5.1 illustrates the four structural components present in many judgments.[3] First, the judge provides notice of the impending judgment. In formal courts, there are ritual means of giving notice of an impending verdict or judgment—for example, the bailiff's announcement that the jury is coming in, followed by the entrance of the jurors. In the absence of such rituals, the judge must use a more conversational strategy to end the testimony and warn the litigants that the pivotal point of the trial is at hand.[4]

Text 5.1

JUDGE: **[Notice]** Sir, **[Decision]** I'm gonna have to dismiss the case **[Explanation]** as grounds are there. The contract ended unless he told you he wanted it renewed. You have no grounds to renew it on your own. **[Advice]** You have
5   ten days. You may appeal it to district court.

Second, the judge announces the decision in the case. This might be viewed as a perfunctory task, but careful examination of the way in which judges perform it is revealing. Consider the question of how a judge addresses the litigants during the announcement and explanation phases of judgment. The judge could (1) speak about both parties in the third person (e.g., "The defendant will pay the plaintiff $50"), or (2) address one party in the second person and refer to the other in the third (e.g., "You will pay the plaintiff $50"). The first alternative conveys greater neutrality and thus might be expected in this context. We have found, however, that judges usually address their remarks in the judgment phase to one or another of the parties. Moreover, the judge usually addresses the "loser," in the sense of the party whose expectations are more frustrated by the judgment.[5] Thus, if the judge's decision is that the plaintiff recover nothing or only a token portion of what is sought, the judgment will be addressed to the plaintiff. In rendering judgments for plaintiffs, judges tend to address their remarks to the defendants.

Two interesting exceptions help to prove the rule. First, in one case discussed later (Text 5.3), a judge avoided deciding which party was more believable by splitting the judgment and awarding the plaintiff exactly half of the amount he sought. In announcing the judgment, the judge referred to both parties in the third person. Second, in rendering complex judgments that contain partial rulings in favor of each party, judges usually alternate addressing the parties, but are consistent in directing remarks that disadvantage either party to that party.[6]

After announcing the outcome the judge provides an explanation of the factual and legal reasoning underlying the judgment. With few exceptions, the judges we observed routinely offer rationales for the judgments reached, even though the laws of their states do not require them to do so. Legally trained judges and more knowledgeable lay judges may be influenced by the requirements of procedural rules applicable in formal courts[7] and structure their judgments according to those requirements. However, in providing to the losing parties the reasons behind their decisions, the judges are also conforming to the everyday conventions associated with the denial of requests.

A final component of the judgment is the giving of advice. The advice may consist of a suggestion to the loser about satisfying the judgment and clearing his name, information for a successful plaintiff about collecting the judgment, or, rarely, a personal comment. We suspect that judges offer advice more often and in more detail to parties with whom they have some common social and cultural background.

THE JURISPRUDENCE OF JUDGES: SOME DIFFERENCES IN APPROACH TO THE LAW

The Strict Adherent to the Law

The strict adherent views the law as a set of inflexible neutral principles. The judge's role is to ascertain what principles are relevant to a given situation and then to apply them straightforwardly. From the strict adherent's perspective, there is little room for discretion in the decision-making process. Rather, the judge must serve at times as an unwilling conduit for the nondiscretionary application of the abstract rules and principles that constitute the law.

Judge Alexander, whom we have chosen to illustrate the strict adherent, presides over the small claims court in a city of about 10,000 inhabitants. The volume of cases and the manner in which they are handled are such that the court is usually in session only one morning per week. The practice of scheduling cases at five minute intervals indicates the court's expectation that trials will ordinarily be of very short duration. In fact, the vast majority of cases brought before Judge Alexander are handled in a few minutes. Judge Alexander had been in office for two years at the time we observed her and is not a lawyer. Her only formal training consisted of a week-long introductory judges' training course given at a state university. Prior to her appointment, she worked in the same city as an assistant court clerk. During that time, she had made it her practice to sit with her predecessor and observe the working of the informal court.

Judge Alexander's conception of the nature of law and her role as a judge are exhibited in her method of rendering judgment. In Text 5.2, Judge Alexander awards a landlord a judgment for back rent and possession of the premises.

Text 5.2

JUDGE: Sir, *I don't have any choice but to go ahead with the judgment* that you be removed from the property and the plaintiff be put in possession of the property described in the complaint plus the plaintiff recover rent which is a
5   total of $432.47 through today, plus costs and interests being at eight percent until the judgment is paid. Sir, you've got until June the tenth. If you are not out of there by then and paid her some money, she can come up here and go through the next legal phase and try to collect the
10   money and try to have you moved out. [emphasis added]

In this judgment, Judge Alexander follows the pattern we noted earlier of addressing her remarks to the losing party, and the details of her remarks show attentiveness to the loser's interests. She conveys to the litigants the message that the outcome of the case is beyond her control. She carefully disclaims responsibility for the decision that she pronounces, attributing it instead to a force external to herself: the law.[8]

Viewed from the judge's own perspective, the disclaimer might be simply a statement of fact—she is indeed evicting the tenant because the law requires her to do so. Moreover, the disclaimer may help to achieve two related ends that the judge likely would view as salutary. First, by calling attention to her lack of control over the outcome, it may deflect away from her any hostility that the losing party may feel.[9] Second, the disclaimer emphasizes to both parties the power and neutrality of the law by reinforcing the notion of "a country of laws, not men."

From an analytic perspective, however, the disclaimer is far more than a simple statement of fact. Instead, it expresses a view about the nature of law and the role of judges in the legal process. To say "I don't have any choice about the outcome of the case" conveys the assertion that the law is a set of immutable principles and that the role of the judge is merely to select the applicable principle and then to announce the result that this process yields. Under this view, the legal process is dispassionate and value-neutral, relatively immune from manipulation by either astute litigants or strong judges. By contrast, much contemporary jurisprudence views judicial decision making as a complex interaction among such factors as malleable legal principles; the effectiveness of the parties' advocacy; and the ability, values, and predispositions of the decision maker. Thus, to the extent that Judge Alexander's approach to rendering judgment succeeds in deflecting hostility and in underscoring the solemnity of the law, it may do so at the cost of oversimplifying and even misrepresenting the legal process to the litigants. Ultimately, whether a particular view of the law is right or wrong is irrelevant to the larger point we seek to make in this chapter, namely, that differences in the attitudes and behaviors of judges affect litigants' perceptions of the legal system and, ultimately, their own attitudes toward it.

Another noteworthy aspect of Judge Alexander's judgmental rhetoric is her tendency to offer advice to the litigants. Her advice is of two sorts, legal and social. On the legal side, she often advises winners about procedures for collecting judgments and losers about their right to appeal and how to clear their record when they have satisfied the judgment. Occasionally, she goes beyond such technical matters to offer personal and social advice to losing parties. For example, in Text 5.2, she advises tenants who are in arrears on their rent about the likely possibility of their eviction and the need to find alternative housing.

Judge Alexander's advice giving has a strikingly self-contradictory quality. In tone, it impresses the hearer as sympathetic, but in content it is perfunctory and of little practical value. In giving advice in this fashion, she manifests the same attitude toward her judicial role as she does in disclaiming any personal responsibility for the judgments she renders. In each instance, she appears concerned about minimizing personal conflict with losing litigants, but her mechanical conception of her role precludes her from exercising any discretion to assist the litigants with whom she purports to sympathize.[10] Other judges with different conceptions of law and their place in the legal process behave very differently in comparable circumstances.

The Law Maker

A contrasting judicial approach is that of the judge who views the law not as a constraint, but as a resource. This type of judge renders judgments consistent with his or her sense of fairness and justice, even to the point of ignoring apparently applicable principles of law or inventing legal-sounding principles to fit the needs of particular cases. Such judges are not capricious in their attitude toward the law; indeed, the results they reach may be as predictable in their own way as those reached by strict adherents. What distinguishes them is their unabashed willingness to manipulate rules of law in pursuit of goals that they value more highly than respect for legal precedent.[11]

Judge Barkley, whom we choose to illustrate this approach, presides in a small claims court in a city of about 200,000 people. She has no formal legal education but has served as a judge for many years. She prides herself on being especially diligent in attending continuing education courses to keep abreast of legal developments, and her colleagues view her as particularly astute.

The judgment set out in Text 5.3 typifies Judge Barkley's approach to decision making. The case from which this excerpt is drawn was brought by a tenant against her former landlord who had withheld $24.02 from her security deposit after she moved out of the apartment. The landlord claimed that this amount was compensation for a damaged refrigerator tray; the tenant denied the damage. The sole contested issue was that of responsibility: did the tenant damage the tray? The only evidence of the value of the tray was that offered by the landlord. The tenant did not question or counter the landlord's statement that it cost $24.02 to replace the tray. Thus, only two judgments could be supported by the evidence: the tenant broke the tray and the landlord can keep all the withheld money; or the tenant did not break it and the landlord must return the money.

Text 5.3

JUDGE: Okay, Mr. Jenkins. The question before the court appears to be whether the refrigerator tray was damaged during Miss Dempsey's tenancy. She says that it was not. Um, Mr. Jenkins says that it was. He has charged her, um,
5   the total sum of $24.02, has shown the court that actually the parts cost $17.05. The $10 labor would have made it $27.06, somewhat larger than what he actually deducted from the security deposit. Listening to the case, I have to weigh the credibility of the witnesses. I have listened very
10   carefully. I have taken numerous notes. I would find that the credibility is, um, as believable on one part as on the other. There are pros and cons in each testimony. Therefore, I am going to split the judgment and say that Mr. Jenkins should pay the defendant, um, the plaintiff,
15   $12.01—that's exactly dividing the $24.02. That he should pay $12.01 plus the $19 for court costs. This is the judgment of the court.

In examining Text 5.3, note both the result that Judge Barkley reaches and the way she expresses it. Finding the testimony of the parties on the responsibility issue to be squarely contradictory, she avoids choosing between them by deciding "to split the judgment" and requiring the landlord to return half the money. The result is Solomonic, and undoubtedly would strike many lay people as eminently fair, but it is extralegal, because a damage award that is totally unsupported by the evidence could be reversed by an appellate court.

The manner in which the judgment is presented is as interesting as the result. First, the language Judge Barkley employs reflects the activism and assertiveness one would expect from a judge willing to impose ad hoc compromises.[12] Unlike Judge Alexander, she makes no effort to disclaim personal responsibility for the result. Instead, after stating the issue and recapitulating the parties' factual positions, she repeatedly emphasizes her responsibility for determining the facts (lines 8–12) and identifying and applying the relevant law (lines 12–17). She asserts her own responsibility for shaping the legal outcome. In her judgment, the law itself is portrayed not as a set of unyielding neutral principles, but rather as a malleable raw material to be employed in the pursuit of objectives defined without reference to legal rules.

Judge Barkley treats her decision as a straightforward, conventional legal judgment rather than an informal solution—which, of course, is what it is. For example, she begins and ends the judgment with such ritual legal phrases as "The question before the court . . ." (line 1) and "This is the judgment of the court." (lines 14–15). Her vocabulary and syntax are highly formal throughout the judgment. Perhaps most important, she states the compromise she imposes in terms that suggest derivation from a rule of law (line 13) and thereby mask its extralegal origins. The decision is thus presented to these litigants as "the law"—but it is a different law from that experienced by litigants in Judge Alexander's court.

In another judgment, Judge Barkley exhibits a subtler form of assertiveness. In Text 5.4, she renders judgment in a case brought by a man against his former fiancée. The plaintiff bought a suite of bedroom furniture which he placed in his fiancée's home in anticipation of their marriage. When they broke off the engagement, he asked for the return of the furniture. The fiancée refused, claiming that it was a gift.

Text 5.4

JUDGE: Alright, I've heard the case and am ready to render a judgment at this point. As far as the findings of fact is concerned, we know that, um, the plaintiff and the defendant, Rena Silver, were engaged to be married. We
5 know that the plaintiff put the bedroom suite in the mother's home, where his fiancée was living—whether they were actually engaged at the time or not—but it was placed in there. The subsequent result was that they did become engaged. The bedroom suite was relinquished;
10 the plaintiff took it back. So, at the onset, whether it was to be stored or whether it was a gift, it was removed and then replaced so whatever conversation took place on that replacement would have been significant. Now, in reality Ms. Silver has shown the court—I have evidence before
15 me—the bedroom suite is not paid for. So, he's not free to give it to anyone, because it is not yet paid for. It was not

20   his to give and still is not his to give. If he fails to make
payments on this bedroom suite, they are going to sue
him for nonpayment and for return of the bedroom suite,
because it's still collateral. It was not his to give. In consideration of all these things and the testimony I have heard,
I'm gonna render for the plaintiff return of the bedroom
suite, $23 court costs. The judgment stands as rendered.

Judge Barkley's resolution of the case is ingenious. A conventional legal
analysis would require her to decide the question of gift versus loan; this in
turn would call for an evaluation of which party was more believable. Instead, she finds a way simultaneously to ratify the end of the engagement
and to avoid commenting on the personal worth of the litigants. Her finding is essentially that since the man never acquired legal title to the furniture, he never had the power to transfer ownership to his fiancée. The result is not extralegal, but it is clearly creative. The furniture might be
covered by an installment sales agreement which prohibits its transfer,[13]
but the only evidence is that it was not fully paid for. It might also have
been bought with a credit card or some other type of unsecured credit,
which would mean that the man acquired legal title immediately.[14] Judge
Barkley is thus an active framer of the outcome at every level: she identifies
a legal principle that will avoid a delicate issue, and then shapes her hearing of the facts so that they articulate tolerably well with the chosen principle.

Once again, the form of the judgment reflects the same activism as its
content. At the outset, she assumes personal control over and responsibility
for the outcome (lines 1–2). She also concludes with a personal statement—"I'm gonna render" (line 22)—not "I'm gonna have to render," as
Judge Alexander might have said. And as in Text 5.3, she surrounds her
decision with an unmistakably legal aura. Note, for example, the abun-
dance of such legal expressions as "findings of fact" (line 2) and her formal
legal syntax. Judge Barkley's clear message is that the fruits of her creativity
are "law."[15]

The Mediator

In contrast to the law maker, who asserts authority by manipulating the substance of the law in pursuit of just ends, the mediator pursues
justice primarily through the manipulation of procedure. For such judges,
mediated settlements are an overriding objective. In almost every case, me-

diating judges seek to identify and recommend to the parties settlement strategies that avert judgments which, for the winners, might be difficult to enforce, and, for the losers, might exacerbate already difficult personal situations. Such efforts to avoid rendering judgments seem not to detract from the judge's authority; on the contrary, the striving for workable solutions conveys a subtle but powerful sense of authority and control.

Judge Caldwell, who represents this approach to judicial decision making, presides over a small claims court in a city of about 200,000 people. She is a lawyer who practiced for several years before becoming a judge. Her mediational approach is well illustrated by a case in which a woman has sued her sister over an unpaid debt. In Text 5.5, the defendant acknowledges the debt and then describes an arrangement she had previously made to pay it. In accord with her preference for mediated, consensual resolutions, Judge Caldwell pursues with the litigants the possibility of ratifying the prior arrangement as a formal settlement of the lawsuit. Her approach leads to a negotiated agreement that avoids the necessity for a judgment as long as the defendant makes the payments.

Text 5.5

DEFENDANT: I told her I was gonna pay her, right, and I just. . . . No, my son kept getting sick and I didn't have any other choice but to go to my son first. And I explained that deal and I told her that I was gonna pay her on dates,
5   but she did tell the truth about it, that, you know, I kept promising her the dates and, you know, how they weren't excuses. They was the truth. But, um, I had made prior arrangement with my mother to, you know, um, since my car is finished paying for, to pay her, um, $58 every
10   month, you know, but I can't afford—
JUDGE: Have you got, have you got any money to pay your sister today?
DEFENDANT: Well, I get paid today, and I get money out of the bank, and I pay my mother and my mother give it to her.
15   JUDGE: You'll pay her $58 today?
DEFENDANT: Uh hum.
JUDGE: Have it paid off in three months?
DEFENDANT: Uh hum.
JUDGE: Is that agreeable to you to let her pay it off in three
20   months?
PLAINTIFF: Uh huh.

JUDGE: Okay, how about if I put down today that your sister
is gonna make you a $58 payment today.

PLAINTIFF: Yeah.

25   JUDGE: And then I'll continue it again until sometime in July
for her to make another payment—

PLAINTIFF: Uh huh.

JUDGE: —and if she makes that payment, you call me and I'll
continue it again for the final payment. How's that?

30

[Judge calculates installments]

JUDGE: Okay, now write this date down. Um, I'm gonna put
down here that the defendant is going to pay $58 today
and a second payment of $58 on the $131 balance by July
11th. Alright, Ms. Williams—uh, this Ms. Williams [*indi-*

35   *cating plaintiff*], the plaintiff. If your sister doesn't make
the $58 payment today, you call down here next week,
alright? This is the magistrate's number, and then we'll
enter a judgment for $170 plus costs of court. All right,
you'll have to make that payment today to keep her from

40   having judgment rendered.

DEFENDANT: Okay, it's gonna be made today.

JUDGE: Now, if July 11th rolls around and your sister hasn't
made a second $58 payment, call down here and we'll
give you a judgment then for the balance plus costs, okay?

In acting as a mediator, Judge Caldwell assumes an extraordinary burden. Since the defendant has admitted the debt, the judge could simply enter judgment for the plaintiff and leave her to her own devices in collecting
it. Instead, she takes an active role in moving the parties toward an agreement, makes sure that both of them have ratified it, and volunteers herself
as collection agent.

Despite her preference for alternatives to immediate judgment in most of
the cases that come before her, Judge Caldwell does render authoritative
judgments when other efforts fail. For example, in a suit by a homeowner
to recover a downpayment from a contractor who failed to begin a construction project within a reasonable time, Judge Caldwell first continued
the case in order to allow the plaintiff to bring an additional witness to
testify about critical issues in the dispute. After hearing the new evidence
at a later date, she rendered the judgment in Text 5.6.

Text 5.6

JUDGE: Well, I'm gonna go ahead and rule on this matter. Mr. Trent [the defendant], I'm gonna find that the plaintiff has proven to me by preponderance of the evidence that, um, he rescinded his contract before you had begun your per-
5   formance. I think that's confirmed by the testimony of his neighbor and his wife that the timbers were not delivered until sometime late in November and not as you testified by November 13th. And since he told you and rescinded the contract prior to the time you took on work, because
10   you told him there was gonna be a delay in your ability to get to the job, then I'm gonna find that he's entitled to a refund of this $280 plus the cost of court.

This judgment reflects an outlook on the law more similar to that of the law maker than the strict adherent. Instead of trying to transfer responsibility to some external authority, Judge Caldwell makes it clear that the forthcoming judgment will be hers (line 1: "I'm gonna go ahead and rule on this matter."). When she explains her factual findings, she introduces them with the phrases "I'm gonna find" (line 2) and "I think" (line 5), which emphasize that purported facts achieve legal reality only through her intervention. Finally, she summarizes her reasoning and then announces the decision, using yet another prefatory phrase that calls attention to her role (line 11: "I'm gonna find").

In the excerpt in Text 5.7, Judge Caldwell further demonstrates her preference for negotiated settlements. In this case, the plaintiff is seeking a refund from an automobile paint shop because of what he claims to be shoddy workmanship. The paint did not begin to peel until months after the paint job was completed. In addition, the car had recently been involved in an accident, making the present condition of the paint irrelevant. Text 5.7 begins at the point in the trial when the parties have completed their testimony and Judge Caldwell begins to explore the possibilities for settlement. Her tactic is to preview for them what her judgment might be in the event that they fail to compromise.

Text 5.7

JUDGE: Well, Mr. Haynes [*the plaintiff*], I'd like to continue this case for sometime, for a couple of weeks, to g've you an opportunity to decide whether or not you're gonna

have the car repaired. [*lengthy pause*] I'm inclined to, uh,
5   allow City Body Shop to repaint the car and maybe give
you some type of damages if I see fit for the time that
you've had the car [*i.e., before the problems with the paint
job became apparent*]. But, I think that in a warranty situation like this, when the other party is willing to fulfill
10   their warranty, then I'm gonna give them the opportunity
to do so. . . . [H]e's willing to go ahead and proceed on
his warranty, then I don't think that's really a rejection. In
the light of that, I'd like to give him an opportunity to try
to correct the situation.

In response to the suggested settlement, the plaintiff continues to press
his demand for an immediate judgment that reimburses him for the paint
job and also recognizes the diminished value of his car. At the same time,
the defendant reiterates his offer to repaint it. Judge Caldwell finally aban-
dons the effort to effect a compromise and enters a judgment which, she
predicts, is not likely to please either side. The clear message of the judgment she renders in Text 5.8 is that parties who fail to reason with her do
so at their peril.

Text 5.8

JUDGE: I do not see where you are entitled to anything near
what you're asking for of $791. For one thing, I find that
the bodywork amounted to $267.07. The paint job you
got was $524.95. The, um, car you drove for about a year
5   before you ever made a complaint, and the warranty essentially terminated because of the wreck in May. So, if
you want to bring in more evidence of damages to go with
the testimony of your insurance agent, I'll be glad to give
you that opportunity and continue the case for a couple
10   of weeks. But, on what I've heard today, I will not award
you damages in any amount near $791.
PLAINTIFF: Well, Your Honor, I would like to put this matter
to rest. I don't want it dr-, drag it on for another couple of
weeks. Uh, will you make an award today for what you
15   deem to be fair and reasonable?
JUDGE: I can make an award today. Okay. Sure, I can do that.
DEFENDANT: Your honor, if I may—
JUDGE: Uh huh.
DEFENDANT: I have indicated that we will repaint the car. Uh,

20   I don't know we, why we should be held liable because
        the car supposedly is wrecked.
        JUDGE: I'm gonna give him a diminished value for what I feel
        like the paint job is worth during the time he was driving
        the car, or when his daughter was driving the car, prior to
25   the work. That's about all I can do. And I'll go ahead and
        do that today. And, um, I don't think either one of you
        are gonna be happy with it. But, um, if he wants a ruling
        today, I'll give it to him. I'm gonna find that, um, the paint
        job is guaranteed for approximately two years. And at the
30   time of the wreck, it had approximately six months left on
        the warranty. But I'm not gonna find that you are respon-
        sible for any warranty from that date forward. I'm gonna
        find that, uh, the plaintiff drove the car for approximately
        a year, without any problems certified in his warranty. He
35   took it in there the first time at about December, Decem-
        ber through May. You, uh, did not, I think, I feel like
        under the warranty he was given, you should have re-
        painted the car at that time and if you then decided in
        accordance with the warranty he was given and intro-
40   duced his considerate fee, then, uh, this probably would
        not be here today and that would have solved the matter.
        I'm finding he's entitled therefore to about a fourth of the
        value of the warranty, which I would put at about one-
        third, $131 plus costs. And if you all are dissatisifed with
45   that, you have a right to appeal it in District Court.

An interesting question is how the litigants perceive this sort of intervention by the judge. Judge Caldwell's behavior presumably conveys a different impression of the legal system than either the passive, "hands-off" approach of the strict adherents to the law or the ad hoc, but still legalistic
approach of the law makers. Litigants often come to informal courts seeking solutions to complex social problems. They go away frustrated when
they find out that the court is a limited-purpose institution which can deal
only with certain kinds of grievances and generally can provide only monetary relief.[16]

In Text 5.5, Judge Caldwell confronts a social problem thinly disguised
as a contract case and defers her legal resolution of the case in an effort to
resolve the underlying social issue. Indeed, her only explicit reference to
the law is a mild threat to enter judgment in the event of noncompliance
with the agreement. She thus provides these litigants with the very sort of

assistance that others seek but rarely receive. She thereby brings the operation of her court into conformance with a widespread lay model of civil justice as an all-purpose problem solving institution.

In meeting this pervasive lay expectation, Judge Caldwell may well be contributing to the satisfaction of the litigants who appear before her. However, in departing from the traditional model of the judge as passive adjudicator, mediating judges may be contributing to the public's misapprehension of civil justice and ultimate dissatisfaction with the way the legal process actually works in the vast majority of cases. Moreover, they may also be imposing their own cultural values on the litigants.

For example, in the case of the disputing sisters, it is clear that the sister who filed the case had already determined that the problem of collecting the money owed to her was beyond negotiation and serious enough to merit judicial resolution. In attempting to mediate a settlement, Judge Caldwell effectively told this litigant that the law was not for her. Although the specifics vary from case to case, a consistent issue arises in the judicial behavior of mediationally oriented judges: by diverting a case from the formal process of adjudication in order to defuse conflict, the judge may actually override the litigant's determination that courtroom confrontation is the more appropriate way to deal with the problem at hand. A judge acting in this way may substitute his or her own culturally based definition of "seriousness" for that of the litigants, at once denigrating their opinions and denying them access to the potential of the law. Thus, a mediating judge may enhance a litigant's sense of well-being at the expense of that litigant's ability to achieve tangible ends through legal means.

The Authoritative Decision Maker

Like the law makers and the mediators, authoritative decision makers emphasize their personal responsibility for decisions. In their actions, they resemble strict adherents in that they follow the law as they believe it to be. However, in communicating their judgments to the litigants, they give no indication that there is any source of legal authority beyond their personal opinions. In addition, such judges often express critical opinions about the in- and out-of-court behavior of the parties, making their approach frequently authoritarian as well as authoritative.

Judge Dexter, whom we choose to illustrate the authoritative decision maker, presides over an informal court located in a city of about 200,000 people. He is a law school graduate and member of the bar but has no experience in law practice. The excerpt in Text 5.9 is typical of Judge Dexter's judicial approach. The plaintiff in this case purchased a used refrigerator from the defendant, an appliance repairman. The plaintiff alleges that the refrigerator did not work properly and that the defendant failed to live up to his warranty obligation to repair or replace it within thirty days. Although the plaintiff eventually found someone to fix the refrigerator for $50, he is seeking $209 in damages, including refund of the price and the value of spoiled food.

Text 5.9

JUDGE: Okay, each of you can have your bills here. If you are not happy with the decision, you are welcome to appeal it. Uh, as far as I can tell, there's a breach of the warranty, uh, to, to repair it within thirty days and get it running
5   right. Uh, you are not entitled to $209 though. You are entitled to your damages and those are what it cost to get it working right since he wouldn't get it right. And that's $50 if you got somebody else out there—

DEFENDANT: I'm willing to pay it.
10 JUDGE: —and fix it.

PLAINTIFF: Your Honor—

JUDGE: If you're not happy with the decision, you can appeal it. You have a $50 bill there, uh, to have it repaired. It is working now, according to your wife. She says it's work-
15 ing now. I'm gonna award you $50 plus the $19 cost of court. You've got your refrigerator working fine now. Uh, that's my decision.

PLAINTIFF: We've also lost $60 worth of food in there.

JUDGE: Uh, I'm not—
20 PLAINTIFF'S WIFE: We were never told that.

JUDGE: Okay. I'm not satisfied that, that, uh, that, that is something that he should be responsible for at this point. Um, you know I think he's got a right to try to come out and fix it and if something there is wrong. But when
25 something goes wrong and you lose the food, that's not, I don't believe that's part of the guarantee. The guarantee is to come out and fix it. Your refrigerator can go wrong. A new one can go bad. Um, I'm gonna award you the $50 right here. I think you did the right thing by, by giving
30 him a chance and then going on and getting somebody else to fix it, to fix it properly. So, he owes you $69.

Several aspects of this judgment make interesting points of comparison with the other approaches to judicial decision making we have considered. First, Judge Dexter shows no interest in mediating this conflict. On the contrary, he prefaces the judgment by telling the parties that they can appeal if they are unhappy with the terms of his decision (lines 1–2). Even though the defendant interjects an offer of compromise (line 9) and the plaintiff attempts to complain about the amount of the damages (lines 11, 18), he is unresponsive to either.

Second, the judgment contains no reference to a body of law that guides Judge Dexter in his decision making. Rather, he emphasizes his personal responsibility for interpreting the terms of the warranty and evaluating the credibility and sufficiency of the evidence. When the plaintiff raises specific arguments about the adequacy of the damages, the judge responds in the first person (lines 19, 21–26), thereby personalizing the dispute between the plaintiff and the court.

Finally, Judge Dexter offers gratuitous, if favorable, assessments about the conduct of the plaintiff (lines 29–31). In doing so, the judge steps beyond the bounds of making a legal decision to evaluate and comment on the behavior of the litigants. Such commentary may on the surface appear to be similar to the advice offered by Judge Alexander in Text 5.2. However, unlike that given by Judge Alexander, this advice is not about dealing with the legal system but about how Judge Dexter believes that the people who bring their troubles to his court ought to reform their lives. This extralegal commentary is dramatically illustrated by Text 5.10, which is taken from an eviction action brought by a public housing authority against a young mother who is separated from her husband.

Text 5.10

DEFENDANT: Uh, the reason we have not paid the rent is because neither one of us is working. The apartment, uh, and we were not working. Uh, my husband found a job, um, about two and a half months ago at State Auto Sales.
5   And they are paid—you know, car salesmen—they are paid straight commission. Lenny worked two months and, eh, and had, you know, he had deals but they were all turned down because of the people's credit which meant he got no income. He got no pay. And he, you
10   know, he was working nine in the morning to nine at night and trying to support me and two, and three children and, and two babies. The babies are both under two

years of age. And so because he was not making any
money and he wasn't getting any income, he felt like he
15   needed to leave there, not to stay there for the purpose of
saying he had a job, you know, but because he needed to
provide for hisself and his family and he couldn't do it
with no income. I was working just part-time because of
my baby—the baby's only five months old. And I was just
20   working a little bit part-time, you know, to try to help out.
[*Baby cries at this point.*] But that wasn't working out too
well with the babysitter. You know, we were having problems with the babysitter. So I needed to be home with my
babies and so—
25   JUDGE: Okay, um, if the rent's not paid, they're entitled to
judgment for possession and the apartment and, uh,
$235.

[*Defendant makes an appeal based on extenuating personal circumstances, the representative of the housing authority testifies,*
30   *and the judge restates his original judgment only to have it challenged again by the defendant.*]

JUDGE: Judgment is for possession. $236 plus cost of court.
You need to get some help fast.
DEFENDANT: It's $221.
35   JUDGE: Plus $15 late fee. You need to get some help from
Social Services or Capital Opportunity so that you can
stay or move and find another place. Straighten out your
employment situation.
DEFENDANT: Well, I don't have any—
40   JUDGE: Straighten out the situation with your husband.
Either stay together, split up. Do something—
DEFENDANT: Mm hmm.
JUDGE: —and see if you can't stay there or move to some-
where else that you can afford.
45   DEFENDANT: Okay, Your Honor—
JUDGE: And make—
DEFENDANT: —but what am I supposed to do? I don't have
any money.
JUDGE: I suggest you then go see someone at Social Services.
50   DEFENDANT: But that's what I'm saying. They don't, they,
they, Social Services doesn't pay your rent for you.
JUDGE: They have been known to. And some of these
churches and charitable organizations—
DEFENDANT: No, they'll pay lighting. They'll pay your utility,

55   but they won't pay your rent. But if I don't have it, what am I supposed to do? If they want, they don't have it, if they don't have any . . . It's not, I ex-, I explained to her before the rent was even due that I didn't have any income. I was working only fifteen hours a week.

60   JUDGE: Well, do you want to know?

DEFENDANT: And my children needed me at home.

JUDGE: Ma'am, do you want to know what you're supposed to do?

DEFENDANT: Uh huh.

65   JUDGE: And you asked me, okay? Stop having kids, get out, and find a job.

DEFENDANT: I don't, I'm not having anymore. I—

JUDGE: Get somebody, get somebody that will take care of your kids for you and then talk to me.

70   DEFENDANT: Do you know how much daycare costs a week?

JUDGE: You're not gonna sit in here and tell me and complain to me that you can't pay your rent because your husband who you can't get along with and you married, okay—

DEFENDANT: Well that has—

75   JUDGE: —is, is, quit a job that was paying, that would support you. But you're not going to stay here for free.

DEFENDANT: I don't want to stay there for free.

JUDGE: Well, then go to one of these organizations that I suggested.

80   DEFENDANT: I just want my rent readjusted to my income. That's all.

JUDGE: Then go see them and get it adjusted.

DEFENDANT: She said, she sent me a letter yesterday saying they were gonna—

85   JUDGE: Then go to her, go to her or your counselor. But that's all for today. It's a judgment for possession.

DEFENDANT: God bless you!

This encounter is not an isolated instance for Judge Dexter.[17] He frequently tells defendants who have failed to pay their rent to pay up or move. In other cases, he reprimanded a defendant who claimed to have sent cash through the mail as a payment for his rent;[18] he instructed losing parties to keep their comments or complaints to themselves and to appeal if they were unhappy with his decisions;[19] and he told unsuccessful claimants that they ought to keep better records of their contracts and transactions.[20]

Authoritative judges present to litigants a different picture of the law and the legal process than judges with other approaches to legal decision making. Law-making and mediating judges also take personal responsibility for their decisions. But authoritative judges use their personal authority to emphasize the finality of their decisions and to suppress dissent, not in pursuit of compromise, and they are frequently authoritarian as well as authoritative. Moreover, "judgment" as rendered by the authoritative judge extends beyond the dispute being adjudicated to the personal problems, and sometimes the personal worth, of the litigants. As revealed to the litigants, the law is thus a more powerful, more arbitrary, and perhaps more threatening institution than it appears to be in the courts of other types of judges.

The Proceduralist

In contrast to the other approaches we have considered, the proceduralists, in apparent disregard of the theory of informal justice, place high priority on maintaining procedural regularity. These judges, all of whom are lawyers, invest substantial time in explaining procedure to litigants. They frequently make lengthy prefatory remarks at the opening of court and do not hesitate to point out procedural violations whenever they occur. Their rhetoric emphasizes informality as the essence of the procedure in their courts. However, their obsessive attention to procedure confuses and frustrates litigants who attempt to follow their instructions about the importance of informality. Proceduralist judges give less attention to substantive legal issues. Although they are explicit in claiming responsibility for their decisions, they rarely, if ever, interject themselves personally into cases by seeking to mediate or encouraging extralegal compromises.

To illustrate the proceduralists, we choose Judge Edwards, who hears small claims cases in a large metropolitan area. At the beginning of each three-hour court session, Judge Edwards collectively addresses the litigants whose cases will be called during the session. In introductory remarks that differ only slightly from session to session, he discusses the purpose of small claims courts and describes the procedures that will be followed. Text 5.11 is an example of such remarks.

Text 5.11

JUDGE: To begin with I usually have some opening remarks about our court and its differences, and our procedure, and such as that. Much of what I might ordinarily say perhaps does not apply today. Uh, and then again some of

5 you have been here before and you're already well familiar with those procedures. I might just briefly run by a few
things though that may be of importance or of interest to
you. We're not as formal as District Court and the procedural evidence and pleading rules do not apply here in a
10 strict fashion, but they do in District Court. Decisions that
are made here though are likewise enforceable, exactly
the same as District Court. There is no difference. We do
have lawyers once in a while as one of the parties. Otherwise presentations in this court are largely up to the lit-
15 igants themselves be they plaintiffs or defendants. That
process, of course, includes your testimony, perhaps witnesses, and also the use of possible exhibits. It's difficult to
underemphasize the importance of exhibits. Sometimes,
of course, one of those may control what happens in the
20 case. Basically an exhibit speaks for itself, provides a lot
of information that maybe we wouldn't otherwise learn.
Also our experience is that an exhibit sometimes is more
to the point and, uh, more specific than what people say
about the exhibit or the controversy. So you're encour-
25 aged to make use of it. Action is sometimes taken when
one or both of the parties are not here. That could be the
case this morning. That could raise some questions. The
absent party in small claims court does have a thirty-day
period to come in if they choose to do so, that is if they
30 want to. Explain why they couldn't make it today and at
the same time ask that whatever happened in their absence be turned around or set aside. If that is your case
and the other party is not here today and does choose to
file that request, the clerk of the court will let you know
35 by mail so that you'll have an opportunity to be here at
the time of the hearing. You can hear the reasons why the
party couldn't make it and you can consent, you can object, that's all up to you. Usually it takes a rather substantial reason. There could be others, of course—a death in
40 the family or hospitalization the day without knowing it
earlier today—something of that type would be considered as illustrations of possible basis for turning something around. There's no waiting period even though
there is that thirty-day period for the other party. Any
45 judgment can be immediately enforced when it's the result of a hearing or a judgment as a result of a default.

Clerk's office can help you take action on those judgments through those doors and to your left. There's limits to the kinds of help you'll get, however. It will not be legal ad-
50 vice. It'll be procedural advice—steps that you can take, the things that you can do now that you do have a judgment. Anyone who is unhappy with what happens here today, if you disagree, certainly it doesn't have to stop here. There are ways that you can appeal and the clerk's
55 office can explain all of those procedures to you as well. In contested matters we do not adopt or borrow what someone else may have already come up with as far as a solution is concerned. We are completely independent of what may have gone on elsewhere. Sometimes we're
60 urged to adopt the thinking of the Better Business Bureau or the insurance company, labor department, police officer at an accident scene. There are lots of dispute-resolving agencies. However, we are not bound by their decisions. We must independently probe into the merits of the claim.
65 While we do proceed informally, one qualification is that we're informal and at the same time orderly. We find that by doing so several things happen and they're all for the good. We get through a little sooner. By being informal and orderly, uh, each party has opportunity to hear what
70 the other one has to say. I get to hear it, of course, and at the conclusion perhaps there's a better basis for under-standing exactly what happened. Usually at the beginning first with the plaintiff over here on my right I'll have a few beginning questions. After a little bit we'll switch to the
75 defendant. Most of the time, not in every case, but most of the time we go back to each of the parties for a con-cluding statement. At that point, of course, you will have heard the other things from the other party, the statement of the other party. You may have thought of something
80 else. There could be some things that you'd like to em-phasize so you will have that opportunity more or less to rebut what's presented by the opposition. You may have other questions. If you do, don't hesitate to ask at any time. The procedural rules, the evidence rules do not ap-
85 ply in this court—as I stated—in a strict fashion but the rules of law do, same as district court. There is no differ-ence. With that we'll call the matters that we have before us at this session. The first being . . .

Judge Edwards's concern with procedure does not end with his introduction. As each trial progresses, Judge Edwards continues to remind litigants of the rules that apply to the presentation of their cases. In Text 5.12, he emphasizes one of these rules: the trial will follow a strictly adversarial model in which each party must present his or her own case, and the judge will not call witnesses or otherwise assist in any active manner.

Text 5.12

JUDGE: The witnesses can be seated until you're called or you can stay there [*i.e., standing with the litigants after the swearing in*]. I don't care whichever way you want to do it, sir. I recognize—I do not call—witnesses. If you want
5   them to testify, you call them at your time. Okay? Your case, sir.

Even such a basic and ostensibly simple principle can cause difficulties for litigants. As we demonstrate in chapter 7, many litigants come to court with serious misunderstandings about such fundamental matters as the adversarial nature of the civil justice system. One litigant spoke for many others when he said, a few days before his trial, "I'll just . . . answer . . . the judge's questions or whatever." As some of the texts in other chapters illustrate, many judges do take an active role in structuring the presentation of evidence. The proceduralists seek to avoid such a role, however, and, as Text 5.13 demonstrates, may become condescending or sarcastic when forced to come to the aid of a confused or unprepared litigant.

Text 5.13

DEFENDANT: Can I get a witn—
JUDGE: Sir, you can call anybody you want. I don't call. Remember?
WITNESS: I don't know how this works.
5   JUDGE: Your name, that's fine. Your name—
WITNESS: Excuse me?
JUDGE: Your name?
WITNESS: Carl Richardson.
DEFENDANT: Do I ask him questions or what?
10   JUDGE: If you want or I can just say, "What happened? Tell me what happened the other day." It'll be a lot easier on you, right?

DEFENDANT: Yeah, right.
JUDGE: Okay, tell me what happened.
15   : [*Witness gives his account at this point.*]

The judgments rendered by Judge Edwards and the other proceduralists tend to be more formulaic and less variable than those of judges in the other categories. As Text 5.14 illustrates, the key elements are: notice of impending judgment (line 1), recitation of the facts as the judge finds them (lines 2–15), brief announcement of the decision (lines 16–17), and a usually perfunctory statement about where to obtain help in executing the judgment (lines 17–18). Given the legal backgrounds of all of the proceduralists, the inclusion of these elements is predictable, since the Federal Rules of Civil Procedure and most state rules require explicit findings of fact leading up to appropriate conclusions of law in the written judgments of formal courts.[21]

Text 5.14

JUDGE: Court has listened to the testimony and the parties
and makes the following findings of fact. The plaintiff's
vehicle was struck by the defendant's vehicle and that, uh,
defendant's vehicle was negligent in the, uh, driving, and
5   that the plaintiff has met the burden of proof necessary for
the court to enter a judgment against the defendant and
the amount of damages totaling $741.31. And the court
is making that finding based upon the fact that from the
description of the accident as set forth by the defendant
10   and his witness that the, uh, door in the court's estima-
tion, the, would not have been damaged. It all would have
been at that stage of the game would have just been two
bumpers and looking at the repair bill here, shows the
effect that the left door was, uh, damaged in addition to
15   the bumpers and that is the basis of the court's decision.
Therefore, a judgment will enter in favor of the plaintiff
against the defendant for $741.31 and costs. If you'll step
outside, the clerks will tell you want to do next.

The extensive findings of fact underscore the importance of the judge's evaluation of the evidence to the outcome of the case. In this respect, the proceduralists' judgments are comparable to those of the law makers, the mediators, and the authoritative decision makers in that "facts" acquire meaning through the interpretive role of the judge. Several stylistic features of Text 5.14 contradict this suggestion of personal responsibility, however, by creating an impression of distance between the judge and the litigants.

The judge speaks not in the first person, but as "the court." He addresses neither party, but refers to both in the third person. In attributing fault, he conveys an impression of neutrality by describing events without reference to human agency as in the phrase the "defendant's vehicle was negligent" (line 4). Finally, in announcing the judgment, he says merely that "a judgment will enter" (line 16) rather than that he is entering judgment or even that the court is entering judgment.

Proceduralists convey to the litigants an impression of law and legal process significantly different from that conveyed by other types of judges. They present the substance of the law as flexible and outcomes as dependent on their discretion. But the source of this discretionary authority is remote and inaccessible—an impersonal "court" insulated by a wall of procedure and unwilling to interact directly with the parties.[22]

In observing and studying the proceduralists, we found that their insistence on procedural regularity is a source of great frustration to litigants, who sometimes lose sight of their substantive objectives in attempting to deal with the judge's concerns. Often, the problem was that the judge's procedural instructions and admonitions were incomprehensible without an understanding of such basic concepts as the adversarial nature of the civil justice system and the limited remedial power of the civil courts. Proceduralists assume this understanding to be part of basic cultural literacy, but it is not, even among the educated and business-wise. This assumption of shared knowledge about the power and limitations of the legal system is a source of frequent conflict between litigants and judges, and of litigant dissatisfaction with the system as a whole. We deal with some of the implications of this conflict in chapter 7.

THE JURISPRUDENCE OF JUDGES: RULES AND RELATIONSHIPS?

The extent of the variation in the decision-making process in informal courts is extraordinary, particularly in view of the fact that we studied only fourteen judges. Judges who theoretically apply the same law—and sometimes sit in adjacent courtrooms—dispense justice in radically different ways. Depending on the judge that a litigant draws, informal justice may mean mediation, enforced compromise, apologetic application of legal norms, authoritative decision making spiced with social commentary, or obsessive attention to points of procedure.

Our examination of what judges say in rendering on-the-spot judgments has revealed divergent conceptions of the judge's role and of the nature of legal decision making. Thus, strict adherents to the law, who rarely deviate from the straightforward application of legal rules, speak of a process in which they are at the mercy of unyielding principles. The law makers, who adapt or even invent rules of law in pursuit of justice as they see it, express themselves in terms that suggest that the law exists to serve their purposes, and not vice versa. The mediators, who treat the adjudicative process as simply an opportunity to effect compromises, put similar emphasis on their central and highly discretionary role in the system. The authoritative decision makers, who render definitive legal judgments and often involve themselves in the personal affairs of the litigants, speak in extraordinarily personal terms in exercising their authority. Finally, the proceduralists, who attend closely and sometimes obsessively to procedural details, paint a verbal picture of a legal decision maker who has discretionary power yet is protected from direct interaction with the litigants by several layers of legal formality. In each category, there is a clear parallel between judges' attitudes as revealed in their unrehearsed speech and their behavior on the bench.

An important question is whether this variation in judicial approaches can be explained in terms of the rules-relationships continuum that we discovered in our observations of litigants. A number of parallels are readily apparent. For example, the strict adherents display a strong rule-orientation, at least superficially. With such statements as "I have no choice, it's the way of the statute," they create an image of the judge as the servant of inflexible legal rules. Strict adherents are not oblivious to relational issues, as their occasional rendering of advice indicates. However, their statement of judgments in rule-oriented terms is almost invariant, even when they are palpably moved by the circumstances of a litigant. Moreover, they tend to respond readily and positively to arguments stated in terms of legal rules, even when the arguments are of dubious legal merit. Thus, to all appearances they epitomize a rule-oriented approach to legal decision making.

Although there are important differences between the authoritative decision makers and the strict adherents, these judges share a fundamental orientation toward legal rules over social relationships. Both types of judges state their judgments in terms of legal rules, but the manner in which they invoke rules differs substantially. Whereas the strict adherents speak of the law as an external force beyond their control, the authoritative decision makers imply that the law, while no less binding, takes on life only through their intervention. For the strict adherents, facts are facts, immutable and nonnegotiable. For the authoritative judges, facts are simply the outcome of the judge's sorting out of the conflicting accounts. Similarly, whereas the strict adherents convey the impression that the selection and application of legal principles is a mechanical process with a high degree of inevitability, the authoritative judges emphasize their discretionary power over the process. The result is that the authoritative judges appear as willing and active collaborators in the dominance of rules, not victims of it. This leaves no room for apologies for the often harsh effect of this dominance. Perhaps the best way to put it is that for strict adherents, rule-orientation is a role that duty requires them to assume. For authoritative judges, however, it is a way of looking at the world.

Nearer the other end of the rules-relationships continuum are the mediators, whose overriding concern is finding a compromise on any basis acceptable to both parties. Accordingly, when litigants present their problems in relational terms, mediators adopt the litigants' agendas in their search for common ground. Occasionally, when rule-oriented litigants have reached an impasse, a mediating judge will force them to rethink the problem in relational terms, as part of the ongoing search for a basis for compromise.

Mediating judges are not oblivious to rules, of course. When mediation fails, mediators may issue judgments that are highly authoritative in tone. Most interesting, however, is their use of rules to promote relational solutions. Recall, for example, Text 5.5, in which a mediating judge adumbrates the likely outcome if the parties refuse to compromise and she is forced into a rule-oriented posture. Such tactics lead to an unusual anomaly: while it is common for relational litigants to be frustrated by rule-oriented judges, in a mediator's court one may observe the unusual situation of a rule-oriented litigant coerced into accepting a relational outcome.

The law makers display an interesting blend of relational and rule-oriented tendencies. These judges are relationally oriented in the sense that they are willing to manipulate, ignore, or even invent legal rules in pursuit of relational objectives. It is significant, however, that even while they show little respect for the substance of legal rules, law-making judges evidence great concern for their form. Their judgments sound like legal pronouncements, not ad hoc, relational compromises. Their language style is highly legalistic, and the results are stated in terms of purported legal rules—recall "splitting the judgment." These tendencies appear to be the product of relationally oriented judges who nonetheless understand the power that inheres in rule-orientation. The law makers are thus hybrids, pursuing a relational agenda while recognizing and deferring, at least superficially, to the power of rules.

The proceduralists are qualitatively different from the other categories of judges we have documented. The others are predominantly rule-oriented or relational in the way that they achieve results. The proceduralists, by contrast, seem to view the legal process as an end in itself; the results that the process yields are almost an afterthought. The ethnographic investigation of their discourse suggests that they are oriented primarily toward maintaining procedural regularity as a means of creating distance between the court and the litigants.

The proceduralists are strongly rule-oriented in that they are constantly announcing rules and requiring the litigants to follow them. However, these are rules of courtroom behavior. They are not the rules for determining responsibility and allocating rights that we have been discussing in connection with the other judges. By contrast, proceduralists may convey an impression of largely unfettered judicial discretion when announcing their judgments. They tend not to state applicable legal rules explicitly, and they show little appreciation for the impact of their judgments on the litigants. Thus, while they flaunt the form of the law's rule-orientation, in confronting substantive issues they seem not so much rule-oriented or relational as simply uninterested.

Accounting for the Variation in Judicial Approaches to Decision Making

A final question is why particular judges take different approaches to legal decision making. We discussed the ontogeny of the rule and relational orientations among litigants in chapter 4 and argued that gender, class, race, and social experience are related to an individual's acquisition of one or the other outlook. Because the distinctions among judges are similar to the rules-relationship distinction, it is reasonable to suspect that some of the same factors affect the distribution of decision-making styles. A sample of fourteen judges is too small to support a statistical analysis of the distribution. Nonetheless, a comparison of the specific judges we chose to illustrate the various styles sheds some light on the question of distribution.[23]

Compare, for example, Judge Alexander, a strict adherent, and Judge Dexter, an authoritative decision maker. Judge Alexander is not a lawyer and has less legal experience than most judges we observed. We found that lack of legal training and experience correlate with the tendency to displace responsibility for decisions onto rules that are beyond the control of the decision maker. Such judges lack the legal acumen and resulting confidence to take more personal and creative approaches.

Judge Dexter contrasts with Judge Alexander in two important ways: Judge Dexter is male and has been trained as a lawyer. Hence, his pervasive rule-orientation is more expected. Judge Alexander is female, has a limited formal education, and, until recently, occupied the traditionally female role of assistant court clerk. Now, she finds herself in the more powerful, traditionally male role of judge. One might expect Judge Alexander to be a fundamentally relational person, but one who is in transition as she adjusts to her new role. This ambivalence is precisely what the linguistic evidence reflects: she drifts back and forth between acquiescing to the institutional demands of the law, as she perceives them, and following the conventions of everyday discourse in a relational world.[24] When faced with a decision, she gravitates toward the most readily available rule. Because of her inexperience, she may choose the wrong one, or may be overwhelmed by a legal-sounding argument that proposes a plausible rule. Because of her lack of confidence, she preempts or responds to complaints by bemoaning her lack of discretion. She does not entirely ignore relational issues however. Almost as an afterthought to her judgments, she offers perfunctory advice on mitigating the social impact of the judgments she believes the law requires her to render.

It is probably not coincidental that the judges who mediate most often are women. They issue rule-oriented judgments only when necessary. One of those we studied, Judge Caldwell, also tends to use the threat of an unfavorable rule-oriented judgment to coerce mediation. A possible interpretation is that the mediating judges derive their relational orientation from their primary socialization as females. Judge Caldwell, with her legal training and experience, has had considerably greater exposure to rule-orientation than Judge Alexander. For Judge Caldwell, however, this exposure has not resulted in rule-orientation superseding the relational one. Instead, she uses her facility with rule-oriented argumentation as a tool to promote the relational agenda that remains her primary concern.

Law makers display a mixture of rule- and relational orientations. They ignore the substance of rules in order to achieve relationally appropriate results, but present their judgments in a rule-oriented form. We lack sufficient examples even to speculate about any patterns in the distribution of this category and, for the present, cannot construct an adequate hypothesis to account for its ontogeny.

Among the judges we have studied, we find strong proceduralist tendencies exclusively among legally trained men. The impression conveyed is that these individuals began with no clear predeliction for either orientation, and then were exposed and attracted to the specific rule-orientation of the law. That exposure has not imbued them with the coherent world view that the law embodies, however. Instead, they focus obsessively on the form of the law to the exclusion of the substantive issues.

At this point in our research, we make two observations about the variation in judicial approaches to decision making. First, it is difficult to generalize because our sample of judges is small. We have described five approaches among the fourteen judges we have studied. We have further suggested that the rules-relationship distinction that we have found among litigants may be at the heart of the differences among judges as well. Further studies of these aspects of judicial behavior are needed to clarify the patterns of variation that exist among judges. Our present expectation is that a larger sample of judges would show even greater variation. This finding in turn would serve to strengthen our conclusion that the legal system is less a system than it is an inconsistent collection of varying styles and approaches to law.

Second, we have made some suggestions about the relation of judicial approaches to the gender and the legal background of judges. These must be taken as tentative suggestions rather than firm conclusions. These connections seem plausible to us because of what we have observed ethnographically and because of what is generally known about how gender and education are related in other contexts to important social and behavioral differences. Our evidence is laid out here before the reader who may disagree, draw different inferences, or conclude that even tentative suggestions about the social coordinates of variation in judicial approaches are premature. In any event, firm conclusions about the significance for judicial decision making of gender and legal education as well as other factors such as race and social class background await further study.

CONCLUSION: THE NEXT QUESTION

In this chapter we have attempted to dismantle the stereotype of "the judge" as impassive arbiter. We have shown that informal court judges are highly variable in their conceptions of law, their views of their role, and their approaches to problem solving. Much of this variation can be explained in terms of the rules-relationships continuum we developed in reference to litigants.

The next question is, what happens when judges and litigants interact? More specifically, what is the nature of the interactions between judges and litigants with similar orientations, or with varying degrees of differences in their orientations? These interactions are complex, and their study yields many significant insights into the nature of law and the legal system. In the next three chapters, we address several aspects of the issue of interaction.

6 Concordant Orientations

The "legal system" consists of innumerable encounters of competing litigants with each other and with the judges who preside over their cases. Accordingly, understanding the dynamics of these interactions is essential to understanding the nature of the system. As we saw in chapter 4, litigants are highly variable. In particular, their orientation toward life and law varies along a rules-relationships continuum. We also saw that in contests between relational and rule-oriented litigants, the latter usually enjoy an inherent advantage because their orientation articulates better with the "official" orientation of the law. However, as the evidence in chapter 5 has also demonstrated, the law is itself variable. In chapter 5, we proposed five categories of judges based on differences in their approach to legal decision making. We argued that, except for the proceduralists, the judges—like litigants—tend toward rule- or relational orientations. Further, we suggested that judges' orientations are not fixed, but may shift in response to differences in case substance, litigants' orientations, and other factors.

Given the variability we have discovered among both litigants and judges, the first step in exploring the dynamics of the system must be to examine the interaction of orientations. Specifically, what happens when a judge with a particular orientation interacts with a litigant of similar or different orientation? Although most cases involve more than a single one-on-one interaction, and the introduction of each new actor adds new complexities, the encounters between individual litigants and judges are the fundamental building blocks of the system.

When a judge interacts with a litigant, there are four logical possibilities: (1) both judge and litigant are rule-oriented; (2) both judge and litigant are relational; (3) the judge is rule-oriented and the litigant is relational; and (4) the judge is relational and the litigant is rule-oriented.[1] In this chapter we consider possibilities (1) and (2), where there is concord between the orientations of judge and litigant. We begin with the simplest kind of encounter, in which a rule-oriented litigant interacts with a rule-oriented judge. We then illustrate the relatively rare situation of concord between relational judges and relational litigants.

EASY CASES: RULE-ORIENTED LITIGANTS AND JUDGES

Rule-rule concord occurs most often in the simplest and least controversial civil cases, those in which a rule-oriented plaintiff presents a rule-oriented judge with a claim that is legally unassailable. The judge is able to assign the case to a legal category easily (e.g., contract, tort, etc.). Text 6.1, from a bill collection suit brought by a hospital, is typical of such cases.

Text 6.1

HOSPITAL REPRESENTATIVE: Okay, Your Honor, on September 6, 1987, Carlton M. Webb was admitted to the hospital for services, received services in the amount of $4628.05. His insurance paid all but $940.60. We've had no payment
5   from Mr. Webb. We request judgment in the amount of $940.60 principal with $48.60 in interest, leaving a balance of $989.20.
JUDGE: Mr. Webb, does that amount sound right to you?
WEBB: Yes.
10   JUDGE: Are you working anywhere where you may be able to go over there and set up some kind of payment schedule with them?
WEBB: I'm still unemployed. I've been unemployed ever since November '87.
15   JUDGE: Alright sir, I'm gonna have to go ahead with the judgment. It's $989.20 plus court costs—$14—and interest from today until the judgment is paid. Sir, as soon as you can, you can go up there and try to set up some kind of payment schedule with them and get this thing paid. If
20   you have not worked out something with them by June 10, they legally could come up here and go through the next legal phase to try to collect the money.

The account given by the hospital representative in Text 6.1 articulates easily with the rule-oriented agenda of the law. The account provides the judge with the information she needs to decide the case: a claim that services were rendered, the dates of the services, the value of the services, the amount of partial payment, the balance due, and the accrued interest. Each item of information is specifically identified, and the account contains no other extraneous information.

The fact that this information is easily processed by the judge is reflected in the highly specific question she poses to the defendant (line 8). Rather than inviting him to give his side or comment on the plaintiff's evidence, she offers him the limited opportunity to challenge the accuracy of the hospital's calculations. When he declines to do so, she enters the requested judgment (lines 15–17), digressing briefly to show solicitude for Webb's financial plight (lines 10–12).[2]

A lawyer might characterize this case as merely an instance of the law working as it should: the hospital is clearly entitled to relief, and it gets what it deserves with a minimum of wasted effort. However, it is important to note that the plaintiff's agenda articulates with the court's in two distinct senses. The hospital's case is noncontroversial in a legal sense because the hospital can show all of the elements of a contractual claim for services rendered, and Webb offers no defense. Moreover, the law gives the judge no alternative to rendering judgment for the hospital in the amount claimed.

It is also a straightforward case from the perspective of discourse. Not only is all the requisite evidence present, but it is packaged to articulate with the rule-oriented discourse of the law. This packaging may be of limited significance in this case, where the dictates of the law are straightforward and the defendant presents no defense. However, both types of fit—with the substance and the discourse of the law—are conceptually distinct,[3] a point that takes on practical significance in more complex cases.

More Elaborated Cases: Relational Litigants and Judges

Even though defendants often advance relational arguments, judges tend to be oblivious to them, to ignore them, or to dismiss them as irrelevant. Sometimes, however, a judge responds to a relational defendant on a relational level. This development may not alter the legal outcome of the case, but it usually has a powerful effect on the discourse that ensues and on the litigant's encounter with the legal system.

Another case illustrates this type of concord. The case is unusual because the defendant, a law school graduate who has been unable to pass the bar exam, displays a grasp of both the substance of the law and the structure of legal discourse. Nonetheless, his orientation is fundamentally relational, and it is on this level that he ultimately engages the attention of the judge.

The plaintiff in this case is the rental agent of a landlord. She seeks to evict the tenant, Evans, from his apartment and to collect overdue rent. In Text 6.2, the agent states her case in a rule-oriented form that the judge can readily grasp.

Text 6.2

JUDGE: At this particular time the court—Metropolitan Real
Estate, if you want to state to the court the reason this
action's been brought against Mr. Evans?

AGENT: We are requesting, uh, possession and payment of the
5   amounts owed in rent from Mr. Evans which has exceeded the amount that this court has authority to deal
with at this particular time,[4] but, uh, the, um, clients we
represent feel that they've waited long enough for Mr. Evans to pay and are asking for both a judgment for and
10   possession of the unit. He is and has been for the last three
years behind in his rent but it's become even more critical
in the last eight months because of his unemployment.
And we have worked with him to the extent that we
could, but we have reached the point where there is noth-
15   ing that we can do.[5]

In Text 6.3, when the judge invites him to respond, Evans offers a relational account of the larger problem behind his failure to pay the rent.[6]
Interestingly, he acknowledges that this information is irrelevant to the
law's agenda, but offers it anyway because it makes him "feel better."

Text 6.3

JUDGE: Okay, Mr. Evans, do you have any statement at this
time concerning this matter?[7]

EVANS: The only statements, uh, that I, uh, could make is
that, uh, I don't think that I owe $1500 which is the ju-
5   risdiction of this court. It's over 1,000, I think a little less
than 1500.

AGENT: Well, I can give you exact—

EVANS: Good, I would like to itemize.

AGENT: I'm sorry, that, it's, uh, 1373.

10 EVANS: Okay, well, okay, like I say, I thought it was less than
the jurisdiction. Okay. Alright. Uh, another thing, uh, like
to say that I appreciate all that she's done in addition to
the, uh, the owner of the property at will, uh, you know,
given my set of circumstances. Uh, she happened to know
15   something was very seriously wrong back when my rent
started falling behind. Uh, and, uh, asked me to confer
with her, you know, on some regular basis, in fact to keep
advising her as to what I was really out here trying to do

in order to get a job. And it's for that reason, you know,
20   that she went along with it, you know, and, uh, this sort
of thing. And she was still prepared to go along with my
latest prospects for a position in that, uh, as I understand
it they were going to allow me to, uh, get a job—job
which I was up for, uh, and expected to get it like I have
25   expected others in the past. I have been nominated for a
criminal magistrate position five separate times by Judge
Leonard Karl over the last eighteen months. I have received the, uh, backing of some of the city bar committee,
from the dean of the law school, from uh, uh, other prom-
30   inent members of the community and for that reason I am
really baffled as to why I can't even get one of those jobs.
But I also want to say that I haven't limited myself, you
know, to just finding a magistrate's job. I've applied for
security guard at, uh, Bladen Chemical, get no response.
35   I don't have a criminal record. Some of these matters I'm
mentioning now, you know, are irrelevant toward the
payment of rent, you know, and, positions, talked what I
felt like was harder to get this out, you know, at least to
make me feel better, in terms of knowing that I have done
40   the best I could with this problem, you know. Uh, my
wife, uh, brings home something like $480 a month after
things have come out for, uh, the credit union thing and,
uh, out of that I would estimate about twenty-five per
cent of that take-home pay goes toward medical treat-
45   ments for asthmatic problems and for the prescriptions.
And so what she—[*Judge is briefly interrupted by a matter
not related to this case*]—I got to say, uh, what she's, uh,
done is try to get me to pay some rent, uh, with, uh, you
know, what, what could come up with in addition to, uh,
50   provide the other absolute basics like food and utilities,
the gasoline for transportation, things like that. Uh, I've
been, uh, working, uh, for the most part as substitute
teacher over the last, uh, two years. But, uh, you know,
uh, you're not going to be able to pay eight, nine, thou-
55   sand dollars a month bills out of $165, you know, just
can't do it, do the best you can, and, uh, that's, that's,
that's what I, that's where we stand.[8]

At this point in his account, Evans raises the possibility of a compromise,
suggesting that the entry of judgment be deferred to give him one last

chance to raise some money (Text 6.4). In a brief response to this proposal, the judge exhibits a relational orientation. As is her custom, she invites the plaintiff to mediate the issue (lines 19–20) and negotiations begin (line 21).

Text 6.4

EVANS: Uh, I'd like to make one request. Uh, is there some way that we and they can, uh, uh, arrest a judgment or continue judgment to allow me until Friday to come, to try to make one last effort and that's before this month is
5   out. July 1 comes in on Sunday. To allow me to see if I can get some people whose paydays come this weekend. Don't know how much, I have no idea, it depends upon, you know, who I can get together and, uh, you know, try to come up with something. That's my only other pros-
10   pects at this time. [*Long pause.*] I try to keep, uh, judgments off me as much as I can in any way, and I have since 1977 [*inaudible*] then. And the reason I'm trying to keep judgments away from me is that it could have some adverse effect on me being hired, you know, with the state
15   or in a position sim-, as well as with the county and other things that I want to take the bar exam one more time. Uh, uh, I want to, I want to give it one more crack. So that's why I made that request.

JUDGE: Okay. Metropolitan Real Estate, you want to respond
20   to that?

AGENT: Yeah, I don't have any authority to request any further, uh, extension or continuance, uh, I've been told what I have to do, and, uh, the only thing that, that I could think of is that if, should you grant the judgment
25   we'd still have another ten-day period, uh, you know, in which we have the right to make some decision and maybe something will happen within that ten-day period. I, I mean it's a matter of me either losing my, yeah, and that, I mean, this is a fairly—

30   EVANS: Do you suppose—

AGENT: It's not just a one-unit deal, and it—

EVANS: Do you suppose if we contact her and explain to her the reason why I would, uh, request a judgment not be entered at this time?

35   AGENT: I don't think it will do any good because she got angry with me for putting it off until today.

EVANS: Okay.
AGENT: So I'm, you know, I just don't, I, I'll, will say this that
should, uh, we get judgment I'm not going to execute it
40   until she advises me to do so. I mean that's all I can do. I,
I, I sympathize with you.
EVANS: I understand.
AGENT: If there were anything I could do, but I have an obligation to carry out.
45   EVANS: Well, I'm not going, bitter, you know, and, uh, uh, uh,
angry or anything like that, I'm just only trying to, uh,
find some way, you know, to, uh, uh, keep [*inaudible*] if
at all possible.
AGENT: I understand that, which is why I called, uh, the mag-
50   istrate and asked her to defer it until today, but then I got
in trouble for doing that.

At this point the judge suggests several social agencies that Evans might contact for assistance. Then she finally enters the judgment requested by the plaintiff (Text 6.5).

Text 6.5

JUDGE: Okay. As much as I would prefer not doing this, um,
I will have to enter a judgment, you know, for posses-
sion—
EVANS: I understand.
5   JUDGE: —as well as $1,000.
EVANS: Nothing I can do, nothing I can do about that.

From a legal perspective, this case is identical to the hospital bill collection case discussed earlier in this chapter (Text 6.1). In both cases, the plaintiff presents a sound legal claim in a rule-oriented format, and there is a precise legal fit between the plaintiff's presentation and the court's agenda. The defendant offers no effective legal defense, and the judge readily comprehends the plaintiff's unassailable position and enters the judgment sought.

Despite its legal similarity to the bill collection case, this case unfolds differently in court. Whereas the first trial was perfunctory, this one is filled with drama. All of the participants are put through a lengthy process of examination of their conduct and motives. The real estate agent is forced to confront the social consequences of her business. The judge must come to terms with the human impact of the law. The defendant finds no practical solution for his troubles, but is ultimately reconciled with his antagonists. Because of their willingness to listen to a story that he acknowledges to be "irrelevant toward the payment of rent," he is neither "bitter" nor "angry or anything like that." He is able to say to both the judge and the agent, "I understand."

What is it that causes this routine eviction case to evolve along such an elaborate pathway? The answer lies in the judge's orientation and its articulation with the defendant's. A strictly rule-oriented judge probably would have interrupted Evans's relational account with specific questions about his ability to pay the rent and moved more quickly to enter a judgment. Such a trial might have looked more like the earlier one. Here, however, notwithstanding the ongoing legal dissonance between Evans and the judge, the similarity of their orientations leads them to deviate from conventional patterns of courtroom interaction.

This judge displays a relational orientation in two ways. First, she permits Evans to give a lengthy and emotional account of his personal dilemma. Second, she invites the real estate agent to participate in her effort to mediate a solution, which requires dealing with Evans's situation relationally. The defendant's lack of legal fit is never overcome, however. The mediation is unsuccessful, and the judge ultimately reaches the decision that the law compels her to make. But because of the concordant orientations of the judge and the defendant, the law has a different face. Although it cannot provide a concrete solution for Evans's problem, it is presented as an institution that is attentive to human needs. For all concerned, the trial has been a different experience from what it would have been if the judge had been oriented only to legal rules.

An additional case further illustrates how relational concord can influence the legal outcome of a case as well as the quality of the litigant's encounter with the legal system. The plaintiff, Mrs. McCall, has been renting an apartment to the defendants, Mr. and Mrs. Ridley. She is suing for two months' overdue rent plus late charges. Mrs. McCall began the testimony in the trial with a rule-oriented account which included a precise statement of the amount she claims. In Text 6.6, Mr. and Mrs. Ridley respond with relational accounts that implicitly admit the debt and focus on the reasons for their failure to pay.

Text 6.6

JUDGE: Just want to tell your side? Okay, go ahead.
MRS. RIDLEY: Okay, well, when I first moved into the apart-

ment, I had recently got married and my husband was not
living with me. And so I was late paying my rent then.
5   Then a couple of months, I told her that my, my husband
is in the County Detention Center, and, and at that point
I was paying all the bills. I had everything. I told her when
he went on work release, I will send her a check around
the twentieth, that's when I will get a check from him,
10   around the twentieth of every month. That's why my rent
was late. And when my husband got out, he went in business for himself and business, business, business been
kind of slow. I still had most of the bills myself to pay. So
I will pay it whenever I could. But, before we received
15   this, um, paper, my husband talked to her husband about
why we were late with our rent. And he told that, you
know, to pay him whatever he could. He wrote it down or
whatever. My husband was with him. And it was—
JUDGE: You want to testify sir?[9]
20   MR. RIDLEY: Yes ma'am. Um, like I, I got out of, out of prison
in October, and, um, I went in January, went into my own
business. And, um, I'm in the same, you know, type business that, um, her husband is in. So lot of time, you know,
we, you know, we talk, you know, and he tells me, told
25   me, you know, how business is up, sometimes it's up,
sometimes it's down. And, um, during the month of April
and May it was kind of like, uh, you know, pretty, pretty,
uh pretty rough month. And I had to, you know, take
some of my, my money and you know, pay my employees
30   off and it kind of threw me way behind. So, um, I went to
Mr. McCall and I explained to him and he told me, he
said, "Well, look, um, if you can bring this amount up
next week and then, you know, from now on we'll just,
you know, you, you pay a certain amount until you get it
35   caught up." And he took and wrote it down on a piece of
paper. I signed it and he put it in the little box. And then
I don't—and then about three days later, you know, that's
when we got the summons to come in court. Now, um,
we've been behind before, and, uh . . .

The account that Mr. and Mrs. Ridley jointly produce in Text 6.6 has
three principal elements. First, Mrs. Ridley describes the compelling personal and economic circumstances that made them unable to pay the rent.
Second, she suggests that Mr. and Mrs. McCall, because of past forbear-

ance, are obligated to tolerate the current failure to pay the rent as well. Third, Mr. Ridley reinforces points one and two, and then makes the specific claim that he and Mr. McCall executed a written agreement to extend the time for payment. (Mrs. McCall subsequently denied any knowledge of this agreement, and Mr. Ridley could not produce it.) Each of these elements reflects a relational perspective on the underlying problem, as well as the expectation that relational matters will be significant to the court. None represents a legally adequate defense to the claim of nonpayment of rent.[10] Nonetheless, the account attracts the attention of the relationally-oriented judge, who mediates a compromise (Text 6.7). However, to enforce the agreement she effects, she uses the rule-oriented devices of setting up a payment schedule, continuing the trial until later in the month, and announcing that if the rent has been paid by the specified date she will dismiss the case, but if not, she will enter judgment for the plaintiff.

Text 6.7

JUDGE: Well, are you willing to take their money and continue it? When could you pay it off? When are you gonna have June's rent?

MR. RIDLEY: I can, um—see, what I've done—uh, my busi-
5   ness had got so slow until I had, I had five employees. I had to lay practically all of them off and things had dropped down 'til, you know, I just decided to let my business go and I went to work, uh, started Wednesday, you know, for another builder, um, you know, making a reg-
10   ular salary at $8 an hour. I just started Wednesday and, um, you know, it wouldn't be that much of a problem to get caught up.

JUDGE: When could you pay June's rent?[11]

MR. RIDLEY: I could pay it, um, I could pay it before the month
15   is out.

JUDGE: Well, could you pay it by the fifteenth, I mean, not the fifteenth, by the twenty-third?

MR. RIDLEY: Yes ma'am.

JUDGE: You'll give her $220 today and pay all you owe on
20   June's rent by the twenty-third?

MR. RIDLEY: I think so.

JUDGE: That'll be $77, that'll be $287 by the twenty-third, $220 today and $287 by the twenty-third.

MR. RIDLEY: That's, uh, when is it?

25   JUDGE: Did you mark it down?

MRS. RIDLEY: Yes ma'am.

MR. RIDLEY: When is the twenty-third, next week?

JUDGE: It's uh, it's two weeks.

MR. RIDLEY: Two weeks?

30   JUDGE: Or almost, just, uh, a week from Monday.

MR. RIDLEY: I think so. I think I can swing that.[12]

JUDGE: Are you willing to take their $220 today and continue it until the twenty-third to give them a chance to pay it all off?

35   McCALL: Yes, I'll, I'll be willing to work with them.

As a result of the judge's relational orientation, a potentially simple collection case is elaborated into a lengthy exploration of the defendants' personal circumstances. A rule-oriented judge might have cut the Ridleys off earlier and insisted that they address the specific question of the overdue rent. But this judge listens to their account in all its relational detail, and then takes an active role in mediating a compromise. The concordant orientations of the judge and the defendants thus influence both the outcome of the case and the quality of the litigants' experience with the legal process.[13]

THE CONTEXT OF CONCORD

Concord in orientation between a judge and a litigant is not a randomly occurring event. Most of the judges we have observed are rule-oriented.[14] In terms of the judicial approaches we described in chapter 5, strict adherents to the law, authoritative judges, and proceduralists are almost invariably rule oriented. Law makers are also oriented to rules, although the "rules" about which they speak are sometimes ad hoc solutions motivated at least in part by relational concerns. Among the five approaches, only the mediators consistently display a relational approach. However, as Texts 6.2–6.5 illustrate, although mediators are sensitive to relational issues, they rarely carry their orientation to the point of ignoring legal rules. Indeed, they frequently use the threat of applying rules to compel attention to the relational agendas they set.[15]

Not surprisingly, most instances of concord involve rule-oriented judges and plaintiffs experienced in business matters. The two plaintiffs discussed in this chapter—a professional bill collector and an apartment management agent—are typical. They deal on a daily basis with contracts and their consequences, and they go to court frequently. Before they go, they are able to make accurate assessments of the strength of their legal positions. In court, they package their cases to suit the predispositions of the rule-oriented judges they typically encounter. Not only are they usually successful, but their presentation is so well attuned to the conventions of legal discourse that the case is completed quickly. To be sidetracked by a relational judge who is willing to listen to a relational defendant is a rare event.

Relational plaintiffs are uncommon. The very act of going to court seems to presume some degree of attention to rules, as well as a belief in personal autonomy and power that is foreign to the relational orientation in general. When relational people do bring cases, their accounts are often unusual and contrast with the cases that ordinarily make up most dockets, as illustrated by Mrs. Rawls's case reported in Text 4.1. Because both relational plaintiffs and relational judges are uncommon, concord between a relational plaintiff and a relational judge is a singularly rare event.[16]

Rule-oriented defendants are also uncommon, at least among those defendants who actually appear in court. We suspect that many rule-oriented defendants who are sued by rule-oriented plaintiffs analyze their cases in terms of the legal issues and rules in much the same way as the plaintiffs already have done. Since both parties approach the case similarly, they are more likely to reach pretrial settlements than litigants of differing orientations. When rule-oriented defendants do appear in court, it is often in response to claims brought by relational plaintiffs. The defendants enjoy a double advantage in such cases. The judges are likely to have difficulty grasping the plaintiffs' claims, irrespective of their underlying legal merit; conversely, whatever their legal value, the defendants' responses are tendered to the court in a familiar package.[17]

The typical trial defendant who appears in court is a relational person responding to a rule-oriented claim. Such a person has analyzed the underlying events in terms of fairness and social equity, and believes that these issues will be of interest to the court. Since the plaintiff and the defendant see the case from fundamentally different perspectives, there is a good chance that they will not be able to compromise.

Assuming that the rule-oriented plaintiff's claim is legally sound, the relational defendant may simply experience summary justice as dispensed by a rule-oriented judge. Occasionally, a judge with some degree of relational sensitivity will express understanding of the defendant's position. The judge may even offer more tangible support by inducing the other side to attempt to mediate a solution. Although these efforts rarely alter the legal outcome, they can have a powerful impact on the relational defendant's encounter with the legal process.

AN UNSYSTEMATIC SYSTEM

The "legal system" is a misnomer, at least at the level of informal justice. Depending on the approach of the judge, the same plaintiff may receive instant satisfaction or be forced to undergo a painful exploration of questions of social equity. Similarly, the same defendant may experience sudden vanquishment or soothing reassurance. The system is not really a system at all, but an aggregation of individual encounters whose quality depends on the orientational alignment of judges and litigants.

When a judge and a litigant have concordant orientations, that litigant receives the style of justice that he or she expects, even if the result is unfavorable. Except in the instance of business plaintiffs, such concord is rare, however. More often, the lay people whom informal courts were originally designed to serve experience ringing discord on a variety of levels. In the chapters that follow, we examine this discord and its consequences for the "system."

7   The Problem of Discord:
What Do Litigants Want?

As the evidence presented in chapter 6 indicates, it is sometimes the case that the litigants and the court share a common view of the nature of the law, the purpose of the legal system, and the appropriate analytic approach to a problem. Such harmony is the exception rather than the rule, however. More often, litigants and judges approach one or more of these issues differently. These differences are sometimes so sharp that each side may be unable even to comprehend the other's perspective. For litigants, the result can be dissatisfaction with the handling of their cases or even disrespect for the law as a whole. Many judges, seeing litigant dissatisfaction but not appreciating its source, develop disdain for what they perceive to be the unreasonableness or stupidity of legal consumers.

In this chapter we begin the analysis of discord between lay litigants and the legal system. We consider the fundamental questions of what litigants want and expect when they turn to the legal system for help and, relatedly, what assumptions the law makes about litigants' desires and expectations. We present evidence of the invalidity of the law's operating assumptions that civil litigants come to court to pursue discrete economic objectives;[1] that people can and do define their problems in financial terms, and are thus prepared to accept monetary solutions; and that litigants have a general understanding of how the civil justice system works, and of the limits of judicial authority.

We analyze several cases, brought by litigants of diverse backgrounds, which reveal three types of fundamental discord between litigants and the legal system. First, misunderstanding and dissatisfaction arise when litigants seek intangible benefits from legal procedures that were designed to process rational economic demands. A second source of discord is the insistence of some litigants on pursuing a noneconomic agenda that the courts may fail to discover and to which they are rarely able to respond. The third problem is that many litigants come to court with unrealistic expectations of the law's authority. The pervasive differences between the courts' concern with rules and the litigants' greater interest in relationships prove to be a significant factor in the discord.

Legal professionals are not oblivious to discord and litigant dissatisfaction; on the contrary, those who practice law are often the system's harshest critics (Burger 1982; Rosenberg 1980–81; Galanter 1983). However, the operating assumptions of most legal professionals lead them to attribute dissatisfaction to such superficial (but nonetheless important) problems as expense, delay, or poor performance by judges and lawyers. In other words, they assume that litigants share their understanding of the nature and purpose of civil justice, and are frustrated by flaws in its delivery (see Trubek 1988). As a consequence, legal reform movements historically have focused on problems of delivery and usually have been evaluated in terms of their ability to solve those problems (Walker 1988; Metzloff and Vidmar 1988). As we will see in this chapter, the sources of dissatisfaction are more fundamental.

PROCEDURAL GOALS: LAW AS THERAPY

Judges and lawyers usually assume that litigants are result oriented: they come to court to win their cases and do not think much about legal procedure unless it gets in the way of a successful outcome. We begin by examining a case that illustrates the simple but significant fact that a litigant can be as concerned with procedure as with the outcome of the case. Indeed, such a litigant may evaluate the outcome with reference to the quality of the procedures that generated it.

The recognition that litigants are concerned with procedure is not new. Experimental research in the procedural justice tradition shows convincingly that litigants sometimes value procedural fairness over a successful outcome in evaluating legal processes.[2] What has been missing in these studies is a means of specifically identifying litigants' concerns about procedure as they develop in actual litigation. The ethnography of discourse is particularly well suited to this task, because litigants identify through their own talk the specific issues that concern them. The evolution of these issues can be followed as the litigants think and speak about them at different points in the legal process.

We begin our examination of discord with the experience of a litigant whose agenda did not articulate with the court's. The plaintiff in the case, Sarah Freeman, is a young graphic artist. She contracted with the defendant, a manufacturer's representative who does business as a one-person corporation, to design a company logo, stationery, and business cards. When she tried to deliver the work and collect her fee, the defendant refused to talk to her. She sued his corporation to collect the fee.

Freeman arrived in court on the trial date with her copy of the contract, her record of correspondence with the defendant, and her portfolio containing the actual work she did for him. The defendant failed to appear. The judge raised an initial question about whether she intended to sue the corporation (the defendant she had served the complaint on) or its owner. Freeman asked the judge what she should do, and he told her that he was not allowed to give legal advice and that she should consult a lawyer if she needed such advice. He excused her from the courtroom to do so. When she returned, acting on the advice of her lawyer, she asked for a default judgment[3] against the corporate defendant. Following the usual practice in default cases, the judge questioned her briefly in order to establish that she had a valid contract case and to verify the amount of her damages, and then entered judgment for the amount she claimed. The entire proceeding took about two minutes.

We later interviewed the judge who had heard the Freeman case. We asked him about default cases in general, and in particular about this case. In Text 7.1, the judge explains his policy for handling defaults and makes specific reference to Sarah Freeman, about whom we asked in particular.

Text 7.1

JUDGE: [W]hat they don't recognize is this—they've gotta be prepared, as if the person is going to be there and defend against the case. But what they don't recognize is the fact that if the person isn't there, that all I've got to do is do
5   what we call a prima facie case. We don't have to get involved with all these details. She got her judgment.
INTERVIEWER: Oh, she got everything she wanted?
JUDGE: That's what I said—she got everything she wanted. And what they don't recognize is why should we take the
10   time to go into all these details just to give her her day in court when she got what she wanted. All she came in for was the judgment.

From the perspective of judicial administration, it is difficult to question the reasonableness of this policy. Out of concern for the rights of the absent defendant, the judge insists that the plaintiff testify briefly to demonstrate that she has a legally valid claim. However, in order to save the time of the plaintiff and those waiting in the courtroom for their own cases to be heard, he hears nothing more than this skeletal evidence before awarding judg-

ment in her favor.[4] He thus balances the interests of justice and convenience in a seemingly appropriate way.

We also interviewed Freeman immediately after her trial was heard and
found her to be one of the most dissatisfied litigants we encountered in
three years of research. In Text 7.2, she gives her evaluation of the procedure the judge followed in her case.

Text 7.2

FREEMAN: I feel like I am furious I didn't get to tell that [*my
story*]. I spent, you know, a good part of my night last
night preparing that, to have the judge not give a damn,
basically is how I felt. I felt he was very short. I felt that
5   he was not, um, let me put it, a little less than professional
in the way that he was dealing with that court today. Personally, um . . .

INTERVIEWER: Could you say what you mean by "a little less
than professional"? What reason . . .

10   FREEMAN: Yeah, he was giving me information. He was jum-
bling things for me so that I didn't understand it. And he
was expecting me to understand what was going on there
like I am a lawyer. I am not a lawyer. He failed to listen to
what I had to say.

15   INTERVIEWER: By "listening to what you had to say," do you
mean the context and the, uh . . .

FREEMAN: My presentation. And there's a reason why I spent
that kind of time putting it together.

INTERVIEWER: Like what would you have said in your presen-
20   tation? What was it all about?

FREEMAN: My presentation just delineated how things developed, that he owed me the money, um, the meetings that
took place, the understandings of how much money he
owed me, um, some other information about the com-
25   pany as well as the payments he made for payments.
Some other things—and I explained it in the presentation.

The most striking aspect of Text 7.2 is the clash of perspectives between
judge and litigant. What the judge sees as efficient, Freeman sees as "short."
What the judge seems to view as a fair balancing of interests, Freeman
views as "less than professional." Most significantly, whereas the judge believed that "all she came in for was the judgment," Freeman never even

mentioned the judgment as mitigating the procedural affront she felt she had received.

The conflict between Freeman and the judge demonstrates that procedure is a powerful influence on litigants' motivations and attitudes toward the legal system. In identifying their objectives in coming to court, litigants may focus not only on ends they hope to achieve, but on procedural opportunities that are of importance to them. Freeman echoed a procedural concern we have heard from many litigants—the desire to tell one's story. In a variety of contexts, litigants have told us that the opportunity to tell their whole story is sometimes more important than the result. Some losers report that the chance to tell their story to the judge made the whole effort worthwhile, whereas some winners, such as Freeman, go away dissatisfied because their story went untold.

The telling of the story seems to be important for two reasons. First, many people treat the litigation process as a form of therapy. As in other kinds of therapy, the central, cathartic element is the chance to relate one's troubles to an authoritative yet sympathetic listener. A related issue is the desire expressed by many litigants for "official" validation of the seriousness of their problems. As Freeman put it, it was devastating—irrespective of the outcome—"to have the judge not give a damn." Other, unsuccessful litigants have commented on how important it was for the judge to show appreciation for the gravity of their situation, even if no legal help was forthcoming. For such litigants, the dominant emotion seems to be relief in learning that someone in a position of authority understands why they are upset.[5]

Freeman's difficulties with the judge can also be seen as another manifestation of the conflict between the rule and relational orientations. The judge has assumed that Freeman shares his rule orientation. He presumes that she has defined her goals with reference to legal rights, and that she will be satisfied with the vindication of those rights. Freeman's outlook is thoroughly relational, however. As she hints at in Text 7.2, she sees the underlying problem with the defendant not simply as a breach of contract, but in terms of their deteriorating relationship. Freeman's "presentation," which dealt with "how things developed," "the meetings that took place," and so forth, is of importance to her because it is the embodiment of her relational concerns. When the judge brushes aside the presentation, he symbolically dismisses her orientation toward life, work, and interpersonal relations. Thus, it is not surprising that in her assessment of the trial the refusal to hear her presentation transcends the questions of outcome that the law deems paramount.

Lawyers and judges with whom we have discussed the issue of litigants' concerns about procedures sometime reject our findings out of hand, observing that the legal system has neither the resources nor the expertise to address litigants' psychological needs. However, the demands that litigants such as Freeman make on the system are often minimal. For example, she acknowledged in the posttrial interview that she understood there was no legal reason for the judge to hear her story. She would have been satisfied if the judge had merely showed some understanding of her dilemma (see Text 7.3). By paying attention to what litigants say rather than acting on assumptions about their objectives and concerns, the law may discover opportunities to bring about material increases in litigant satisfaction in exchange for minimal commitments of time and the resources.

Text 7.3

FREEMAN: He could have explained it in a different manner. He could have said to me, "The case is decided, period, no matter what you have to say from here on out. I'm sorry that you wasted your time on your presentation."

5　INTERVIEWER: Some sort of . . .

FREEMAN: That would have taken care of it.

SUBSTANTIVE GOALS: FINDING THE HIDDEN AGENDA

In some respects, Sarah Freeman seemed less concerned about the legal outcome of her case than about the treatment she received from the court. Even when a litigant focuses on the outcome of the case (as judges and lawyers assume), the specific outcome sought may deviate substantially from what the law expects. In all jurisdictions, informal court litigants are required to fill out a complaint form when they file their cases. On their own or with the assistance of a clerk, they make a short statement of what they want from the defendant—typically, money or the return of property. The law assumes that this is the end of the inquiry into litigant objectives: they are indeed pursuing the rational economic ends recited in the complaint, and the job of the system is to facilitate the quest. Once again, the ethnographic investigation of discourse suggests that the underlying reality may be more complex.

Analysis of the case of *Mottley v. Newell* illustrates the elusiveness of litigant objectives. The plaintiff, William Mottley, claims to have "cosigned"[6] an installment sales contract to enable the defendant, Shirley Newell, to buy some furniture. Newell has failed to make the payments, and Mottley has paid two monthly installments at the demand of the furniture store.

Mottley now seeks to enforce Newell's alleged promise to be responsible for the payments.

In Text 7.4, the plaintiff gives the first indication of what he wants. Interestingly, this colloquy takes place before the judge has sworn in the litigants, and is thus technically not part of the evidence. Nonetheless, there can be no doubt that Mottley's objective is clearly communicated, even if not, as we will see, clearly understood.

Text 7.4[7]

JUDGE: Is William M-O-T-T-L-E-Y here?
MOTTLEY: Yes
  [*Judge calls the defendant, Shirley Newell.*]
JUDGE: Before you start, sir, um, what are you seeking here
5   this morning?
MOTTLEY: Um, possession of my furn-, of the furniture.
JUDGE: Possession of furniture?
MOTTLEY: Yeah.

After swearing in the litigants, the judge invites Mottley to tell his story. In Text 7.5, Mottley gives a lengthy account of his arrangement with Newell and his efforts to collect the payments from her.

Text 7.5

JUDGE: Mottley versus Shirley Newell. If you will, sir, you
  may begin. Court's in session at this time.
MOTTLEY: Um, Shirley New-, Newell, I don't know her before. Her girlfriend is my friend. I went to school with her.
5   She [*Newell's friend*] introduced me to her [*Newell*] as her
  friend. So she [*Newell*] asked me, one, if I could cosign for
  her to get some furniture from Rhodes Company, which I
  agree. I told her, I said, "I don't want to do it then, I don't
  want to do it then. Later on it will be trouble, but if you
10   trust yourself that you would make the payment, I will
  help you."

  [*He describes meeting Newell at Rhodes Furniture*]

  I signed the lease for her to get a dinette set and I left.
  When I left, she and Nicole [*Newell's friend*] went behind
15   me to room furniture and added more items to, to the
  furniture. We, I think that that amounted to $820. So

---

when I got the first bill, because it is cosigned in my name,
so they, they mailed the bill to me. So when it got, when
20   it, when I got the first bill, I was mad. So I got mad. I went
to her, I said, "Look, what you did is not good, that frau-
dery. I could take you to court. But anyway, since we are
all friend, if you make your payment, it's okay with me.
Just make sure you make your payment." She said, "I'll
25   make my payment. I always make my payment." I said,
"You saying that now, but when time come, it will be
trouble." So the first payment [*bill*] came, the first payment came to me. I took the stuff [*bill*] to her house. She
didn't even want to open the door. I had to, she opened
30   the door. I gave it to her. I said, "I only brought this payment stub which is $44 a month. It, it'll give you seven-
teen days to pay." I gave it to her at the beginning part of
the month. So she said, "I'll pay my bill," and I left. After
the seventeenth, about two weeks later, I call her one
35   night. I said, "Have you made a payment?" She said, "Yes,
I made my payment." So when I looked this, on the
month end of the second, the, uh, second bill came. I saw
on it $88. I said, "But how come? She told me she made
her payment." Then I went to her house. When I went to
40   her house, she said, "I have made a payment." I said, "To
who?" She lie to me. She called somebody who does not
even work at Rhodes Furniture—she said she made payment to a girl.

[*Mottley goes on to describe a lengthy discussion among Newell, Nicole, and himself, as a result of which Newell paid him $88*]

JUDGE: She gave you how much money?
MOTTLEY: She gave me $88 for the first $88 I have already
    paid.

Several aspects of Text 7.5 are notable. First, it is striking that Mottley
begins his testimony by responding to an accusation—that he knew Newell "before"—that no one has made in court.[8] The implication is that
Mottley views his courtroom testimony not as a discrete episode with a
clear beginning and end, but as part of an ongoing, although discontinuous, conversation. He and Newell are the principals in this conversation,
with Nicole, the judge, and others drifting in and out as bit players. The fact
that Mottley picks up this conversation in mid-stream, by responding to an

accusation made at another time and place, also suggests that he has more in mind than the legal remedies of collection and repossession. In particular, his fixation on his continuing dialogue with Newell suggests that the specific legal problem he brings to court is symbolic of the larger problems in their relationship.

Relatedly, note the extraordinary personal and dramatic quality of his account of the transaction. He continually uses direct quotation, reporting not only his conversations with Newell but even his soliloquizing on passing events (line 38: "I said, 'But how come . . . ?'"). He sometimes steps out of his performing role to make evaluative comments about the characters in the drama (line 20: "I was mad"; line 41: "She lie to me"). He thereby underlines his emotional stake in what purports to be a business transaction with a person whom he did not know "before."

The judge's single interruption in this lengthy account indicates that his focus is on the narrow issues of specific legal relevance rather than on the unfolding personal drama. The interruption is particularly interesting because it seems gratuitous: can the judge possibly have missed the twice-stated point, "She gave me $88"? One is tempted to interpret the judge's interruption not as a question, but as an emphatic statement about the limits of the court's interest and power.

In Text 7.6, Mottley continues his account in the same fashion, replete with performance and personal commentary. He repeats his description of collecting the initial $88 payment, and then recounts his receipt of the bill for the third month. Once again, the judge interrupts, ostensibly to clarify issues of legal relevance.

Text 7.6

MOTTLEY: Last month, the stuff came. When I, the stuff came. When I took the stuff to her house, she won't open the door.

JUDGE: Let me ask you a question, sir. Where is the furniture
5   at this time?

MOTTLEY: She, she, she had it to her house.

JUDGE: Now, inasmuch as you are saying that, um, Ms. Newell has this furniture that you cosigned for . . .

MOTTLEY: Yeah.

10   JUDGE: Now, how about the deal with, uh Rhodes Furniture Company? Who is taking care of that?

MOTTLEY: I am taking care of it now.

JUDGE: So, you are paying this bill?

MOTTLEY: On my own now.
15   JUDGE: On your own, to Rhodes Furniture Company?
MOTTLEY: Yeah, yeah—because it's in my name.
JUDGE: Yeah, I understand.
MOTTLEY: And I don't want my credit to spoil.
JUDGE: I understand, you cosigned for Ms. Newell.
20   MOTTLEY: That's right.
JUDGE: Thank you very much.
MOTTLEY: I'm not through.

After recapturing his speaking turn at the end of the judge's interrogation, Mottley recycles some of his account, returning to his description of Newell's refusal to open the door. He tells of filing the suit for the third and fourth month's payments, and his difficulties in obtaining service of the complaint. Then, in Text 7.7, he concludes his presentation by reiterating his opening demand for repossession.

Text 7.7

MOTTLEY: I went back and make another payment again before I file to her working place. There were they—I think
that where they got her—that why she been, she been
hiding. And then two month and she had not pay, so I, I
5   had paid it two months. I want to repossess the furniture.
I will take over the, if I don't need it, I need it, but I, I will
take, I will take care of it.

The judge turns to Newell for her version of what happened in Text 7.8. She responds directly to several of Mottley's accusations, and offers explanations for her behavior, but does not address the basic question of whether she owes him the money.

Text 7.8

JUDGE: Um, Ms. Newell, you have heard the testimony coming from the gentleman here. If you have something, the
court will honor it at this time.
NEWELL: Yes, I do. First of all, Mr. Mottley knew exactly what
5   I was getting, because Jack Roy, the salesman at the store,
told him, showed him the paper in which what was written on there, that I was getting. They said there was no

way that anyone could go and add anything on his account, because it's in his name—he did not cosign. It's in
10   his name, period. Mr. Mottley came to my house before
the seventeenth. The bill is past due on the seventeenth of
the month. I told him at that time I had gave my money
to my friend to go pay for me because I had no transportation . . .

[*She explains why she has no receipt for the payment*]

As far as him saying that I was dodging the sheriff, Mr.
Mottley and Your Honor, I have not been in my home
since June 10th, due to the simple fact that I had no lights.
20   I was with my mother. On June 21st, we went to
Lancaster, South Carolina for a funeral.

At this point the judge intervenes and begins to move the parties toward
a settlement. Before ultimately succeeding, he encounters resistance from
each of them. Newell continues to avoid his direct questions about the
debt, insisting instead on repeating her denials of Mottley's allegations
about her behavior. For his part, Mottley continues to press for repossession of the furniture, but never elicits a direct response from the judge.

Text 7.9

JUDGE: Sir, how much money, uh, does Ms. Newell owe you
at this particular time?
MOTTLEY: Um, at this particular time, she owe two month
rent. She—
5   JUDGE: And the payments are how much a month?
MOTTLEY: $44 a month.
JUDGE: $44 a month?
MOTTLEY: Yes.
JUDGE: And she's two payments behind at this time?
10   MOTTLEY: Yeah, yeah.
JUDGE: Ms. Newell, do you have any intention of paying this
money, uh, to this gentleman here in relationship to him
having paid it already?
NEWELL: As I said, your honor, I have been out of town. My
15   great-grandmother has passed away.
JUDGE: Well now, I can understand that, but I'm asking you—
NEWELL: When I returned to my home on the first, the office

manager and the neighbor told me that Mr. Mottley was at my door They had to fix my door in which I have to
20 pay for, because he kicked it.

MOTTLEY: No, I didn't.

NEWELL: Yes, he did.

MOTTLEY: [*Laughing*].

JUDGE: Now let me ask you a question, um, Ms. Newell—

25 MOTTLEY AND NEWELL: [*Both laughing*].

JUDGE: Did you intend to pay this amount of money that's owed on this furniture at this time?

NEWELL: I had every intentions to pay. When I returned, I called my job. They told me that the sheriff had been
30 there. I called downtown in which I talked with the sheriff of car 619. He told me that he had a paper for me and I told him exactly where I was. I gave him the phone number. I had no reason to hide.

JUDGE: Ms. Newell, when do you plan to pay this money
35 that, uh, was owed to this gentleman here?

NEWELL: He can have it tomorrow if he wants, but, if he wants his furniture, he's—

JUDGE: I'm asking a question: when do you plan to pay him the money that's owed at this time?

40 NEWELL: I had planned to pay him when I returned from out of town.

JUDGE: Then Mr., uh, sir, would you be willing to accept the payments that are due at this particular point from Ms. Newell?

45 MOTTLEY: Um, sir, to, to, to ease her problem, I would, I would, I wouldn't regret past payment. I would just like to possess the furniture. Then, I don't have to be bothered with nobody at this point of time. She owe me two months' money, it's okay, I will, I need it.

50 JUDGE: The question that I'm asking you, inasmuch as, um, Ms. Newell does owe you this money—

MOTTLEY: Uh-huh.

JUDGE: —are you willing to accept this money that she owes you, uh, to Rhodes on this bill?

55 MOTTLEY: Yeah.

JUDGE: You are willing to do that?

MOTTLEY: Yeah.

JUDGE: Ms. Newell, when do you plan to pay this money to, uh, this gentleman here?

60 NEWELL: That's what I'm trying to explain. As I said, I was

willing to pay him when I left. And when I returned, and
then when I came back to a job, which I was fired from,
because of the sheriff.

JUDGE: Well, when do you plan to, when do you plan to pay
65   the gentleman?

NEWELL: I can pay him next week.

JUDGE: What day next week can you pay him?

NEWELL: What's the date, the 13th? Round the 24th.

JUDGE: After listening to the testimony from the plaintiff and
70   the defendant, in relationship, sir, to what was said by Ms.
Newell here that she was gonna pay you this amount of
money that's owed in order to bring this account up to
date on the 24th of this month, I'm gonna continue this
case until June the 27th, June 27th, '86 at 11:00 a.m. Now,
75   if this, uh, money has been paid to you in that period of
time—

MOTTLEY: Uh hum.

JUDGE: —of course, you can call me at my office and I'll be
able to handle the situation at that point. Now, if this is
80   not done on the 24th, I'm gonna hear the case on the 27th
of June '86. at 11:00 a.m., and I'm gonna enter a judgment
at that time.

By most objective measures, this outcome would be deemed a success—
for the plaintiff, the system, and even the defendant. The plaintiff has the
defendant's agreement to pay what she owes, backed up the court's threat
to enter judgment if she fails to do so. The judge has ignored Mottley's
claim for repossession, but there is no clear evidence that he is legally entitled to get the furniture back.[9] Mottley thus appears to have secured a
legal victory, along with some practical help in collecting his money. The
result also seems ideal from the perspective of the judicial system. Rather
than simply pronouncing judgment, the judge has used his authority as
leverage in moving the parties toward a consensual resolution, with an
attendant increase in the likelihood that the parties will comply.[10] Presumably, a plaintiff who both wins and gets paid will be a satisfied customer of
the system. The outcome is positive even for Newell, given the fact that she
never denies the agreement with Mottley or her failure to pay. She keeps
the furniture, she has two more weeks to pay, and, if she does so, she avoids
a judgment against her. Moreover, she has an opportunity to defend her
conduct and denounce Mottley's, an opportunity that seems to have been
important to her.

There is evidence, however, that the judge's decision entirely misses the point of the dispute as the parties see it. Recall, for example, that Mottley began the case by denying a legally irrelevant accusation about his relationship with Newell that she must have made at another time and place (Text 7.5, lines 3–4). For her part, Newell ignored the legal thrust of his case, even when the judge demanded that she address it, and insisted on justifying her conduct during the relationship. Note also Mottley's repeated demands for repossession, and in particular his comment that "I would just like to possess the furniture. Then I don't have to be bothered with nobody" (Text 7.9, lines 46–48).

In separate interviews immediately after the trial, Mottley and Newell elaborated on these hints and shed further light on their hidden agendas and the degree of their satisfaction with the outcome. In Text 7.10, Mottley responds to a question about whether he was satisfied with the trial. He focuses more directly on his interest in repossession as a way to end his dealings with Newell, and asks the interviewer, almost plaintively, if she appreciates the point that the judge apparently missed.

Text 7.10

MOTTLEY: Well, with the judge running this, he spoke about, it would be too much for me. You know, my main point is, if I could possess my furniture.
INTERVIEWER: Is that what you really wanted to do?
5   MOTTLEY: Yeah, I would be, I would, I don't have to be bothered with her, I would be okay. You see?
INTERVIEWER: Uh huh.
MOTTLEY: You see, that's all I want.

Finally, in an interview a few minutes later, Newell solves the mystery of the hidden agenda. Text 7.11 begins in the middle of Newell's retelling the story of Mottley coming to her home to collect the payments.

Text 7.11

NEWELL: There was a lot—the day he said he came by and I wouldn't let him in, the man wanted me to open the door naked. I was getting out of the shower, and he expected me to jump up and run down to the door. But he got in. And he was nasty. And the reason I refused to argue with him [*in court*], 'cause he was lying. And I knew that judge knew he was lying. And the fact about he didn't know

what was on that stuff [*the Rhodes documents*], he [*Mottley*]
knew. And I started to tell the judge the exact truth as to
10   why he decided to come to court—
INTERVIEWER: Why is that?
NEWELL: —but I felt that it was like personal.
INTERVIEWER: Right.
NEWELL: I turned him down.
15   INTERVIEWER: Oh yeah?
NEWELL: And that stuff was bought as a gift, alright.
INTERVIEWER: When you first, like, bought the stuff, did you
think you'd have to pay him at all?
NEWELL: Uh uh [*negative*]. But then I told him that my inten-
20   tions was wrong as far as except, um, letting him give, and
I would prefer to pay him, because he was expecting a
little more, and I wasn't going to give him no more
[*laughter*].

[*Newell comments further on Mottley's aggressive behavior, and explains that her
friend introduced Mottley to her "to get him off her back"*]

INTERVIEWER: Did you want the furniture to begin with, or is
it just something that he got you? I mean, now that you've
got it, do you want to go ahead and pay for it, or . . .
NEWELL: The truth?
30   INTERVIEWER: Yeah.
NEWELL: I was hoping he'd tell that man he could have his
stuff.[11] I really was. Because he's a pest. He is a home pest.

Newell's revelation finally explains the enigma of the parties' trial tactics.[12] Mottley's repeated demands for repossession now seems less a property claim than a request for what amounts to a divorce, a divorce to which
Newell would consent. Those aspects of their testimony that seemed so
out-of-place in a contract case—for example, his response to a preexisting
accusation about the start of their relationship, and her insistence on constantly justifying her conduct—are appropriate in the context of a domestic
relations case. Indeed, such issues are essence of a domestic case.

Seen in this light, the result reached by the judge looks far less successful.
Its substantive terms are unresponsive to the real objectives of the parties.
From a procedural standpoint, the judge's effort to get them to compromise

seems to be exactly what the parties do not want or need. They are tired of dealing with each other and have looked to the court for a termination of their relationship that they seem unable to bring about by themselves. Instead, the court extends the relationship for at least two more weeks.

The case is a complex instance of conflict between rules and relationships. From one perspective, it is a straightforward instance of conflicting orientations. The parties have come to court with a relational problem thinly disguised as a legal dispute. The judge, influenced by his own rule-orientation, fails to penetrate the externalities, and predictably disposes of the matter on the basis of the applicable legal rules. The litigants go away dissatisfied because the judge has been unable to appreciate their relational agendas.

When the dispute is viewed from another perspective, however, the conflicting orientations are reversed. Although Newell and Mottley have a relational problem, they want it resolved in a discrete, rule-oriented manner. They want the judge to decree an absolute divorce. But the judge, even though he defines the problem in terms of rules, tries to resolve it through relational means. He mediates rather than adjudicates, and calls on the parties to continue their relationship in an effort to work out their difficulties. The case thus presents the unusual spectacle of litigants who seek a rule-oriented remedy to a relational problem confronting a judge who is rule-oriented in his definition of the problem but relational in his choice of procedures to deal with it.

Misunderstanding the Power of the Court

For some litigants, such as Sarah Freeman, discord and dissatisfaction arise because they expect the court to be attentive to their feelings as well as their tangible economic needs. For others, such as William Mottley, the problem is a relational agenda concealed within what appears to be a straightforward case of rules. Frustration can also arise when litigants come to court with mistaken assumptions about the power of the civil justice system. Problems typically occur when litigants attribute to the court unlimited authority to seek out and punish wrongdoers. Two additional cases illustrate different aspects of this phenomenon.

The plaintiff in the first of these cases, Harvey Johnson, earns his living doing odd jobs. The defendant owns a lawn care business. Johnson agreed to work for the defendant cutting lawns. The defendant agreed to pay him $35 per day, which Johnson assumed referred to an eight-hour work day.

The first day, the defendant picked him up early in the morning, drove him from house to house, and brought him home at the end of a thirteen-hour day. He paid Johnson $35. The next day, they started early in the morning and worked nine hours. At that point, Johnson said he refused to work until eight at night again, and the man responded, "We're gonna be here as late as we were yesterday." Johnson quit on the spot and demanded to be paid for the time he had worked, but the defendant refused. Johnson took the bus home from the house where they were working.

Johnson then went to the State Labor Board. They advised him that he was entitled to be paid an hourly wage for all the time he had worked, with time-and-a-half for any hours in excess of eight in a given day. They also told him that they could not collect his money for him, so he should go to small claims court. He did so, and we interviewed him as he came out of the clerk's office after filing his case. As it turned out, he was never able to have the complaint served on the defendant. The sheriff's deputies, who serve papers only during normal business hours, could not find the defendant, and Johnson did not want to serve the complaint himself. As a result, he ultimately had to drop the case.

As Johnson explains in Text 7.12, he has brought the case because of a failure on the part of "the state," which "couldn't catch up with" (lines 12–13) the defendant and told him to try small claims court. As an avid viewer of "The People's Court" television program,[13] Johnson is familiar with the small claims process in general and Judge Wapner's judicial behavior in particular.

Text 7.12

JOHNSON: I went by and and asked him for my money a few
days later. He said that he didn't owe me anything. So,
I've been watching uh, Judge Wapner.
INTERVIEWER: [*Laughter*]
5   JOHNSON: He said, "If you have a case—
INTERVIEWER: "The People's Court?"
JOHNSON: Yeah, "People's Court." And uh, so I decided to
bring him to court. Well I took him to the state but the
state can't catch up with him. He keeps his equipment in
10   one place and he lives in another place.
INTERVIEWER: Um huh.
JOHNSON: And it's hard to catch up, the state couldn't catch
up with him 'cause they told me to bring it to sm-, small

15	claims court. But the problem that I think I'm going to have is serving the papers, serving him.

In spite of, or perhaps because of, what he had learned from "The People's Court," Johnson was unpleasantly surprised by the real civil justice system, in which litigants bear the entire burden of prosecuting their cases. In particular, as he explains in Text 7.13, his responsibility for serving the summons on the elusive defendant runs contrary to his view of how "the law" should function.

Text 7.13

JOHNSON: And, well I probably know several guys that I could get to go around and just catch him, and give him the papers, but, uh, it's all left up to me.
INTERVIEWER: Right.
5   JOHNSON: And um, I thought the law was supposed to be, you know, if you have a case against someone, hey, I think the law, the deputy sheriff should be able anytime up until midnight, anytime, to serve papers.

The reason for Johnson's dissatisfaction with the legal system's passivity is itself interesting. As he acknowledges in Text 7.13, he knows "several guys" who might be able to find the defendant. Nonetheless, he states in Text 7.14, he is reluctant to see the defendant until the court date. Johnson wants their ultimate confrontation to be mediated by the state.

Text 7.14

JOHNSON: I'll just have to get someone early in the morning or late at night and just wait on him—
INTERVIEWER: Yeah.
JOHNSON: —to serve the papers. That's the problem, that's the
5   thing I don't like. See, I don't want, I don't want—he know what I'm doing to him. See I don't want to have the, I, I don't want to be seeing him until court.

In Text 7.15, Johnson discloses the source of his reluctance to confront the defendant—his bad feelings toward him—and makes the point that this is the only grievance he has thus far with the small claims process.

Text 7.15

> JOHNSON: And I, I don't, I don't, that's, the only thing that I don't like about the courts to start with, is serving him the papers.
>
> INTERVIEWER: Have you ever uh . . .
>
> 5　JOHNSON: See I don't, I don't feel good towards him at all.

In some respects, Johnson's expectations reflect a model of civil justice that would be more appropriate for the criminal system. He believes that "the law," as it does in the criminal context, should seek out the defendant and bring him to justice while the plaintiff remains anonymously in the background until the trial. Later in the interview, in Text 7.16, he suggests the source of these expectations.

Text 7.16

> INTERVIEWER: Have you ever uh, you know, gone to a court before like that?
>
> JOHNSON: No, not to claims, not to small claims, not suing anybody.
>
> 5　INTERVIEWER: Uh huh.
>
> JOHNSON: When I've ever been to court, I've always been behind the gun in the courtroom, DUIs, disturbing, and things like that, I've always been behind the gun.

Even though Johnson has been influenced to some extent by "The People's Court," his only personal experience with the legal system has been as a criminal defendant. He has seen the active, inquisitorial arm of "the law" at work. He generalizes from this experience, and expects this power to be put at his disposal when he is the complaining party. He is predictably dissatisfied when this formerly omnipotent law suddenly pleads helplessness and tells him to solve his own problem.

Johnson's problem is not that he fails to appreciate that the law operates according to rules, but that he misapprehends those rules. His rules all derive from his mistaken belief that the law, and indeed the government as a whole (recall his experience with the State Labor Board), is a unified entity with limitless power. This belief is in turn based on and validated by his experience as a person who is in many respects "behind the gun." He has thus built a model of legal rules inductively, from the ground up. He misses the distinctions between courts and administrative agencies, and between civil and criminal justice, because fine lines in the power structure are not apparent or even relevant to him. Because his social experience has little in common with that of the people who make and administer the law, his model is inaccurate, and is a source of discord and dissatisfaction.

The plaintiffs in a second case, Mr. and Mrs. Winner, sued "some old friends" who failed to repay a loan. The full details of this story are unclear, but it appears that the defendants had a recent history of moving around the country, living with friends and borrowing money. The defendants were living in Arkansas until the Winners suggested that they would help them find jobs if they moved to their city. The defendants came, and lived with the Winners until, as they put it, "We kicked them out. . . . We starved them to death." Then Mr. Winner inherited some money, and he and his wife lent or gave the defendants $390. After a couple of months passed without repayment, the Winners prepared some type of loan document which the defendants signed, although they admitted while signing that they could not repay the money. The document apparently required the defendants to make a $50 payment by June 17. On June 24, having heard nothing from the defendants, the Winners sued. They sought the $390, plus $110 for their expenses in bringing the suit. According to Mr. Winner, the purpose of claiming the additional damages was to "make it hurt." The defendants did not appear for trial, and the Winners received a default judgment for $400. Although they later located the defendants, they were unable to collect their money.

In a pretrial interview, the Winners revealed that they, like Johnson, came to court with a fairly detailed, rule-oriented model of how the system works. In Text 7.17, for example, they claim to have some knowledge of the small claims process, derived largely from watching "The People's Court."

Text 7.17

INTERVIEWER: How'd you know to do, do small claims? How'd you think of it?

MRS. WINNER: I don't know. We just told them you know, if they didn't pay us, we'd take them to court.

5   INTERVIEWER: Uh huh.

MRS. WINNER: We watch Judge Wapner on TV.

INTERVIEWER: Oh yeah. People, a lot of people find out about you know small claims, you know, through that.

MR. WINNER: Yeah.

10   INTERVIEWER: 'Cause if not, you really wouldn't know where, what to do I guess, so.

MRS. WINNER: That's right, that's right. And we wouldn't know to, um, you know, charge them for lost wages and stuff. . . .

The Winners are also aware of the significance the law attaches to written contracts, particularly those sworn to before a notary. Thus, when their ex-friends failed to repay the loan, the Winners made them sign a sworn document, and advised them of the potential legal consequences of continued failure to pay (Text 7.18).

Text 7.18

MR. WINNER: They're some old friends of ours. And took them a couple of months to finally make payment arrangements with us so I wrote up a contract and they signed it in front of a notary and everything, to pay me $50 a

5   month and, uh, by the 17th of this month and they haven't done so.

INTERVIEWER: Uh huh.

MR. WINNER: And I told them I'd take them to court, no hesitations. And they've done this—

10   INTERVIEWER: Sure.

MR. WINNER: —they've done this to people before, so.

As is evident from Text 7.19, however, the Winners were also aware before they came to court that the defendants simply did not have the money they owed (recall that the defendants so admitted when they signed the loan document.)

Text 7.19

MRS. WINNER: She didn't think we would do it, I don't think.

INTERVIEWER: Oh yeah? So um, do you think she, they have it?

MRS. WINNER: No.

5   MR. WINNER: They don't have it.

INTERVIEWER: Yeah, so . . .

MRS. WINNER: They're gonna have to go to court, ah ha ha.

The obvious question is why these plaintiffs, sophisticated in some respects about law and procedure, are wasting time and money in the pursuit of debtors who will be unable to pay the judgment ("judgment-proof" defendants, in lawyers' jargon). Text 7.19 provides one clue. Mrs. Winner says, in a mocking tone, "They're gonna have to go to court, ah ha ha," suggesting that she and her husband may intend to punish the defendants with the inconvenience and humiliation of a court appearance. Later in the pretrial interview, however, in Text 7.20, the Winners provide evidence for a different interpretation.

Text 7.20

MR. WINNER: You know, I figured I can go up for $390 but I'm
losing time from work. I gotta pay these fees and—
· INTERVIEWER: Sure.
MRS. WINNER: —gas to get down here and everything else.
5 INTERVIEWER: Yeah, yeah.
MR. WINNER: I'm gonna make it hurt.
INTERVIEWER: Mmhm.
MRS. WINNER: [*Laughter*]
MR. WINNER: Feels good.
10 INTERVIEWER: Yeah. Well, I understand. Probably can use
some money.
MR. WINNER: Yeah, we sure could.

In Text 7.20, Mr. Winner says, in reference to his inflated damage calculations, "I'm gonna make it hurt" (line 6). The clear implication is that the increased damages will inflict more pain on the defendants, though they lack the resources to pay even the $390 amount of the loan. Mr. Winner then concludes the interview by responding to the interviewer's "Probably can use some money" (lines 10–11) with "Yeah, we sure could" (line 12), suggesting some measure of economic motivation in bringing the case.[14]

If the Winners' motivation is at least partially economic, it rests on an erroneous assumption about the power of a civil court. In fact, the court merely furnishes a piece of paper called a judgment, and then provides a mechanism for the successful plaintiff to collect it against the assets, real estate, bank accounts, stocks, etc., of a defendant who will not pay voluntarily. If the defendant refuses to pay and has no property which can be sold off, the plaintiff is out of luck. The Winners seem to assume, however, that the court will somehow force the defendants to produce money they do not have or perhaps will punish them for their penury. They thus attribute to the civil court some of the power of the American criminal system, or of some hypothetical inquisition.

The Winners' erroneous expectations contribute to their ultimate dissatisfaction with the process. In a posttrial interview, Mrs. Winner described the trial itself as "real fair," "real easy with them not being there," and she did not complain about the amount of the judgment. However, she became increasingly vitriolic when discussing her belief that "the court should be able to go after them." She progressed from "We're pretty unhappy with the overall system," to "It just stinks," observing that her husband "was pretty pissed off about the whole thing." It is significant that for these litigants, dissatisfaction has arisen not because they "lost" in a normative sense, nor because the system failed to perform up to its capabilities, but because it lacked capabilities that they erroneously attributed to it.

The Winners' dilemma can also be analyzed in terms of rules and relationships. On one level, they are consistently rule-oriented. In dealing with their former friends, they set up a rule-oriented structure of written agreements. When the defendants failed to live up to the agreement, the Winners presented the problem to the court in a rule-oriented format, suggesting that they understand the law's logic. In the end, they get the judgment they sought and express satisfaction with the court's procedure.

On another level, however, the Winners are just as consistently relational. Although they act as if they understand the court's rule-oriented agenda, they expect more. In particular, they expect the court to go beyond legal rules and exact some sort of penalty from the defendants for abusing a relationship. The court's failure to involve itself in their problems at the relational level is the ultimate source of their dissatisfaction with the legal system.

The Winners thus live simultaneously in two worlds. They have learned deference to rules in dealing with others on money matters and in interacting with institutions such as the court. But when rules fail them, they revert to interpreting events and shaping their expectations of others in terms of deeper relational concerns.

How Does the System Maintain Itself?

The picture that emerges from this chapter is one of considerable discord. At least three varieties of discord are prevalent. Some litigants, typified by Sarah Freeman, seek emotional benefits from legal procedures. Others, such as William Mottley, pursue hidden agendas that the courts are ill prepared to detect and even less well equipped to deal with. Finally, many litigants are confounded by their misapprehension of the authority of the civil courts and the basic operating assumptions of the civil justice system.

All of these sources of discord can be seen as manifestations of the conflict between rules and relationships. Litigants who seek therapy are asking the courts to depart from their rigid rule-orientation and address the relational aspects of their problems. Hidden agendas often consist of relational problems packaged as rule-oriented disputes. The issue is even more complicated in some cases, where what the litigant really wants is a rule-oriented solution to the hidden relational problem. The court is typically relieved to find the rule-oriented package, and is thus unlikely even to investigate its contents. The experiences of those litigants who misunderstood the civil justice system can often be explained in terms of a conflict between a superficial appreciation of the law's rule-orientation and a more fundamental tendency to interpret events in relational terms.

Irrespective of the source of the discord, all of these litigants have one thing in common: they come to court with demands that the system cannot or will not satisfy, and go away frustrated. This frustration is no secret; on the contrary, there are few more popular media themes than the problems of the legal system. Yet people keep coming, bringing their unrealistic expectations that the court will find a way to solve their problems.

Why do they keep coming? How does the system maintain any semblance of credibility in the face of such dissatisfaction? We turn to these questions in the next chapter where we begin by exploring another, even more subtle form of discord. We find in it the key to the apparent contradiction of public faith in a system that seems to satisfy so few public needs.

8 Managing Discord

The evidence presented in chapter 7 shows that the courtroom experiences of many initially optimistic litigants end on discordant notes. The disappointments of litigants like those we considered in chapter 7 are part of popular folklore about the law. Yet the system perseveres and even flourishes in the face of this discord. An ever-increasing number of litigants turn to it for solutions to an ever-wider array of problems (Galanter 1983; Burger 1982). In this chapter we examine how it is possible for the system simultaneously to frustrate popular aspirations and maintain a modicum of public confidence.

We seek an explanation for this apparent contradiction by examining legal ideologies. We define a legal ideology as a system of beliefs about the nature and purpose of law which guide those who hold them in constructing meaning in the legal environment.[1] We explore the discrepancies between popular ideologies of law and the "official" ideology promulgated by representatives of the legal system. The ethnographic evidence we present reveals both the ideology of the law as practiced in the courts and the diverse, often conflicting ideologies held by litigants. Analysis of this evidence offers some insight into the mechanisms whereby litigants manage this ideological dissonance, and the role that these mechanisms play in maintaining the integrity of the system.

We draw inferences about lay ideologies of law from three categories of evidence: what litigants say about the law, the choices they make in structuring and presenting their cases, and their reactions to their experiences with the legal process. We have chosen a series of texts that provide a basis for examining the management of discord. As these texts demonstrate, there is no unified lay ideology of law, but a range of lay perspectives on the nature and purpose of law and the legal process. The texts also suggest the complexity of the interaction between lay ideologies and the "official" ideology as expressed by judges.

COPING WITH THE SYSTEM: THE LEAKY ROOF

We consider first several texts drawn from a case brought by Higgins and Andrews, two young men who are joint owners of a house. They hired Riva Roofing Company to fix a leak in their roof, signed a contract, and paid a $500 deposit. According to the plaintiffs, the roofers removed the leaky segment but then simply covered the area with tar paper and aluminum siding, which made the leak worse. When Higgins and Andrews called the company to complain, they were told that the work had been done by subcontractors, and that Riva would refund only half the deposit.

After a demand letter proved unavailing, Higgins and Andrews went to small claims court. Following the local procedure, they were interviewed by a court clerk who inquired about the case, made sure that they had the relevant documents, and then wrote out a complaint form, including a brief narrative description of their claim, for their signature. We interviewed them in the hallway as they walked out of the clerk's office.[2] In Text 8.1, Higgins responds to a request for "general comments on what brings you to court."

Text 8.1

HIGGINS: My—basically a wrong has been done to me and I
 want it righted.
INTERVIEWER: Yeah.
HIGGINS: I put out money to someone to provide a business
5 service. The person did, first of all, a faulty job, uh, didn't
 come in when they were supposed to have come. The
 people that they subcontracted to, I've no idea.

In these opening remarks, Higgins makes two points which are striking on their own as well as by virtue of their juxtaposition. First, he begins with a forthright, powerful statement of values. He has come to court not to get his roof fixed, nor to collect money, but to right a wrong. If this is indeed why he has come to court, then he presumably believes that the court shares his interest in righting wrongs, and has the power to do so.[3]

Second, having expressed his expectations of the legal system, he moves directly to state his legal theory of the case. He made a contract by giving money in exchange for a promise of future services, and the other party breached the contract by failing to render the services in satisfactory fashion. Higgins also anticipates Riva's possible defense by disclaiming any knowledge of or assent to their subcontracting agreement. In coming to this understanding of the legal elements of his case, he has undoubtedly benefited from his conversations with the clerk and, as we shall see, his brother, who is a law student.[4] What is particularly interesting is that in this brief commentary Higgins reveals an insider's knowledge of some of the legal technicalities of his case coexisting with an ideology of law that insiders would probably regard as naive. This combination of realism and idealism becomes a major theme as the interview continues.

In Text 8.2, Higgins explains the factual background of the case. There is no explicit statement of ideology comparable to that in Text 8.1, but a number of inferences can be drawn from the way in which he selects and emphasizes particular facts.

Text 8.2

HIGGINS: Okay, the contractor that did come, came up, nailed, first of all, took off my barge board, nailed up some aluminum siding right to my wall—which if you don't know anything about roofing, you just don't—I mean, it just
5   doesn't work that way. The water seal is not there, nothing. Then they proceeded to roll some, uh, asphalt tar paper down and nail that to the roof and by this time it took like an hour, okay. My roommate decides it was done 'cause I was at work—I told him to stay home, make sure
10   the work was done—which they also went over the contract before they even started. Okay. So first of all, they were two hours late when they got there. Two people came, they had no barge board in the truck which was in the contract, "new barge board." He [*the roommate, An-*
15   *drews*] complains that, "Look, you know, aren't you supposed to put the barge board on?". The man started saying obscenities to him.

As in Text 8.1, Higgins again displays considerable sophistication about the law as it actually works. Apparently aware of the legal significance of the precise terms of the contract, he notes that the parties went over it before the work began, and emphatically quotes the contractual reference to "new barge board." At the same time, however, he reports other details that reflect a concern with breaches of social convention to which the court is unlikely to attach any meaning. He relates, for example (and stresses with the preface "first of all," line 2), that the roofers were two hours late (line 12),[5] and concludes these remarks with a reference to the roofers' obscenities (line 17). Thus, his perspective is simultaneously rule oriented and relational. He is attentive to the law's agenda even as he stresses his own social agenda. He implies, consistent with his explicit statements in

Text 8.1, that although he understands the "official" ideology of the law, his personal beliefs presume a legal system with a broad interest in social justice.

At the end of the interview, Higgins and Andrews describe the interaction with the legal system that has brought them to their present understanding of its objectives and limitations. In Text 8.3, they respond to the question, "How did you think to come to small claims?"

Text 8.3

HIGGINS: Uh, well, first of all, just from common knowledge. Second of all, my brother's a law student.

ANDREWS: Oh, okay. He's a, a interna-, uh, insurance lawyer for a multinational insurance company.

5 INTERVIEWER: Uh huh.

HIGGINS: Okay. And, and he basically guided me as to the steps that were necessary to do, like send the cer-, send in the letter, send in the certified letter—

ANDREWS: Which is very difficult for the average citizen who's

10 never done it before.

HIGGINS: Exactly.

INTERVIEWER: Yeah.

ANDREWS: We've been here [*to the clerk's office*], we were here three times before we got it correct.

15 INTERVIEWER: Oh, okay.

ANDREWS: We came the first time, the guy said, "Well, you need this—"

HIGGINS: Three, three copies of everything.

ANDREWS: So we went back and we got—

20 HIGGINS: So we got three copies of everything.

ANDREWS: Then we came back and they said, "Oh—"

HIGGINS: "You don't have specific—"

ANDREWS: "—you really should get that organized." So we got that, and today they almost said the same thing to us.

25 HIGGINS: Luckily, we have the original.

ANDREWS: She [*another clerk*] pulled out another piece of paper that we didn't know about last time. So it's difficult for the lay person to deal with.

Because of their discussion with Higgins's brother, the law student, Higgins and Andrews came to the legal system considerably better prepared than "the average citizen who's never done it before" (lines 9–10). In particular, they were forewarned about the law's concern with such details as certified letters (line 8). Nonetheless, even they had to show extraordinary persistence to find their way through the procedural maze of the small claims court. Their belief in the law as an agency for righting wrongs seems to have been challenged at every turn. They repeatedly encountered an institution whose apparent purpose was to limit access only to those with an unusual combination of technical knowledge and perseverance. One might consider their faith in the system survived this experience, such that they still saw themselves as invoking the law to right a wrong.

It is interesting to consider the way in which Higgins and Andrews manage the dissonance between the beliefs they brought to the system and the beliefs they found to be guiding the operation of the system. Rather than abandoning their naive idealism about the law, they draw a distinction between the law as a symbolic abstraction and the law as an everyday reality. Their comments suggest that they retain their belief in the abstract law as a force for righting wrongs, while developing cynicism about the day-to-day practices of legal administrators. Instead of challenging the fundamental legitimacy of the law, Higgins and Andrews direct their frustration at those who administer it. Ultimately, they modify their behavior to meet the administrators' needs. The result is that they are able simultaneously to espouse one ideology while doing business with another.

When their case went to trial, the evidence was essentially as Higgins had predicted. Higgins and Andrews stressed the terms of the written contract and Riva's failure to live up to its obligations. Riva acknowledged that there were problems, but blamed them on the subcontractor. The judge took the position that Riva was responsible for the actions of the subcontractor. She found for Higgins and Andrews and awarded them $425.

In a posttrial interview, Higgins virtually repeated the principal points that he had made in the initial interview. He said that after the trial, he "felt vindicated and righted by law." He found the judge to be fair and "very objective." He would "most certainly" go to small claims court again in the event of a similar problem.

Despite this overall satisfaction with the outcome and the process, a number of things troubled Higgins. As in the pretrial interview, he was particularly concerned that "the average person" would be unable to fight his way through the procedural morass that the system presents.[6] Higgins resolved the dissonance between the images of law as an instrument of vindication and an instrument of limitation by distinguishing between the abstraction of law and the reality of its daily practice. In both pre- and posttrial interviews, he strongly criticized the clerks and other functionaries, calling them "bimbos . . . who couldn't give a shit." His device of personalizing the shortcomings in the system is so effective a means of redirecting his dissatisfaction that his faith in the system as a whole remains undiminished, and perhaps even strengthened, as a result of his experiences with the courts.

MANIPULATING SYMBOLS: THE SUPER FIXER-UPPER

A set of texts from a second case provides a different perspective on the discrepancy between lay beliefs about the law and the functioning of the legal system. Analysis of the interaction between the judge and the litigants during the trial demonstrates the process of constructing, manipulating, and managing meaning in court, as well as the difficulties that emerge when litigants and the court approach the case from different ideological perspectives.[7]

The plaintiffs, Mr. and Mrs. Sutter, express a relational outlook on society and a belief in the law as an institution that actively seeks out and corrects social iniquities. The defendants, Mr. and Mrs. Ross, have a rule-oriented perspective. They view the law as passive and oriented exclusively toward rights and obligations created by mutual consent. The judge shares the Rosses' belief, with the result that those things that are of greatest concern to the Sutters have little impact on the development of the case. In a posttrial interview, Mrs. Sutter recognizes and attempts to resolve this discrepancy.

Mr. and Mrs. Sutter rented a somewhat dilapidated house—they termed it a "super fixer-upper"—from Mr. and Mrs. Ross. The Sutters had an option to buy the house in six months if they could get a mortgage. They anticipated doing considerable work on the house to bring it up to local building code standards before they would be able to get a mortgage. Their legal claim is that the Rosses misled them about the extent of the work that needed to be done. Only after they had spent more than $1,000 on repairs did they conclude that they would never be able to afford all the work that would be necessary to meet the requirements of the building code. They seek $1,500 in damages (the limit of the court's jurisdiction), consisting of a full refund of their $500 security deposit and $1,000 in partial reimbursement for improvements they made. The Rosses' position is that they owe the Sutters nothing because their so-called repairs were so poorly done that they caused more than $1,500 damage to the house. From the court's perspective, the critical legal issue is whether the Rosses concealed or misrepresented the problems with the house, or whether the Sutters had an adequate opportunity to inspect the house and discover the problems for themselves.

Text 8.4 is Mr. Sutter's initial courtroom account of the situation. He begins with a number of personal factors: the Sutters' need for a house and a home, their desire to establish and maintain social relationships, and his wife's need to maintain her animals (she works for the local animal protection society and often keeps strays). Then he addresses several problems with the house, including the amount of insulation, the cost of heat, and the condition of the foundation. Two things are significant about this portion of his testimony. First, even though this is his initial statement to the court, he says little of an affirmative nature. He largely limits himself to responding to things the Rosses have said in correspondence to the Sutters prior to the trial or earlier in the trial itself.[8] Second, on each point Mr. Sutter does not directly dispute what the Rosses have said. He admits that he has no personal knowledge of what was said about insulation, and that the Rosses told him that, because of heating problems, they had moved into a single room in the house when they lived in it. He also acknowledges that the holes in the foundation are small, as the Rosses have contended.

Text 8.4

MR. SUTTER: Um basically, um what the situation is here is
that we needed a home, a house to live in. It looked like
a good opportunity for one. I wanted to be close to town,
so that we could be close to our friends and neighbors.
5   Nan needed a large yard for her animals. Uh, this is why
we looked at the Rosses' home. Okay, now, um, as for
insulation, I have no—I was not told anything about the
insulation. I noticed that they had high ceilings. I heard
that they put in the new windows. I realize that they said
10   it would cost about $150 a month to heat the house in
the winter time, but they had one bill that, um, was at
worth—exceeded $300 for one month during winter
time. They had mentioned that they had at one time
blocked off the rooms and lived in one room of the house,
15   okay. That's—now what I had heard or what I had understood from the situation was that they were working to
complete, to fix up the house so it wouldn't cost so much
to heat. They put in these double windows. My wife and
sister-in-law both say that the house was presented to

20   them as being fully insulated. When we walked around to
the outside of the house and I did indeed, did indeed notice the holes in the foundation. They are small holes basically where Mr. Ross needed to get under or to cut holes
to see what he was doing to put in the electrical work.
25   Okay, I assume that was done before we moved in the
house in the winter time. So that was not a problem in
heating the home. The pictures my wife showed you of
the foundation here—this one for instance—now I don't
know that the Rosses were the ones who put on this
30   uh. . . .

Mr. Sutter includes in his testimony several details about his personal
situation that he believes will be important to the court. The implication is
that he sees the law as an institution that will take an interest in the personal needs of litigants, and perhaps be inclined to help those whose actions are motivated by sound values. He then addresses the Rosses' factual
allegations, largely admitting their truth. From a legal perspective, a plaintiff in a misrepresentation action does not help himself by listing things that
the defendants did not misrepresent to him. His approach is understandable, however, if viewed from the perspective of one who sees the law as
oriented toward solving human problems in human terms. By acknowl-
edging that he cannot challenge the defendants' position on several important factual issues, he presents himself as an honest and forthright person,
willing—indeed, going out of his way—to sacrifice strategic advantage for
principle. His factual presentation harmonizes with the personal details
with which he begins the testimony, since a forthright acknowledgment is
just what would be expected from a person who values home life, friends,
neighbors, and kindness to animals.

It is clear from other portions of the trial that the presiding judge does
not share this understanding of the law's interests. In Text 8.5, for example,
Mrs. Sutter is showing the judge a series of photographs that illustrate the
condition of the house.

Text 8.5

MRS. SUTTER: This is here a picture of the backyard and the
fence, showing that none of the drains or anything has
ever been attached. This is one of the chimney, showing
that both the chimney foundation and the house is falling

5   away from the house and is falling apart. The part—
       JUDGE [*interrupting*]: Did you not have a chance to inspect
       the property before you bought it?
       MRS. SUTTER: Uh, we didn't really know what we were look-
       ing for at the time. We had never, you know—
10   JUDGE [*interrupting*]: If it is so obvious from these photo-
       graphs, I wonder how you didn't catch it?
       MRS. SUTTER: Well, we weren't looking for it. But when we
       moved into the house, we were in a predicament at the
       time. We had formerly been renting a house in the coun-
15   try. The lady that we were renting from had been living in
       Florida, and she moved back to our place instead of, uh,
       moved back to [*unintelligible*]. And so we were in a bind.
       We had only one month to find another house to move
       our . . . [*Mrs. Sutter stops talking and waits for the judge, who
20   examines the photographs at length, to speak*].

Text 8.5 portrays succinctly the contrasting ways in which the lay plaintiffs and the judge assign meaning to events.[9] For the Sutters, events take
on meaning in the context of their human impact. In their testimony, both
Mr. and Mrs. Sutter suggest their belief, or at least their hope, that the judge
will share their values. With just two questions (lines 6 and 10), however,
the judge confounds this expectation. For her, the law is not concerned
with predicaments, friendship, and neighborliness. In her view, the law operates in a context of competent, autonomous, and economically self-
interested individuals who make informed judgments and commit them to
written contracts. Those who seek relief from the terms of their contracts
thus bear a heavy burden of demonstrating the reasonableness of their conduct. Accordingly, she focuses on the single issue of what was visible at the
time of the inspection, putting aside such factors as the personal situations
of the litigants.

The Rosses' presentation is much more closely oriented to the agenda of
the court. Their focus is on what was disclosed, what the Sutters had an
opportunity to inspect, and the terms of the parties' written contract. They
ignore the human and social considerations that are so important to the
Sutters. The Rosses' approach to the case is epitomized by the excerpts in
Text 8.6, which are drawn from their cross-examination of the Sutters.[10]

Text 8.6

MRS. ROSS: Did you not, excuse me, did you not state that you wasn't worried about the heat, because you was going to heat with a wooden stove?

MRS. SUTTER: Yes, I did. I stated that to her also.

5 MRS. ROSS: Okay. So you wasn't worried about the heat to begin with?

MRS. SUTTER: That's right.

[*further questions about heating*]

MR. ROSS: When you, when y'all come up to look at the
10 house, did you not know the reason why the holes was in the foundation?

MRS. SUTTER: I didn't. My husband is shaking his head yes, but I didn't know the holes, why the holes were in the foundation.

15 MR. ROSS: Did we not state why?

MRS. SUTTER: Not to my knowledge. Again, maybe when my husband gets up—he's nodding yes, but, uh, to my knowledge, no, I don't recall that.

[*Judge explains that Mr. Sutter can be cross-examined after he testifies*]
20
MRS. ROSS: Uh, did you not state to me that you noticed the chimney's being ready to fall in at the time, that you was getting the one outside the bedroom, the master bedroom?

MRS. SUTTER: I probably did. Uh, yes. We weren't—

25 MRS. ROSS: Okay.

MRS. SUTTER: —going to use it at all. You told me that was closed off, and that it was unusable, correct?

MRS. ROSS: Yes, ma'am. Did we not state to you that neither fireplace was in satisfactory condition to use—that they
30 was, it was an old house and the fire inspector refused to let it be used?

MRS. SUTTER: Yes, you did. And that's why the furnaces weren't attached to the fireplaces.

MRS. ROSS: That's all.

In rendering judgment at the end of the case (Text 8.7), the judge confirms that the outcome has turned on the inspection issue. She turns the "predicament" argument on its head, suggesting that the plaintiffs should be grateful that their predicament is no worse that it is. She then focuses on the provision in the lease that all repairs are to be done at the tenant's expense, suggests that the Sutters can avoid its effect only by proving "gross misrepresentation" (lines 11–21), and concludes that this is an impossible task, given the opportunity for inspection. Finally, she declines to order the return of the security deposit, apparently agreeing with the Rosses that the Sutters' repair efforts did more than $500 damage to the house.

Text 8.7

JUDGE: I listened long and carefully to all the testimony. This is an interesting situation. I'm, I am sure that the plaintiffs in this action are thankful that they did not buy the property for $15,000, that they first rented it for six months
5   with the option to purchase, because you found these things that caused you to decide, so your losses are minimized to some extent by reason, uh, by virtue of the fact that you did not actually close the deal on the very day that you signed this lease agreement. You could have been
10   paying her $15,000 and you would have been stuck with what you have here. Uh, on the other hand, on examination of the lease, there is a section in it—Section D— "The lessee shall use the demised premises for residential purposes. Lessee shall keep the premises, including but
15   not limited to the plumbing fixtures, in a clean, safe, sanitary, and presentable condition. The lessee shall be responsible for mowing of the grass, watering the plants as needed. The lessee shall make all repairs that are required to the premises at his own cost and expense and all repairs
20   shall be made in a good, workmanlike manner." I cannot see, um, gross misrepresentation here. I believe that you as tenants had a chance to inspect the property but there were some visible flaws, that you expected to get a really good deal and if it had worked out for you, it would have
25   been a very good deal. Uh, it is the burden of the plaintiff to prove to the court that you're entitled to the amount that you are suing for. I don't feel that the plaintiff has carried this burden in this action, therefore the case is dismissed. You each have suffered the losses far above, um,
30   the $500 security deposit. You're gonna have to get work done on the house to bring it up to standard, um, they put the chain-link fence up, which is to your advantage, but

your losses are large and I think one more or less cancels
the other out. That is the judgment of this court. Case dismissed.

It is interesting to imagine how this case might have been handled by a
judge with an ideology more consistent with that of the Sutters. This judge
might have started from a view of society which stressed interdependency
rather than individual autonomy, with the written contract the exception
rather than the rule in the structuring of relationships. Such a judge might
have identified as relevant other legal principles in addition to those of contract and misrepresentation. Similarly, this hypothetical judge might have
taken a broader view of the relevant facts, perhaps paying more attention
to the Sutters' predicament in evaluating the reasonableness of their failure
to notice the defects in the house. With respect to the specific legal issue of
the meaning of the lease, it would have been possible to construe the
phrase "all repairs that are required to the premises" (lines 18–19) as referring only to ordinary maintenance, and not to major structural repairs.

The result reached in this case was not inevitable. Legal results do not
flow ineluctably from raw facts, but are strongly influenced by the way in
which the judge and the parties weave a fabric of meaning out of the
strands of the events that led to the dispute. There is little or no connection
between the Sutters' approach to the construction of meaning and that of
the judge. As a result of this ideological dissonance, the plaintiffs and the
judge talk past each other, each framing events in terms that are of little
interest or meaning to the other.

In a posttrial interview, Mrs. Sutter offered a remarkably incisive analysis
of the "meaning gap" that developed between the judge and her husband
and herself. Her remarks in Text 8.8 are in response to a question about
what she wished she had done differently at the trial. Her general point is
that the "damage" the judge attributed to the Sutters involved items that
the Rosses would have had to repair anyway in order to meet the building
code.

Text 8.8

MRS. SUTTER: Yeah, after we left the courtroom and stuff and
on the way home, we were thinking, "Well, we should
have said it this way, or we should have been more clear
here, or clear there, or something."

5   INTERVIEWER: Where do you think those areas were? I mean,
          any specific ones that you can remember?
      MRS. SUTTER'S SISTER: I don't think we come right out—
      MRS. SUTTER: Well, we didn't.
      MRS. SUTTER'S SISTER: —and told the judge, you know, this
10   stuff—
      MRS. SUTTER: —had to be done anyways.

Note Mrs. Sutter's emphasis on their failure to state the problem explicitly. She recognizes that facts are not self-evident, but acquire meaning through a process of negotiation between speaker and listener. As the interview continues, she also displays grudging admiration for the Rosses' ability to package the facts in a way that was seductive to herself and appealing to the court.

Text 8.9

      MRS. SUTTER: Um, and so they seem, they portrayed a big
          Christian family, you know, um, just uh, you know, dainty
          and particular and, "We would never do this."
      INTERVIEWER: Right.
5   MRS. SUTTER: And so I guess I, it suckered me in. I just assumed what they said was gospel and—
      INTERVIEWER: Uh-huh.
      MRS. SUTTER: —let it go at that. And then they come to court
          with these half-pictures of these different things—
10   INTERVIEWER: Right.
      MRS. SUTTER: —and these half, different, uh, just the whole
          thing is, was—totally misled from anybody that had ever
          seen the house or would see the house—
      INTERVIEWER: Uh huh.
15   MRS. SUTTER: —wouldn't know. So I was mad at them for
          that, but what could I do?
      INTERVIEWER: Yeah.
      MRS. SUTTER: You know?
      INTERVIEWER: Yeah.
20   MRS. SUTTER: I can't say, uh, "Well, this picture is not what it
          is," Okay, you know, . . .
      INTERVIEWER: Right.
      MRS. SUTTER: "It shows a nail there, yeah, but—huh-huh-the
          nail, yeah, we did put the nail there, but this is why."
25   "Well, let me see the picture to prove it."

Ultimately, in Text 8.10, she shifts some of the responsibility for this communication failure from herself to the judge.

Text 8.10

    INTERVIEWER: What did you feel about the judge? Um, do you
      think she was fair, or . . . ?
    MRS. SUTTER: Well, the more I thought about it as the fact, I,
      I didn't think so, because . . .
5   INTERVIEWER: Uh huh.
    MRS. SUTTER: I, I guess I thought that she is a judge. She
      should have a lot of common sense and she should have
      thought of those things even if we forgot them at the time.

In other words, Mrs. Sutter concludes, it is the duty of a judge to understand the perspectives and experiences of litigants, and to be able to bridge the gap between lay and legal systems of meaning. Simply put, her view seems to be that judges should conform more closely to her expectations about how the legal system should operate. As Mrs. Sutter put it later in the interview, "Somebody in that position should have been around the block a few times and thought of some things."[11]

THE NATURE OF IDEOLOGICAL DISSONANCE

Much of the dissonance we have described can be summarized by drawing a fundamental division between those who view the law as an enabling mechanism and those who view it as an instrument of limitation. Among litigants, those with a legal ideology of enablement tend to be those with a philosophy of social governance that we characterize as relational. In speaking about their cases in and out of court, these litigants emphasize status and relationships rather than contracts, documents, and legal principles. Their accounts of events are filled with background details that are presumably relevant to them, but not necessarily to the court. They seek to apportion rights and responsibilities according to need and social worth rather than rules of law.

Like Higgins, these litigants see the law as a force for the righting of wrongs. Like Mrs. Sutter, they expect the law's agents to pursue this objective aggressively. They expect judges to "have been around the block a few times and thought of some things," and thus to be willing and able to recognize social rectitude when they see it and to use the law to insure that it is appropriately rewarded. In stressing social issues to the court, these litigants suggest that they expect that their own ideology of enablement will be the dominant ideology of the legal system.

It is the ideology of limitation, however, which is the "official" ideology of the legal system. Its adherents, as exemplified by the "bimbo" clerks that Higgins described, focus on the limited capacity of the law. In their words and actions, they emphasize that the law is limited to dealing with violations of specific rules of narrow applicability. Moreover, far from seeking out wrongs to right, the legal system responds only to claims that are framed in appropriate terms. Litigants who share this ideology, or—like the Rosses—are able to come to terms with it, enjoy obvious practical advantages in dealing with the system.

Often, but by no means always, litigants who espouse an enabling ideology see their faith confounded. Some, like Higgins, encounter procedural mechanisms that function to limit access to the system. Higgins manages to emerge from this encounter with his ideology intact. It is as if he sees "the law" as an entity separable from those who carry it out. Court clerks and law students may present a picture of the law as an institution that thwarts those seeking justice by the erection of procedural barriers, but he looks past those barriers and continues to see the "real" law as receptive to those seeking to right wrongs.

Mr. and Mrs. Sutter experience a subtler kind of ideological dissonance. There is no direct effort to deny them access to the enabling potential of the law. Indeed, the system "enables" them to provoke a confrontation with the Rosses and demand a response to their grievance. They are frustrated, rather, by the court's passivity. In the posttrial interview, Mrs. Sutter acknowledges her own failure to construct meaning in a way that would have articulated with the court's agenda, but at the same time decries the failure of the judge to come forward and do the necessary reformulation of the raw materials she provided. Mrs. Sutter's recognition of the reasons for their failure in court, and her rueful admiration for the Rosses' ability to manipulate symbols and meaning, suggest that she, at least, has forsaken her ideology of enablement in favor of a more cynical view of the law. However, her posttrial comments reflect disappointment not in the law itself, but in the judge as an unworthy representative of the law. It is possible that Mrs. Sutter, like Higgins, sees the ideology of limitation that she encountered not as the dominant ideology of the law, but as a heresy espoused by an errant functionary. Her ideology of enablement survives, perhaps to be tested another day against the behavior of those who carry out the law.[12]

THE SOCIAL COORDINATES OF IDEOLOGICAL DISSONANCE

Two further issues transcend the problems of individual litigants: the distribution of legal ideologies in American society, and the significance of the management of ideological dissonance for the maintenance of the legal system. The distribution of the ideologies of enablement and limitation appears to parallel that of the relational and rule-oriented perspectives of which they are a part. Thus, the distribution of the two ideologies seems to be influenced by a number of factors, including gender, class, and race, in the manner we described in chapter 4.

For example, the ideology of enablement is clearly a naive one with class associations, but it is not solely a class-based phenomenon.[13] It is undoubtedly more common among working-class people than the ideology of limitation, but we have observed both ideologies among people of varied social, economic, and educational status. In particular, wealth and social position do not seem to correlate directly with rule-orientedness and espousal of the ideology of limitation. Rather, these attitudes appear to derive specifically from experience with the culture of law and business. This experience is differentially distributed among the population, of course, but the distribution does not follow clear class lines. Moreover, the obvious parallels to Gilligan's (1982) comparison of male and female moral reasoning suggest the influence of gender.

The ultimate social issue is the way in which the management of ideological dissonance serves to maintain the credibility of the law in the face of dissatisfaction that is both wide and deep. In our study of informal justice in America, we have rarely seen the conscious manipulation of ideology to deny rights, stifle change, or defuse discontent. Instead, as we noted above, we see a subtle process whereby litigants rationalize their experiences by separating the ideal of the law from the reality of its implementation. Their future legal behavior may be co-opted by the ideology of limitation, but they retain a belief in the law as an instrument of enablement. The more sophisticated become competent players in the game of law and business, achieving enough satisfaction in small victories to distract them from the larger issues that originally brought them to the legal system. The officials of the legal system rarely play an active role in this process; on the contrary, they provide the evidence which persuades many naive litigants of the existence and power of the ideology of limitation. Nonetheless, it is hard to imagine a more effective mechanism for maintaining the status quo.

9 Conclusion

THE VOICE OF LEGAL ANTHROPOLOGY

THE VOICE OF LEGAL ANTHROPOLOGY

As we assess what we have learned from studying the encounters of lay litigants with informal courts in America, we begin by returning to our starting point: the anthropological tradition which guided our initial forays into the discourses that comprise the law. We have profited from our skepticism about the conventions within legal anthropology for the representation of voices, the use of the case as the proper analytic unit, and the focus on conflict rather than accord. We have learned new ways to listen and have heard a great deal. Consequently, we give a different kind of account of people and their relationship to the law than has been customary in legal anthropology.

A fundamental concern of anthropology throughout its history has been the effort to understand and represent people's lives in the terms in which they think about them. The effort to generalize across societies and cultures has necessitated comparative categories and terminology, but anthropologists have sought to avoid projecting the maps of their own cultures onto others. This effort, although worthy and valiant, has never really succeeded. Indeed, contemporary anthropology is deeply occupied with the very question of just how confounded our ethnographies and theories may really be (Stocking 1983; Marcus and Fischer 1986). As creatures of culture, we can never get far enough away from it to view it from a distant or disinterested perspective. Moreover, we are ultimately limited by our native language and professional categories, which are themselves interdependent with our own culture.

Legal anthropology is no different from the larger discipline of anthropology, but the particulars of its subject cast these general issues in a special light. In investigating the legal systems of other societies, anthropologists of law have sought to explain the local means whereby people maintain order and resolve disputes. This has often required consideration of procedures that appear to bear little resemblance to the institutions of Western law (Comaroff and Roberts 1981). It has also involved searches for the norms that manifest each society's own sense of right and wrong, good and evil, justice and injustice. Legal anthropologists have championed the view that these matters are not universal or fixed, but rather are variable and cultural in nature. The focus has thus been on the comparative study of the substance and procedures of law in its very broadest sense.

Moreover, it has been a goal, sometimes stated but always operative, that legal anthropologists above all others interested in law represent the world as it appears to those who live in it. Hardly any anthropologist uses *worldview* as a part of his or her professional vocabulary nowadays, but the underlying visual metaphor persists. We talk of the legal system as seen from the *perspective* of the native, but seldom as expressed in his or her *voice*. As we demonstrated in chapter 1, even the champions of sensitivity to indigenous categories and concepts have not fully empowered the people they study to speak for themselves. And it does not seem that we have always understood the nature and consequences of the choices we make in representing those about whom we write. Treating language as instrumental and transparent has prevented us from examining the discourse of law as fully as we might have (Brenneis 1988; Turton 1975; Bloch 1975).

In addition, legal anthropology has imported into comparative legal studies the unit of analysis so fundamental to thinking about law in our own society—the case. It is almost impossible to find any serious writing about law by anthropologists that is not conceived and presented in terms of cases. We, too, repeatedly refer to cases, even as we argue for other units of analysis. This approach, which has served well at home, has also been useful in other cultures. Indeed, other specialties in anthropology have longed for a similar degree of clarity to guide studies of such aspects of the cultural system as economy, religion, and family. Transactions, beliefs, and relationships are simply not sturdy analytic categories like cases. What we have not fully appreciated is the degree to which this way of conceiving of other legal systems reflects a fundamental failure on our part to hear others and their discourses about life, its meaning, and its difficulties. We have instead built a subfield of anthropology around the effort to search out the details of other people's lives and analyze them in terms of the way we conceive these issues at home.

Finally, the most pernicious problem of all may be the assumption inherent in the very conceptualization of legal anthropology as the cross-cultural study of conflict and its resolution. Where is the subfield that studies social accord? And, when phrased in this manner, why does the topic seem inherently less interesting? The discourse of legal anthropology has set limits on its subject matter and approaches. This discourse has voiced some issues and perspectives stridently but has ignored others. Reformulating the questions we ask around a deeper understanding of the consequences of our thinking does not lead to the hopeless conclusion that we can never understand other systems of ideas. Rather, it raises the possibility that by hearing better we may understand more.

MISSING VOICES IN THE LAW

The constituent institutions of the American legal system have been similarly selective in hearing, reporting, and preserving voices. Through this process of selection, legal institutions shape both the questions they address and the answers they provide.

The official discourse of the law comprises two major subcategories: a professional discourse about how the law is or should be applied in specific instances, and a more general discourse about the nature of law. The first of these discourses is recorded in statute books, decisions of appellate courts, and scholarly commentaries on particular legal issues; the second is archived in jurisprudential writings. Professional legal discourse finds its raw materials, indeed, its very reason for being, in the everyday discourse of disputes. Thus, at its most fundamental level, the voices of litigants are expressed and presumably heard. But, through a process that is remarkable as well as largely unremarked upon, the law selects among these voices, silencing some and transforming others to conform to legal categories and conventions. The more abstract discourse of jurisprudence has only recently begun to recognize the potential relevance of everyday discourse to its concerns. But this increased attention to voices that historically have been suppressed or ignored has created a new, practical problem: that of finding and hearing them.

The problem of missing voices in the official discourse of the law can readily be seen in the process of case adjudication in America. Two or more people engage in a dispute in which words are likely to be the principal, if not the exclusive, weapons. The parties originally wage the dispute in the terms of everyday discourse (or perhaps in some specialized language that they share, as, for example, the terminology of a particular business or trade).

When the dispute enters the legal system and becomes a "case," its expression is transformed. Lawyers listen to the participants' stories and decide which ones or parts of them to include within the bounds of the case. The lawyers reformulate the accounts selected to conform to the requirements of the legal categories applicable to the particular case as well as to the general conventions of legal discourse that apply to all cases. Thus transformed, the voices of the participants are represented to the court prior to the trial in briefs and preliminary arguments.

At the trial, the disputing parties ostensibly speak in their own voices as they testify. But the lawyers, informed by both legal definitions of relevance and tactical constraints, decide which topics the witnesses may discuss and the order in which they will talk about them. Everything witnesses say is framed by the lawyers' questions. And when this narrowing process is complete, the law of evidence may place further constraints on both the form and the content of what gets said.

This rarified version of the voices of the participants is recorded by a court reporter. If the verdict is not appealed, the court reporter's stenographic notes and/or tapes will be retained for a short period and then destroyed. The original voices of the participants in the case are irretrievably lost, subject at best to partial reconstruction from episodic mentions in judicial orders or lawyers' briefs. If the verdict is appealed, the court reporter prepares a transcript of the trial, perhaps editing what was actually said in the interest of making the testimony more readable.[1] The lawyers undertake another round of transformation in writing briefs and arguing the case to the appellate court. Ultimately, the court issues a written opinion that reduces all the preceding discourse to a terse "statement of facts."

Thus, even under the best of circumstances, the permanent record of the case yields only a distant echo of the living discourse of the dispute as it evolved. Most voices are silenced; those that survive do so in a barely recognizable form. It is as if they have been found objectionable and thus stricken from the historical record. For those interested in finding the missing voices in traditional legal sources, the problem is insurmountable.

The more abstract discourse about the nature of law has shown little interest in these missing voices. In the tradition of Anglo-American legal philosophy, to discuss an actual statute or appellate decision in detail represents a noteworthy descent to empiricism.[2] The conventional legal view is that when the law speaks authoritatively, it does not adopt the actual voices of its constituents or practitioners, but uses a voice of its own which is separate, distinct, and neutral.

Although not stated in these terms, much recent jurisprudence represents a critical investigation of the law's voice. Both critical legal scholars (e.g., Unger 1975; Kennedy 1976) and feminists (e.g., West 1988) reject the contention that the law can have a voice apart from the voices of the participants. In their view, legal decision makers choose among contending voices, representing their choices as the voice of a higher order of authority. And they do so along lines of class, gender, and race. The purported voice of legal authority is in fact the voice of social power.

Although critical jurisprudence has identified some of the people who have not been heard, it has not provided a systematic means of listening to their voices. In much of the literature, the reader hears only the voice of the scholar asserting the putative position of women, minorities, the working class, the poor, etc. Thus, critical scholarship has given us representations of a new set of voices, but the voices themselves remain muffled.

The absence from legal discourse of the voices of the law's constituents raises an interesting question of cause and effect. One might conclude that this absence is simply a methodological issue, an unintended effect of the law's record-keeping practices. But the boundary between the method and the substance of any investigation is obscure. The choice of a method is both biased and biasing, simultaneously reflecting the preconceptions of the investigator and influencing what issues will emerge from the investigation. Thus, in considering the law's treatment of voices in the light of its recording practices, we are left with this dilemma: is legal discourse unconcerned with the voices of the law's constituents because it cannot hear them, or is it unable to hear them because it is unconcerned?[3]

DISCOVERING VOICES

In our search for missing voices in the legal process, we have focused our investigation on the most fundamental component of human interaction: talk. We have examined talk at the level of interactions, accounts, and narratives, rather than at the more microscopic stylistic level that characterized our research on institutional language (and that of most other investigators) a decade ago. This shift in focus has resulted in the discovery of some previously unnoticed aspects of language in legal settings. It has also prompted the recognition of discourse-level manifestations of phenomena previously investigated at other levels.

Our research has led to a number of observations about both the form and content of talk in legal contexts. We recognize, of course, that form and content are ultimately inseparable, at most two dimensions of the same phenomenon. But despite its artificiality, the distinction is useful in analyzing the interactions of litigants with the law.

How Litigants Talk

By listening to litigants as they move through the legal process from filing a case, to litigating it, and finally to reflecting on their experiences, we have learned that their accounts vary considerably and in relation to the environment and point in the process where they are given. At the time they file their cases, most litigants describe their difficulties as relatively straightforward matters. Many do not appreciate that at trial the opposing party will present an alternative, often contradictory version of the dispute. During the trial, litigants typically give elaborated accounts that are responsive to the interaction with the judge and the opposition. A "story" does not exist fully developed on its own, but only emerges through a collaboration between the teller and a particular audience—which may be a sympathetic neighbor willing to listen, a research interviewer asking questions, a judge presiding in an informal court, a lawyer talking with a client, or any number of other possibilities.

This point is reinforced by the findings of researchers working in the conversation analysis tradition. Their studies have shown that many aspects of everyday interaction are structured in such a way that a part of an interaction sequence has a usual and expected second part. For example, a request carries the expectation that the addressee will either fulfill or deny it (Pomerantz 1984). Similarly, it appears that the giving of accounts entails certain expectations about the behavior of those to whom the account is given. In particular, account givers expect that their audiences will acknowledge comprehension and request elaboration from time to time. Failure to comply with such expectations may result in account givers withholding details that listeners might consider appropriate or relevant if they were to hear them.

In the informal court environment, some judges actively request elaboration of accounts whereas others do not do so. Consistent with the findings of conversation analysts, it is clear that the behavior of judges strongly influences the nature of accounts given in informal court trials. Thus, it is wrong to consider an account as simply that of a litigant. Rather, the audience is in some respects as important to the form of an account as the "facts" being recounted.

A further finding concerns differences between the conventions for giving accounts in legal and nonlegal environments. The conventions for giving accounts in everyday situations run up against a variety of legal conventions that, for many litigants, are counter-intuitive and confusing. Many rules of evidence that apply in formal courts are in effect rules about telling one's story. These rules specify both what may be told and how it may be told. For example, the hearsay rule, which limits reporting of what another person has said, has no counterpart in everyday conventions. When people talk outside court, they emphasize some parts of their accounts by reporting them in greater detail, to the point of "replaying a tape" (to use Erving Goffman's term) of what they claim the various parties to have said. Under many circumstances in formal courts, such evidence is disallowed. When this occurs, many litigants are confused because the hearsay rule confounds the usual practice of emphasizing and detailing some parts of an account through the use of quoted speech.

Perhaps the most common complaints of litigants at all levels of the legal process are that they did not get a proper opportunity to tell their story and that the judge did not get to the real facts in their case. This troublesome situation arises in formal courts as a result of the rules of evidence and the management of account-giving by lawyers, and in informal courts because many judges do not pursue litigants' stories to the point where the litigants believe they have told all that is worth knowing. This suggests that lay and legal conceptions of adequate accounts differ in ways that have practical as well as theoretical significance.

The ethnographic investigation of the form of accounts given in legal contexts thus sheds light on lay notions of storytelling, on the epistemological beliefs encoded in legal conventions for giving accounts, and ultimately on reasons why many litigants are unhappy about the treatment they get in court. In addition, these findings suggest that researchers who have investigated storytelling in experimental and laboratory conditions should reconsider the degree to which their results are conditioned by the environment they have created. Likewise, research based on assumptions about rules of storytelling thought to apply in all contexts should be viewed with greater skepticism.

What Litigants Say

Even more compelling is what we learn when we listen to the content of the accounts that lay people give in and out of court. Many litigants speak of their place in a network of social relations and emphasize the social context of their legal problems. They assign legal rights and responsibilities on the basis of social status and adherence to social conventions, and expect the courts to do the same.

By contrast, the official discourse of the law is oriented to rules. This orientation is typical of all forms of official legal discourse, including both the discourse among legal professionals and the talk that characterizes the interaction of lawyers and judges with lay people. This dominant discourse of the law treats rules as transcending the social particulars of individual cases. It thus rejects the fundamental premise of the relational orientation.

For this reason, lay people and legal professionals often hear each other as speaking different languages.

The rules-relationships continuum can also be understood in ideological terms. Relational speakers espouse an ideology of enablement which holds that the law is an instrument of vindication with a broad mandate to right wrongs. Legal officials are expected to take an active interest in the problems of litigants, to seek out just solutions to these problems, and then to take whatever steps are necessary to punish wrongdoers and compensate victims. By contrast, the rule-oriented approach is consonant with an ideology of limitation which considers the law to be a limited-purpose institution, existing to provide clearly defined remedies for people whose problems fit into certain narrow categories. Legal officials are seen as having the negative function of excluding those claims which do not satisfy the categorical prerequisites.

The distribution of these orientations is not random, but is socially patterned. The discourse of relationships is the discourse of those who have not been socialized into the centers of power in our society. Gender, class, and race are deeply entangled with the knowledge of and ability to use the rule-oriented discourse that is the official approach of the law. Thus, it is no surprise that the agenda of relational speakers is often at variance with the agenda of the law.

We have come to suspect that the relational orientation may be the discourse-level manifestation of the powerless speech style we identified in our earlier research program conducted in formal courts. We found that the powerless style, which significantly impairs the speaker's credibility, is typical of women, the poor, the uneducated, and others traditionally denied access to sources of social power (O'Barr 1982; Conley et al. 1978). It now appears that the relational orientation and the powerless style are two components of a pattern of thinking and speaking that typifies those on the fringes of power. It is our expectation that when experimental research is conducted on the effects of these alternative ways of talking about problems, it will confirm that the relational orientation affects a speaker's case in a similarly negative way as the powerless speech style. Accordingly, the overall pattern is probably both a cause and an effect of an individual's relegation to the social periphery.

Finally, we are struck by the parallels between the rules-relationship continuum and Henry Maine's century-old distinction between status and contract. We, like him, see a fundamental distinction between legal arrangements predicated on social status and those premised on contractual arrangements between autonomous individuals. Maine saw this distinction as a tool for discriminating among societies. He argued for a pattern of evolution from status-based legal systems to contract-based systems like that of his own Victorian England. While we dissociate ourselves from Maine's evolutionary thinking, we find continuing vitality in the status-contract distinction. However, we see the analogous rules-relationships continuum not as a basis for distinguishing among societies, but as evidence of a fundamental cleavage that exists within our own society.

THE INTERACTION OF VOICES

In analyzing the interaction of voices within the informal justice system, we discover both concord and discord. In the simplest form of interaction, a rule-oriented plaintiff presents a legally adequate, rule-oriented account to a rule-oriented judge. The case typically proceeds quickly to a predictable result. The judge, aided by the familiar form of the presentation, quickly identifies the decisive legal issues and the facts that are relevant to those issues. Rather than inviting a discursive account, the judge is likely to focus the defendant's attention on the specific issues raised by the plaintiff's account. The plaintiff's voice is readily heard, whereas the defendant may never have the opportunity to speak in his or her own voice. This pattern is often found in so-called collection cases, where a landlord, merchant, or collection agent experienced in the language and formulas of law and business sues an individual debtor.

We have also observed concord between relational litigants and relational judges. The relational litigant is almost invariably a defendant. The analytical and procedural steps required to file a suit demand a degree of attention to rules that may be beyond the capacity of many relational people, so relatively few relationally-oriented plaintiffs actually make their way into court. Concord between a relational judge and a relational defendant usually emerges when the defendant offers a relational response to the plaintiff's account. Rather than focusing the defendant on the rules that the plaintiff has put in issue, this judge listens. The judge may turn both parties in a relational direction by attempting to mediate the dispute. In rendering judgment, the relational judge is likely to show some solicitude for the personal feelings and social needs of the parties. This concord may or may not yield any tangible benefit to the defendant in the form of a favorable outcome. However, as our texts repeatedly demonstrate, the opportunity to have one's voice heard can have a profound impact on a litigant's sense of personal well-being and satisfaction with the system.

Discord between judges and litigants is at least as common. Relational litigants may find their voices silenced from the outset. In other instances, rule-oriented judges give them an opportunity to speak, but are unable to comprehend what they are trying to say because they do not conform to the law's discourse conventions. In another type of discord, rule-oriented litigants may find themselves diverted to mediation by a relational judge.

As a result of these kinds of discord, the court may fail to appreciate a legally meritorious argument, or may unwittingly add gratuitous insult to an adverse legal judgment. Judges are typically oblivious to the existence of the discord and the communication problems it can create. On an institutional level, the law has failed to take these problems into account when it assesses the reasons for litigant dissatisfaction with the system and contemplates procedural reform. Unaware of the fundamental problem of discordant orientations, the law continues to concentrate its efforts on such issues as expense and delay. These factors undoubtedly contribute significantly to litigant dissatisfaction, but the law's exclusive focus on them compounds the difficulty of discovering the underlying problem of discordant voices.

The most interesting conceptual issue that emerges from the analysis of dissonance is the question of how litigants manage the discord they experience. Relational litigants are routinely frustrated by a rule-oriented legal system. They find their expectations confounded by the perspective and behavior of judges and other legal officials. But many are able to maintain their idealized outlook on the law and their respect for the institution. Moreover, even though the frustrations of litigants have entered the public consciousness, there is no shortage of new customers, people bringing their problems to the courthouse and expecting to find justice.

The key to managing dissonance appears to lie in the ability to distinguish the concrete from the abstract. Even after unsatisfactory personal experiences, many litigants continue to believe that "the law" shares their ideals, understands their concerns, and is interested in hearing their voices. They write off the frequent frustrations of dealing with the courts as the work of errant officials: ill-tempered clerks, lazy deputies, and inept judges. Rather than generalizing from their experience and concluding that the law is no better than the sum of it its unsatisfactory parts, these litigants retain a belief in the abstraction of the law as distinct from its everyday reality. Ironically, they join the discourse of traditional jurisprudence in accepting the proposition that the law speaks with a separate voice that is impartial and fair.

By managing dissonance in this way, litigants contribute to the stability of the legal system. The law can operate as an instrument of limitation without being perceived as such. At best, litigants learn to deal with the everyday reality of the legal system; at worst, they go away dissatisfied. But rarely do they sense a need for fundamental change in its ideals and objectives. Instead, they accept the law's own view that modifying daily practice will constitute adequate reform.

IMPLICATIONS FOR THE LAW

The law historically has been unwilling or unable to incorporate the voices of everyday discourse into its official discourse. It is remarkable that the legal community has not been more concerned about their absence. Most lawyers spend most of their time trying to understand problems stated in lay terms and transform them to meet the requirements of legal discourse. That lawyers have not felt the need to investigate their constituents' modes of thought and expression says a great deal about the insulation of the legal system from the larger culture.

Having found a way to listen to the voices of the law's constituents, we discover, not surprisingly, that they are saying a number of things that should be of specific interest to the legal community. Most importantly, it is clear that the legal thinking of lay people is neither random nor illogical, as lawyers often claim. The relational thinking that is so common among lay litigants is not unstructured, but rather structured according to different precepts than the rule-oriented thought process that dominates legal reasoning.

Lay people are also expressing expectations of the legal system that deviate greatly from what the system is prepared to deliver. For example, there is widespread belief that the civil justice system functions in an inquisitorial fashion. People expect that if they simply appear at the courthouse, the judge will figure out their problem, agree with their position, and then dispatch the police to find the guilty parties and compel them to do whatever is necessary to right the wrong. Many litigants have never thought about the burdens they bear in an adversarial system: locating documents, procuring witnesses, presenting their cases, and, if they win, finding ways to collect their judgments. Moreover, litigants tend to see the rectitude of their own positions as absolutely self-evident. The idea that there will be a second, competing version of the story (which the judge may favor) simply does not occur in advance to some people.

Similarly, lay litigants have theories of evidence, proof, causation, blame, and responsibility which differ markedly from the official legal versions. The law's preference for information that is acquired visually rather than aurally, its insistence that a story be told from a consistent perspective, and its effort to draw a sharp line between fact and opinion all run contrary to the conventions of everyday storytelling. The legal standards for establishing responsibility and causation are equally foreign to many litigants. Whereas the law undertakes a deductive, mechanistic inquiry into these issues, following precise rules, lay litigants are often more concerned with who "ought" to bear responsibility for whom in the larger social scheme.

Lawyers with whom we have discussed our findings inevitably ask, what should the law do with such information? We respond on several levels. Our fundamental position is that greater understanding of the law and the legal process, freely available to both consumers and professionals, cannot be a bad thing.

On a second level, we suggest that these findings have specific utility for those interested in reforming legal practice. For example, if the concern is promoting the consensual resolution of disputes, then our findings about the therapeutic value of telling one's story to someone in a position of authority indicate that sympathetic listening should be part of any settlement procedure. Satisfaction with the trial process can probably be enhanced by expanding the opportunity for unconstrained storytelling. Win or lose, people seem to be happier if they have such an opportunity. Finally, by better understanding the thought processes of their clients and witnesses, lawyers can improve their communication skills and perhaps gain some insight into the ways that lay jurors hear stories and construct meaning (Bennett and Feldman 1981). This understanding can in turn be incorporated into legal education to insure its dissemination and perpetuation in the legal community.

But this potential for "reform" raises troubling questions on another, more significant level. At first glance, promoting conciliation, enhancing satisfaction, and improving communication are all unmixed blessings. However, reform at the level of legal practice may serve to mask or even exacerbate a more fundamental problem: the recurrent incongruity between the law and the larger culture. Underlying all the practical problems in the delivery of justice is a definitional one. Because of its history as an agency of the politically and economically powerful, the law has come to define the problems of ordinary people in ways that may have little meaning for them, and to offer remedies that are unresponsive to their needs as they see them.

Reform along the lines suggested might eliminate much of the conflict and tension that the legal system engenders. However, would improving the comfort level of litigants represent a solution to their problems, or merely a distraction from them? In our judgment, the law would best use our findings not to deny people the opportunity to achieve change through confrontation, but to enable more people to make better use of that opportunity.

POSTSCRIPT: QUESTIONS FOR FUTURE RESEARCH

As we bring this project to a close, we are left with a number of unanswered questions. We conclude by noting some issues that we have identified as subjects for future research, whether by ourselves or others.

1. What is the precise distribution of the phenomena we have observed? In particular, how are the rule and relational orientations of litigants distributed? In chapter 4, we offer some tentative conclusions about the correlation between orientation and class, gender, and life experience. Given the prevalence and apparent significance of the rules-relationships continuum, it is essential to develop a more precise answer to the question of social distribution.

2. What is the effect of a speaker's orientation on the audience? In the context of a trial, the question is whether a witness's orientation affects credibility. A number of subsidiary questions follow from this one, including whether the presence or absence of any of the specific storytelling conventions that we have identified influence the audience's evaluation of the speaker. For example, does the elimination of legally irrelevant details or the law's prohibition on reported speech make a story less credible? These would seem to be interesting and manageable topics for experimental study.

3. Is the rules-relationships continuum significant at other points in the legal process? We have used the continuum as an analytic tool in exploring the interactions among litigants, and between litigants and judges. Does it have any relevance to the study of jury deliberations? Does the discourse of jury deliberations reveal a similar continuum? If so, experimental research might reveal whether one of the orientations is associated with enhanced authority in the jury room. The continuum may also prove to be useful in studying the discourses of lawyers, social workers, law enforcement officials, and others involved in the legal process.

4. What is the source of the lay jurisprudence we have discovered?

Where do lay people get their general outlooks on the law, as well as their specific ideas about the legal process? Civics classes, television shows with legal themes, and the news media are all obvious candidates, but more precise comparison of the potential sources and the ideas that people express is needed.

Appendix I
A Note on Quantification

Some colleagues and readers have raised a number of quantitative questions about the rules-relationships continuum. Some have urged that we code our textual data and develop statistical profiles of the two orientations. Others have suggested that we quantify their frequency and distribution, perhaps correlating orientation with such variables as gender, race, or class.

Although this had not been our original goal, we were receptive to these suggestions in order to attempt to provide information that readers wanted. Neither of us is quantiphobic: one of us (WMO) has edited a book on survey research, and the other (JMC) is co-author of a book on forensic statistics. However, our research project had been designed as an ethnographic investigation, not a deductive test of particular hypotheses. Accordingly, the investigation and the data collected did not lend themselves to simple counting of frequencies and descriptions of distributions. Nonetheless, we began to review all of the litigants' accounts given in trials and interviews in an effort to find a way to quantify certain aspects of the analysis. Our objectives were to establish the frequency of the rule/relational orientations among both judges and litigants, and to gain a more precise understanding of distribution. We thought that we might ultimately be able to identify a number of discrete markers for coding purposes, especially since we had had considerable success doing similar kinds of analyses in an earlier study of the speech styles of witnesses in formal courts (O'Barr 1982; Conley et al. 1978).

We were frustrated from the outset. Initially, we tried to make a tentative assignment of each judge and litigant to the rule-oriented or relational category. However, we were constantly distracted by several problems we had identified during our original, qualitative analysis of the texts. Most significant is the fact that few litigants are exclusively rule or relationally oriented. Most have a predominant tendency, but they usually also have some capacity to understand and articulate the other perspective.

Shifts in orientation are often related to context. For example, a litigant may take a relational view of a problem in a pretrial interview or when giving a lengthy narrative account in court, but may become increasingly rule-oriented in response to the judge's questions. Additionally, both judges and repeat litigants may exhibit different orientations toward different kinds of cases. As we have argued throughout the book, the critical practical factor for litigants is the ability to produce a rule-oriented account when circumstances demand.

As a result of all this variation, we found ourselves unable to make even a preliminary assignment of many litigants and judges to one of four boxes in a rules-by-relationships contingency table. We (and our colleagues in the analytic sessions) agreed on the existence of the two orientations and their significance in influencing access to justice, and almost always agreed on the analysis of particular segments of text. However, we disagreed so often over a single label to be affixed to a person's speech over the course of an entire case that we ultimately concluded that such labeling would mislead more than it would inform.

Working from the specific to the general did not resolve the dilemma. We have been unable to decide on a set of coding conventions that would permit a statistical judgment to be made about the orientation of a particular judge or litigant. Certain discrete features are typical of one orientation. For example, rule-oriented litigants tend to refer more often to leases and contracts, and to be more specific in discussing time and amounts of money. By contrast, relational litigants make more frequent references to personal problems and social relations.

Coding such references has proved to be an intractable problem, however. For example, a litigant may cite a contract but interpret the terms of its impact on his personal life. Similarly, a litigant may make multiple references to an adversary's personal status, but only for the purpose of dismissing it as irrelevant. We also noted some instances in which a litigant analyzed a problem from one perspective for a considerable period of time and then made a brief comment from the other perspective which had far greater strategic significance in the case. We have concluded that the rules-relationships continuum, unlike the speech style continuum we studied ten years ago, lacks consistent and reliable indicators suitable for coding. Accordingly, a quantitative profile would be no less interpretive than the ethnographic analyses we have presented, but it would conceal the element of interpretation behind a misleading veneer of precision.

Excerpts from two cases will illustrate the difficulties we have encountered in our efforts at quantification. In the first case, McCann Auto Parts is suing Robert Sherman, Jr. for payment for supplies sold to Sherman's dragstrip. In Text AI.1, Sherman responds to a succinct, rule-oriented statement of McCann's claim. He proceeds with his own rule-oriented argument that the supplies were purchased by a corporation and not by him personally.

Text AI.1

> JUDGE: Mr. Sherman, what you got to say about that?
> SHERMAN: Uh, first of all, I'd like to just see the invoice that
>   he's talking about. [*Pause*] Are these the original invoices?
> PLAINTIFF: Yes, they are.
> 5 SHERMAN: Your Honor, here's the deal, the whole thing on, in
>   a nutshell. The, it's, there's money owed to McCann, I'll
>   agree to that. But I don't owe McCann any money per-
>   sonally. County Dragway, which is owned by a corpora-
>   tion, owns, owes McCann. And I'm asking Your Honor, if
> 10 you don't mind, please to dismiss this, because they don't
>   have the people involved in here for suit. They're in, they,
>   they're suing me, Robert Sherman, Jr. They need to sue
>   the corporation. And it's no signatures or anything on any
>   of these tickets, but I'm not trying to get out of anything
> 15 that's owed. I want to pay 'em what's owed. But they need
>   to sue the corporation.

To this point, there would be little controversy about labeling Sherman as primarily rule-oriented. He makes some reference to his personal desire to see the bill paid, but spends the bulk of his time checking the invoices for signatures and arguing for corporate rather than personal liability. It might also be possible to quantify this interpretation using such markers of rule-orientation as the reference to the invoices, the signatures, and the corporation.

A few minutes later, however, in Text AI.2, Sherman takes a somewhat different perspective. After the plaintiff has finished his rebuttal presentation, Sherman makes the following statement.

Text AI.2

> SHERMAN: Your Honor, I'm not saying that the, the corpora-
>   tion don't owe them money. And for the record, we'd like
>   to try to work out some way to pay them. Right now the
>   corporation's in a financial bind and it owes a lot of
> 5 people. We've only had two who sought legal action, that
>   won't work with us to give them a little money along. But
>   the thing I'm saying is I don't want my name brought up
>   and a judgment put against me when it, when he lent that
>   money to a corporation. If you'll look at the invoices

10   there, it's got County Dragway on 'em. Then why sue me?
          That's my only argument in, and if I can get this dismissed,
          if uh Mr. Drummond would like to, uh, entertain an idea,
          I'd be glad to sit down to try to work out a deal to pay
          McCann his money. But I don't want a judgment against
15   me personally.

What orientation does Sherman exhibit in Text AI.2? He continues to stress the legal distinction between individual and corporation. But he puts at least equal stress on his personal concerns and his desire for mediation and settlement. Any coding scheme that we can conceive of will yield a similarly inconclusive interpretation. Moreover, the ambiguity present in Text AI.2 casts doubt on the overall categorization of this litigant. Is Sherman a rule-oriented litigant who adds a relational afterthought to his case, or is he a fundamentally relational person who puts a rule-oriented gloss on his presentation? It is difficult to see how quantification or categorization can improve on the simple observation that Sherman is a litigant who can simultaneously pursue relational ends and state his case in terms of legal rules.

A brief excerpt from an eviction case illustrates the same point. In Text AI.3, the tenant responds after hearing the landlord testify that she is two months behind in her rent.

Text AI.3

JUDGE: Ma'am, what have you got to say about that?
TENANT: Um, I, um, realize that I am behind in my, um, my
          rent, but it's because I got fired off my job at Glenmoor
          and I was supposed to been, um, to be giving him some
5   money, you know, because I got a job at University Tem-
          porary, but the job didn't last long enough for me to get
          my bills covered and I just started on a job today. But, um,
          you know, if he wants me to move I guess I got to try to
          get it moved.

Until the last sentence of Text AI.3, the tenant's approach is clearly relational. She explains her failure to meet a contractual obligation by reference to her personal difficulties. In the last sentence, however, she acknowledges that the court cannot save her from the consequences of her violation of a contractual rule. Once again, how should this account be categorized? More importantly, what would categorization or quantification add to our understanding of the litigant and her situation? The significance of the account lies in the poignant tension between the two orientations, and that tension cannot be resolved by statistical analysis.

Difficulties such as these have led us to abandon the effort at quantificative analysis. We have concluded that quantification would add little to the description and analysis of the textual data. On the contrary, it would detract from the presentation by suggesting a degree of precision which is not there. Others may wish to subject our data to such analysis, or to elaborate on our work by making a new and more narrowly focused data collection effort. This project was designed as a descriptive ethnographic study, however, and we remain firmly convinced that it is best presented as such.

Appendix II
Case Summaries

This appendix presents a brief summary of each of the informal court cases discussed in the book and some background information on the litigants and the judges. We do not believe that this information is essential to the linguistic arguments we have developed, and for that reason have not included it in the body of the book. However, questions we have received in response to articles and conference presentations suggest that these matters will be of interest to many readers.

We discuss the cases in the order in which they appear in the book. (We do not discuss a few cases from which we have excerpted only a brief fragment). Each case is identified by text number. The number of every text taken from a particular case is listed. The nature of the case, the contentions of the parties, and the outcome are then described. Finally we describe the litigants and the judge with reference to sex, race, apparent age, and, where available, occupation and other background factors (for example, we learned that one litigant was a law school graduate who had repeatedly failed the bar exam). Because we did not interview every litigant and, in a few instances, present texts from cases we did not personally observe, the extent of the background information is variable.

Text 3.1: The plaintiff, Norris, sued NDE Company, owner of a dry cleaner, and Feldman's, a clothing store. Norris alleged that he bought a new suit at Feldman's, wore it once, and took it to NDE for cleaning. When he picked it up, the fabric of the jacket was damaged. In his case, he alleged alternatively that Feldman's sold him a defective suit or that NDE damaged it during cleaning. Norris sought the replacement cost of the suit plus expenses incurred in prosecuting the case. NDE produced a report from the International Fabricare Institute stating that the material was defective. The judge accepted this report as conclusive. She did not enter judgment, however, but continued the case in order to allow Feldman's a chance to obtain a refund from the manufacturer. There is no indication that the case got back on the court's docket, suggesting that the parties arrived at a solution.

Norris is a black man in his early twenties. He is a skilled industrial worker. His wife accompanied him to court. The two defendants were represented in court by their respective managers: for NDE Company, a middle-aged white man, and for Feldman's, a black man in his twenties.

The judge is a black woman of about forty who has no legal training. We characterize her as a mediator.

Texts 3.2, 4.1: The plaintiff, Rawls, and the defendant, Bennett, are neighbors who own adjoining property. Rawls claimed in her suit that Bennett allowed weeds on his property to grow over the property line, damaging her bushes. She also charged him with general harassment over an extended period. The judge dismissed the complaint.

Rawls is an elderly white woman who lives alone. Bennett is a middle-aged white man and a minister. Thomas, the witness in Text 3.2, is Rawls's son. Bennett's son also testified on his behalf. The judge is a white male lawyer in his sixties whom we characterize as a proceduralist.

Text 3.3: The plaintiff, Ferry, and the defendant, Devlin, were involved in an automobile accident. Devlin's moped struck the rear of Ferry's car as Ferry was turning left into a parking lot. Ferry claimed that Devlin was not paying attention and ran into her car; Devlin alleged that Ferry failed to look before turning and cut her off. Ferry sought to recover her uninsured repair costs. The judge dismissed the complaint, finding that both parties were negligent (a plaintiff's contributory negligence is a bar to recovery under the relevant state law).

Fisher, the witness in Text 3.2, is Ferry's boyfriend. Ferry, Fisher, and Devlin are all white and in their late teens or early twenties. Ferry's father owns a restaurant where Fisher works; Devlin is a university student. The judge is a white male lawyer of about fifty-five whom we characterize as an authoritative decision maker.

Text 3.4: The plaintiff, Harrell, sued the owner of a garage from which she had bought a reconditioned car engine. She claimed that the engine was defective, consumed huge quantities of oil, and ultimately stopped running. Because she lacked transportation, she lost her job and was ultimately reduced to living in her car. She sued for the cost of the engine, the cost of oil, and other expenses she incurred. The judge awarded her a refund of the purchase price, which the garage owner had already offered.

Harrell is a white woman in her forties. In court, she appeared disheveled and distraught. The garage owner is a white man in his thirties. The judge is a black woman of about forty without legal training whom we characterize as a mediator.

Texts 3.5, 3.6: The plaintiff, Allen, sued a moving company for damage to his antique brass bed. The company's representative, Harry, testified that the movers may have caused a small scratch, but that the bulk of the damage resulted from the negligence of a refinisher to whom the moving company sent the bed for repairs. Allen brought the bed to court for the judge to inspect. The judge awarded Allen a portion of the damages he sought, but denied him the replacement cost of the bed.

Allen is a middle-aged white man. Harry is a white man in his twenties. The judge is a white male lawyer in his sixties whom we characterize as a proceduralist.

Text 3.7: The plaintiff was involved in an automobile accident with the teenaged son of the defendants, Mr. and Mrs. Floyd. The son was driving his parents' car at the time of the accident. The plaintiff alleged that the son caused the accident and that she incurred expenses of over $900 to repair her car and rent another car while hers was being fixed. The Floyds did not contest that their son caused the accident, but argued that they should not be responsible for his conduct. The judge disagreed, and awarded the plaintiff just over $500.

The plaintiff is a young white woman. The Floyds are a middle-aged white couple. The judge is a white male lawyer in his sixties whom we characterize as a proceduralist.

Text 4.2: The plaintiff, Webb, formerly worked as a sales representative for the defendant, Instrument Supply Company. Webb alleged that after his resignation the defendant refused to pay him a bonus commission that he had earned on a particular sale. Hogan, a sales manager who represented the defendant in court, claimed that the company had made it clear that the bonus did not apply to the sale in question. The judge dismissed the complaint.

Webb is a white man in his thirties, and Hogan is a white woman of about the same age. The judge is a white male lawyer in his sixties whom we characterize as a proceduralist.

Texts 4.3, 4.4, 4.5: The plaintiff, Broom, is a commercial landlord. The defendant, Grumman, is a handyman who rented an unfinished space in an industrial building which Broom later acquired. Grumman then signed a lease with Broom. Grumman used the space as both a residence and a shop. After Grumman left at the end of the lease, Broom sued for unpaid rent, late charges, cleanup costs, and the cost of replacing a heating system that Grumman had installed. Grumman claimed that the matter of the unpaid rent had been resolved in prior negotiations and that the new heating system was actually benefit for which he should receive credit. The judge awarded Broom the judgment he sought.

Broom and Grumman are both middle-aged white men. The judge is a white lawyer in his sixties whom we characterize as a proceduralist.

Text 5.3: The plaintiff, Dempsey, was a tenant in an apartment owned by the defendant, Jenkins. After Dempsey moved out, Jenkins deducted $24.02 from her security deposit to cover the cost of a refrigerator tray that he accused her of breaking. Dempsey sued to get the money back, claiming that she did not break the tray. The judge ordered Jenkins to repay half the money ($12.01) plus court costs.

Jenkins is a middle-aged white man. Dempsey is a young white woman. The judge is a middle-aged white woman whom we characterize as a law maker.

Text 5.4: The plaintiff and the defendant, Silver were engaged to be married. In anticipation of the wedding, the plaintiff bought a bedroom suite and had it delivered to Silver's mother's home. The details of the transaction were not made clear, but it appears that the plaintiff was making installment payments to the furniture store. When the engagement was broken off, the plaintiff asked Silver to return the furniture. When she refused, claiming that it had been a gift, he sued her. The judge found that because the furniture was not yet paid for, the plaintiff was not free to give it away, and ordered Silver to return it.

The plaintiff and Silver are white and in their twenties. This case was heard by the same judge as the preceding case (Text 5.3).

Text 5.5: The plaintiff and defendant, both named Williams, are sisters. The plaintiff lent money to the defendant, which the latter did not repay. The defendant did not deny the debt, but claimed extenuating circumstances relating to her son's illness. There apparently had been at least one prior arrangement to pay the debt in installments. At the time the plaintiff filed the suit, $170 remained unpaid. The judge mediated an agreement whereby the case would be continued in order to permit the defendant to pay off the debt in installments. We have no information on whether the payments were actually made.

The plaintiff and defendant are black women in their twenties. The judge is a white, legally trained woman in her late thirties. She practiced law for several years before becoming a judge. We characterize her as a mediator.

Text 5.6: The plaintiff is a homeowner who hired the defendant, Trent, to do some repair and remodeling work. The plaintiff gave Trent a $280 deposit. Trent delivered materials, but failed to start the work for several weeks after the promised date. The plaintiff finally cancelled the contract and requested return of the deposit. Trent refused, claiming that he had not been given a reasonable time to start the job and that he needed the money to pay for supplies that he had already bought. The judge agreed with the plaintiff and ordered Trent to refund the $280 and pay court costs.

The plaintiff is a middle-aged white man. Trent is a white man in his twenties or thirties. This case was heard by the same judge as the preceding one (Text 5.5).

Texts 5.7, 5.8.: The plaintiff, Haynes, paid the defendant, City Body Shop, $791 to repaint and perform body work on a car driven by his daughter. The defendant gave a one-year warranty on the work. Almost a year after the work was done, Haynes complained that the paint was peeling. City offered to repaint the car, but Haynes refused, demanding a refund of the entire $791. Haynes then sued for that amount. It came out at trial that the daughter had been in an accident before Haynes complained about the peeling paint. After unsuccessful efforts to work out a settlement, the judge awarded Haynes $191 dollars in damages, which she described as one-fourth of the portion of the $791 attributable to the repainting.

Haynes is a white man in his fifties; his daughter, who accompanied him, appeared to be in her twenties. City Body Shop was represented by its owner or manager, a white man in his forties. This case was heard by the same judge as the two preceding cases (Texts 5.5 and 5.6).

Text 5.9: The plaintiff and his wife bought a used refrigerator from the defendant, who owns a small appliance shop. The plaintiff claimed that the refrigerator failed to maintain a sufficiently cool temperature, and the defendant failed to repair it as required by the thirty-day warranty. Although the plaintiff ultimately found someone else who fixed the refrigerator for $50, he sued the defendant for $209, which included a refund of the purchase price and compensation for spoiled food. The judge agreed that the defendant failed to live up to the warranty, but awarded damages of only $50 plus court costs.

The plaintiff and his wife are black and in their twenties. The defendant is a middle-aged white man. The judge is a white male lawyer in his early thirties whom we characterize as an authoritative decision maker.

Text 5.10: The plaintiff, a public housing authority, sued to evict the defendant from her apartment for failure to pay rent. The defendant is the mother of two young children and is separated from her husband. Her defense was that because her husband had lost his job and she was now on welfare, she was entitled to a rent reduction under the applicable housing law. It came out during the course of the trial that her husband had actually quit a job as a car salesman because he was not earning any commissions. The judge found that the housing authority was not obligated to reduce the rent and ordered the defendant to move. He advised her to seek assistance from various charitable organizations.

The plaintiff housing authority was represented by an employee, a black woman of about forty. The defendant is a black woman in her twenties. She had an infant and a toddler with her in the courtroom. This case was heard by the same judge as the preceding one (Text 5.9).

Text 6.1: The plaintiff hospital sued the defendant, Webb, to collect $940.60 that his insurance did not cover. Webb did not deny owing the money, but was unemployed and could not pay. The judge awarded the hospital the amount sought plus court costs.

The hospital was represented by a middle-aged white man who works in its collection department. Webb is a middle-aged black man. The judge is a middle-aged white woman without legal training whom we characterize as a strict adherent to the law.

Texts 6.2, 6.3, 6.4, 6.5: Metropolitan Real Estate sued to evict its tenant, Evans, and to recover unpaid rent. Metropolitan initially sued for $1,500 in unpaid rent—the jurisdictional limit of the court—but reduced its claim to $1,373 when Evans questioned the amount. Evans explained his desperate financial circumstances but did not dispute the claim, and the judge awarded the relief sought.

Metropolitan was represented by one of its agents, a middle-aged black woman. Evans is a black man in his forties. He is a law school graduate who has failed to pass the bar exam on several occasions. The judge is a black woman of about forty who has no legal training. We characterize her as a mediator.

Texts 6.6, 6.7: Mr. and Mrs. Ridley, the defendants, lived in an apartment owned by the plaintiff, McCall. McCall sued for two months' overdue rent plus late charges. Mrs. Ridley explained that her rent had been late in the past because her husband had been in prison. He added that that when he was released he had started his own business which failed, but recently had gotten a new job. The Ridleys also claimed that they had made an agreement with McCall's husband to forgive previous missed payments, suggesting that the McCalls were obligated to make similar arrangements now. The judge mediated a settlement agreement pursuant to which the case was continued as long as the Ridleys adhered to a specified payment schedule. We do not know whether there was further litigation.

Mr. and Mrs. Ridley are black and in their twenties. McCall is a middle-aged white woman. The judge is a white female lawyer in her late thirties whom we characterize as a mediator.

Texts 7.1, 7.2, 7.3: The plaintiff, Freeman, is a graphic artist. The defendant, a manufacturers' representative who does business as a one-person corporation, hired her to design a logo and some stationery. When Freeman tried to deliver the work and collect her fee he refused to talk to her, so she sued his corporation. The defendant failed to appear for trial. The judge raised a question about whether she really intended to sue the corporation or its proprietor. After discussing the question with the judge, she left the courtroom to call her lawyer and then returned to press the claim against the corporation. The judge asked her to testify very briefly about the work and the amount of the damages and then awarded the judgment that she had requested.

Freeman is a white woman in her late twenties or early thirties. The judge is a white male lawyer in his sixties whom we characterize as a proceduralist.

Texts 7.4, 7.5, 7.6, 7.7, 7.8, 7.9, 7.10, 7.11: The plaintiff, Mottley, and the defendant, Newell, had a relationship of some sort, but its nature and duration were never made entirely clear. This dispute began when Newell acquired over $800 worth of new furniture. According to Mottley, Newell was the purchaser, and he simply cosigned the installment agreement for her; she agreed to repay him if he had to make any of the $44 monthly payments. According to Newell, Mottley initially gave her the furniture as a gift, and then demanded it back when she rejected his romantic advances. The contract documents that might have resolved the question of who bought the furniture were not put into evidence. Mottley brought this suit to recover the furniture. He cited two monthly payments that he claimed he had made and for which Newell had refused to reimburse him (he said that she had reimbursed him for two earlier payments). With the apparent consent of both parties, the judge continued the case and set up a schedule for Newell to reimburse Mottley. He did not deal with Mottley's demand for repossession.

Mottley and Newell are both black and in their twenties. Mottley speaks with a strong accent, perhaps West African. The judge is a middle-aged black man with no legal training whom we characterize as a strict adherent to the law.

Texts 7.12, 7.13, 7.14, 7.15, 7.16: The plaintiff, Johnson, is a handyman and casual laborer. The prospective defendant operates a yard care business. Johnson agreed to work for him cutting lawns, and he promised to pay Johnson $35 per day. The first day, the defendant picked up Johnson early in the morning, drove him around from job to job, and brought him home at the end of a thirteen-hour day. He paid Johnson $35. On the second day, they started early in the morning and had worked for nine hours when Johnson announced that he would not work until eight at night again. When the defendant responded that they would be working as late as the preceding day, Johnson quit on the spot and demanded to be paid. The defendant refused, and Johnson took the bus home.

Johnson went first to the State Labor Board. According to Johnson, the people there told him that he was legally entitled to be paid an hourly wage for all the time he had worked, with time-and-a-half for any hours in excess of eight in a given day. They also told him that they could not collect the money for him, and advised him to go to small claims court. These texts are taken from an interview with Johnson immediately after he filed his small claims case. According to the court records, he never succeeded in having the complaint served on the defendant, so the case was never scheduled for trial. We attempted to interview him several months after the first interview but he had moved and we were unable to obtain a new address. Johnson is a black man of about forty.

Texts 7.17, 7.18, 7.19, 7.20: The plaintiffs, the Winners, sued a couple whom they characterized as "former friends." The defendants were living in Arkansas when the Winners suggested that they would give them a place to live and help them find jobs if they moved to the Winners' city. The defendants, along with at least one child, moved in with the Winners and stayed for some period of time until the Winners put them out. Later, Mr. Winner inherited some money and he and his wife lent or gave the defendants $390. When the defendants failed to repay the money after a couple of months, the Winners drafted a loan document which called for repayment in installments. The defendants signed, but admitted that they could not repay the money. A week after the first installment was due, the Winners sued for the $390 plus $110 for the expenses they claimed to have incurred in bringing the suit. The defendants failed to appear for trial, and the Winners obtained a default judgment for $400. The Winners were unable to collect the money. They saw the defendants on the street sometime after the trial, but apparently did not attempt to speak to them.

Mr. and Mrs. Winner are white and in their thirties. The case was heard by a white male lawyer in his sixties whom we characterize as a proceduralist.

Texts 8.1, 8.2, 8.3: The plaintiffs, Higgins and Andrews, are co-owners of a house. They hired the defendant, Riva Roofing Company, to repair a leak in their roof. They signed a contract and gave Riva a $500 deposit. The roofers cut out the leaking segment of the roof but then merely covered it over with tar paper and aluminum siding, which made the leak worse. When Higgins and Andrews called to complain, Riva said that the work had been done by a subcontractor for whom Riva was not responsible. Riva offered to refund half of the deposit, an offer which Higgins and Andrews rejected. After getting no response to a certified demand letter, Higgins and

Andrews sued for a refund. At trial, the judge found that Riva had breached its contract and rejected its contention that it was not responsible for the work of subcontractors. She awarded Higgins and Andrews a judgment for $425.

Higgins and Andrews are white men in their twenties. The judge is a white female lawyer in her thirties whom we characterize as a mediator. Because we were not present for the trial, we do not have information about Riva's representative.

Texts 8.4, 8.5, 8.6, 8.7, 8.8, 8.9, 8.10: The plaintiffs, Mr. and Mrs. Sutter, rented a house from the defendants, Mr. and Mrs. Ross. The Sutters gave a $500 security deposit. The house was in need of substantial repairs. The Sutters also obtained an option to buy the house in six months if they could get a mortgage. They knew from the outset that they would have to do extensive work in order to bring the house up to local building code standards, a prerequisite to a mortgage. After they had moved in and spent more than $1,000 on repairs, they decided that they would never be able to afford all the work that would be necessary to meet code requirements. They sued the Rosses, alleging that they had been misled about the extent of the defects in the house. They asked for $1,500 in damages (the jurisdictional limit of the court), which included a refund of the $500 security deposit and $1,000 in partial compensation for the repairs they had made. The Rosses took the position that they had disclosed everything and that the Sutters' incompetent "repair" work had caused more than $1,500 damage to the house. The judge found that there had been no misrepresentation and dismissed the complaint.

The Sutters, who recently moved to this city from another part of the country, are white and in their late twenties or early thirties. Mrs. Sutter works for the local animal protection society. Mrs. Sutter's sister, who also testified, is a white woman in her forties who works for an exterminating company. Mr. and Mrs. Ross, who formerly lived in the house in question, are white and in their thirties. The judge is a middle-aged white woman with no legal training. We characterize her as a law maker.

Notes

1. Bohannan has been the most articulate proponent of the position that an anthropologist must guard against the ever-present tendency to interpret other cultures in the terms of categories of one's own. In 1957, he defended this position at a Wenner-Gren Burg Wartenstein Conference where Gluckman argued that the categories of Western law can usefully assist in the comparative analysis of legal systems. This debate, published in Laura Nader's volume, *Law in Culture and Society* (1969), put Bohannan on record as arguing for the necessity of making one's best effort to describe the legal practices of another culture in that culture's own terms:

> It is my opinion that every ethnographer owes it to himself, the people he studies, and his colleagues not to blunt the edge of his material. He must, of course, translate as much as possible; he must gauge the point at which difficulty of reading becomes impossibility of reading. But there is an analogous point at which the gloss method leads to even greater difficulty, because it stimulates understanding through the use of a familiar word. Such stimulation leads—almost inevitably, I think—to an assumption of comparability of everything called by the same word—and this is a difficulty that is almost impossible to correct (Bohannan 1969, p. 403).

2. In 1964, Bohannan claimed that the "literature in legal anthropology is small and almost all good" (p. 199). Two decades later, Laurence Goldman (1986, p. 349) took issue with Bohannan and argued that, while still a relatively small literature, it is almost all bad from the perspective of offering texts of what litigants and legal decisionmakers actually said. He found little that could be analyzed in the light of the new anthropological concerns about the language of disputing. Although Goldman did not put it this way, the essence of his remarks is that the discourse of legal anthropology has not conventionally included within its purview the study of the discourse that makes up the very stuff of law in practice. Thus, all of us schooled in the classics and the conventional approaches to comparative law have been instructed, in effect, in both what to include and what not to include as a part of our considerations. This amounts to looking for the local institutions in each particular culture that are the equivalents of law in our own culture. It also means focusing on cases, or whatever it is that we determine are their equivalents.

3. Bohannan comments on these limits in the preface to *Justice and Judgement:*

> By other techniques, such as sound recording, it would have been possible to get fuller transcriptions of the cases. I am not sure that it

would be desirable, for I have found, in trying to use it, that gadgetry so absorbs the attention of the field worker that it is very easy for him to forget that he must gear his life to the people he is studying, not to his gadgets. He is introducing a false note into the flow of social life much more strident than his own mere presence: he soon begins to "produce" and "direct" the social action and the actors to comply with the limitations of his gadgets. The only sensible gadget for doing anthropological field research is the human understanding and a notebook. Anthropology provides an artistic impression of the original, not a photographic one. I am not a camera (1957, p. vii).

When these issues were discussed in a presentation during the session on "The Credible Witness" at the 1988 Annual Meeting of the American Anthropological Association, Bohannan, who was present, elaborated on the difficulties he encountered in his fieldwork. In 1953, when he conducted his study of Tiv law, using a tape recorder would have meant running it with a gasoline or diesel generator. The noise it made would probably have rendered the tapes useless.

4. Parmentier (1986) suggests that the words supposedly emanating from God as reported in the Bible carry more weight when quoted directly rather than in a paraphrased form. In a similar vein, Tannen (1984) argues that the audience blames the attributed source, not the reporter, for personal criticism.

5. Linguists and folklorists refer to reports of speech as "performed" when the narrator takes on the persona and/or voice qualities of those whose speech is reported.

6. Hymes (1981) and Bauman (1984) have drawn this conclusion from the study of myths and the circumstances under which they are told. Briggs (1988) has drawn a similar conclusion from his study of dispute mediation ceremonies in a Venezuelan society.

7. Briggs argues that "direct discourse has an important evidential function . . . in so far as it is used in demonstrating that one was present at the events that gave rise to the dispute." This is important, he explains, because the conflict resolution forum he studied is one in which testimony is criticized unless there is evidence that the reporter is giving an eyewitness account (1988, p. 21).

8. Philips (1986) argues in her study of reported speech in American trials that directly quoted testimony tends to be reserved for evidence that is directly related to the most critical issues that have to be proved to the court. Anglo-American law in general displays its concern about the significance of reported speech in the hearsay rule, which prohibits the reporting of speech except in circumstances where the report is deemed especially reliable (see pages 13–19).

9. We have not yet arrived at the point in the history of scholarly reporting—which, incidentally, we hope will come—when books of this sort will routinely contain tape recordings so that the readers (listeners?) can recreate events more fully and draw their own inferences and conclusions.

10. These are simply examples. Almost every line in Text 1.4 contains a reference to a speech act.

11. The recent work of Elizabeth Mertz (1988) is an important exception to this generalization. She has analyzed the narrative structure and "voices" represented in such landmark cases as *Plessy v. Ferguson* and *Brown v. Board of Education* as they are reported in appellate decisions.

12. In law school courses, particularly in the first year, appellate decisions such as *Pennoyer v. Neff* are the student's primary source of information about law and law making, suggesting that teachers believe they are an adequate source. These jurisprudential issues are discussed more fully in Conley and O'Barr (1988, pp. 468–70).

13. Fineman (1988) goes farther than others toward addressing this problem. In her analysis of child custody disputes, she reviews the professional discourse of social workers and mediators, and provides glimpses of the discourse of the disputants and their legal and therapeutic interlocutors.

14. A "witness" is any person who testifies during a trial. A "litigant" is a plaintiff or defendant in a case. A witness may or may not be a litigant. Litigants are usually, but not always, witnesses in their cases. "Party" is synonymous with "litigant."

15. Throughout this book, we use the term "account" to describe the totality of the telling of a particular witness's version of the events at issue, even though it may occur as an interrupted rather than a coherent sequence within a trial. We restrict our usage of "narrative" to refer to a relatively uninterrupted telling. We do not use "story" in any technical sense.

16. These rules are thought to promote accurate fact finding. The law of evidence presumes that cross-examination of witnesses will resolve most questions about testimonial reliability by allowing the judge and jury to evaluate the witness's credibility and the plausibility of the witness's account. When a witness testifies only about personal observations, the witness may be cross-examined about everything that is reported. When a witness reports what someone else has said, however, the cross-examiner can only investigate whether the present witness is reporting the other person's statement accurately. The original speaker's factual accuracy and state of mind cannot be probed.

17. Lay opinions and conclusions are most often permitted when there is no concrete way to describe a particular event easily: for example, a lay witness will usually be permitted to offer the opinion that another person appeared drunk without reciting all the observed physical characteristics that prompted that conclusion. Witnesses who qualify as experts are allowed to give opinions about matters that are within their fields of expertise.

18. In this instance, the witness's "Anyhow" suggests that she means something like "I didn't understand what you said, but I will continue with what I was attempting to say." This interpretation is supported by other instances of witnesses reacting to objections with such comments as "Can I answer?" and "I beg your pardon?"

19. Atkinson and Drew report similar findings in their study of English courts. They report that objections "seldom include any explicit reference to the legal rule of procedures which occasioned them" (1979, p. 209), and that "objection sequences appear very unfamiliar when considered in relation to conversation" (1979, p. 210).

CHAPTER TWO

1. The formal court systems of most states are multi-tiered. At the bottom are two levels of trial courts. In many states, these are called the district and superior courts. The former hear criminal misdemeanors and smaller civil cases; the latter, felonies and larger civil cases. Litigants who lose at trial can appeal to an intermediate appellate court and then, in limited circumstances, to the state supreme court. Under even more limited circumstances, the United States Supreme Court will hear appeals from the highest court of a state.

2. In some jurisdictions, a case filed in small claims court may be diverted to mediation if all parties agree. The mediation may be conducted in the courthouse under the supervision of a volunteer lawyer. If an agreement is reached, the court will enforce it by judgment if necessary; cases that cannot be settled are sent back to court. In other jurisdictions, the local court, lawyers, and social agencies sometimes refer disputes to a community-based mediation center staffed by volunteers of diverse backgrounds. Such mediation is usually purely voluntary, but in some criminal cases the court gives the defendant the choice of submitting the underlying dispute to mediation or standing trial. This might occur in a case where a series of arguments between neighbors has led to a criminal assault. For a discussion of the dynamics of mediation, see Silbey and Merry (1986). They describe the strategies that mediators typically bring to their cases, and arrange mediating styles along a continuum ranging from "bargaining" to "therapy."

3. Even in these jurisdictions, litigants who represent themselves in court may consult with lawyers outside of court.

4. For earlier reviews of this literature, see Yngvesson and Hennessey (1974–75) and Abel (1982).

5. These statements are consistent with the observation of Arno (1985) that, for some disputants, the opportunity for structured verbal interaction with a person in a position of authority is the most important aspect of the disputing process.

6. The rates at which cases are dropped or settled appear to vary from jurisdiction to jurisdiction. The question of why this variation occurs is an interesting one, but one that we have not addressed.

7. The jurisdictional limit is the maximum amount of the claims that the court is authorized to adjudicate. Currently, most informal courts in this country have jurisdictional limits in the $750–$1,500 range.

8. In reporting our research findings, we strive to balance our concern for protecting the privacy of the litigants and court officials we studied against the need of readers to have sufficient information to evaluate our findings. We have concluded

that in most instances the names of cities and other items of information which might serve to identify judges or litigants are not relevant to the arguments we develop in this book. Accordingly, we provide such information only where it is specifically relevant.

9. In all the jurisdictions we studied, plaintiffs having claims falling under the jurisdiction of the informal courts were not required to file them there, but also had the option of going to formal court.

10. Several examples illustrate the brief and often cryptic nature of the complaints:

"The Defendant owes me $35.00 + 286.00 *for the following reasons:* For Damage received to my automobile on Nov 11, 1983 in the Arena Parking lot. Plus the cost of Filing in Adams & Burke counties 35.00 total"

"The Defendant owes me $256.50 for the following reasons: I worked for the defendants as line cook for one week at (est 57 hours) rate of $4.50 per hour during 6st week of August 10, 1984. I have one witness that was told I would get $4.50 an hour and that I was a line cook. Plus 50% $128.25"

"The Defendant owes me $400 for the following reasons: At the beginning of June, 1984 defendant took our Queen-size brass headboard for repair after damaging the finish. Headboard has not been refinished nor assembled properly as of this date. It is in the possession of Student Movers or their agent in this matter. It has not been delivered to me in either proper repair or reassembly. I am seeking replacement headboard of identical type and manufacture."

"The Defendant owes me $200.00 for the following reasons: Damages to my car '73 ply duster."

"The Defendant owes me $500.00 for the following reasons: payment of phone bill." (The italicized clauses are printed on the complaint forms used in the jurisdiction from which we took these examples.)

11. We discuss the nature of litigant accounts more fully in chapter 3.

12. There has been considerable discussion both inside and outside the legal profession regarding the heavy case load in American courts in recent years. Former Chief Justice Warren Burger (1982) is perhaps the best-known exponent within the legal profession of the view that Americans file too many cases. Galanter (1983) presents a balanced assessment of both sides of the debate. It is our opinion, however, that this discussion has been preoccupied with the number of cases per se, paying too little attention to the fact that a relatively small number of cases occupy a great deal of the courts' attention.

13. We could not observe these interviews because the interviewing rooms were too small.

14. In two of the research sites the courts make official recordings of trials, and we were able to obtain copies of these tapes. In the other four cities, where they do not, we used our own recording equipment.

15. We also obtained tape recordings for twelve days of trials during which we were not present.

16. In courts with limited volume, a single session (morning or afternoon) is scheduled on a given day. Busier courts often schedule multiple sessions on a single day. Litigants are instructed to report at the start of a particular session.

CHAPTER THREE

1. Our research on speech styles is discussed in Conley et al. (1978) and in O'Barr (1982). Atkinson and Hertiage (1984) and Levinson (1983) provide introductions to the field of conversation analysis for those unfamiliar with its objectives and methods.

2. In the 156 trials we transcribed and studied, we observed an evidentiary restriction being imposed only once, when a judge excluded a document as hearsay on his own initiative.

3. Deictic markers are linguistic features that speakers use to anchor themselves in discourse with respect to place and time (e.g., Fillmore 1971; Jarvella and Klein 1982). Our earlier research in formal courts revealed that witnesses frequently orient themselves by using such contrasting deictic pairs as *here* and *there*, *this* and *that*, and *come* and *go*, often to the apparent confusion and consternation of the court. (Much of this confusion may stem from judges' concerns about producing a clear and unambiguous record in the transcript.)

4. Although Abelson uses the term "point of view" to mean the perspective from which the narrator tells the story, we use the term "vantage point" in order not to confuse this aspect of a narrative with what is commonly referred to as point of view in literary studies (e.g., omniscient first-person narrative, third-person interior monologue, etc.).

5. "Breakthrough into performance" refers to the situation in which a narrator shifts from third-person reporting to enactment of a story by speaking the parts of the characters rather than merely reporting what they said.

6. It is true that the trial process depends in large part on the spoken word. However, the logic of the law and its concern with records and written precedent are clear evidence of its association with a literate cultural tradition. It is no accident that the early development of modern English and French legal procedures in the twelfth and thirteenth centuries coincided with the spread of literacy among the upper classes.

7. We are indebted to Gabrielle Spiegel for correcting our earlier usage of the term *chronological* to refer to what is more appropriately called *sequential*. Sequential accounts cover events in the order in which they occurred, whereas chronological ones cover a defined period of time from beginning to end and account for what occurred within it. This distinction has been important for scholars who, like her, have attempted to account for the history of narrative practices in medieval French and other literary traditions. In reflecting on this distinction, it occurs to us that it is also instructive in thinking about the differing requirements of contemporary civil law, in which the sequence is often at issue, and criminal law, where it is often

critical that defendants be able to account for all their actions within particular periods of time.

8. One of us (WMO) also serves as a mediator in a community dispute settlement center. Similar difficulties are common in mediation sessions. Mediators comment that parties often start "in the middle" of their stories. On being invited to give their side of the case, disputants often ask for guidance with questions such as, "How far back do you want me to begin?" In this particular center, mediators are taught to respond to such inquiries with a noncommittal answer such as "As far back as you think necessary," leaving the decision up to the narrator.

9. Two additional transcribing conventions are used in Text 3.3. First, discernible pauses are indicated (in tenths of seconds) in parentheses throughout the text. Second, rising intonation is marked with an upward arrow at the end of the phrasal segment containing the intonational contour.

10. A lawyer presenting this case in a formal court probably would have laid out the theory of the case in the written complaint. This woman's complaint is much like her testimony. It is full of detail but contains no explicit theory of responsibility. It reads in full as follows: *Bought car engine from defendant. Motor no good. One week later had to install new gaskets for oil leakage in, around & under motor. Kept using oil and still does. Has damaged transmission, causing transmission not to change correctly. Cost of motor oil, time having other mechanics checking damaged property, mileage, etc. has taken toll on livelihood. Transmission may cost more than estimated.* She requested $1,000 (the jurisdictional limit of the court) but indicated that the real amount owed might be greater.

11. Some lawyers have reacted to this case by saying that the differences in presentation are irrelevant: the woman had a bad case and got what, in a legal sense, she deserved. On a superficial level, this is true. However, this reaction begs the interesting question, what does it mean to say that someone has a bad case? Did this woman have no facts and arguments available to her? Or was her problem that she could not articulate her case in a way that the court could understand? Did she have the elements of a successful case but was unable to relate them in a way that was meaningful to the court?

12. Jefferson (1980, 1985), has also conducted extensive analyses of how talk about troubles occurs in nonlegal everyday contexts.

13. Attribution of responsibility in the courtroom context can also be seen in Texts 3.1–3.3. In Text 3.1, the witness is attempting to deflect responsibility by explaining his action as a response to a request by another person rather than a result of his own volition. In Texts 3.2 and 3.3, the witnesses seek to place responsibility for potentially important information on those who told it to them. In these instances, the interactive setting of the courtroom—clearly different from the everyday contexts Pomerantz describes—prevents the diffusion or deflection of responsibility and requires individuals to take responsibility for their actions and knowledge.

14. The wife's behind-the-scenes role in the case seems crucial. One might conclude from the plaintiff's account that but for the domestic discord his inaction was provoking, there would have been no case. Instances such as this support Abel's (1982) suggestion that small claims proceedings often distort social reality by forcing litigants to view multifaceted problems as simple disputes between the parties who are actually in court.

15. Lawyers often advise clients not to talk about their cases, particularly with their adversaries. Usually, the advice is based on the effort to avoid legally damaging admissions. Here, the defendant's attempt to settle has no legal effect, but it has an unanticipated practical effect on the thinking of the plaintiff.

CHAPTER FOUR

1. We are indebted to Craig McEwen for reminding us that our terminology, if adopted without this caveat, might fail to convey to some readers the notion that relational accounts are oriented with respect to social, rather than legal rules.

2. The switch from "you had installed" to "he installed" is apparently a self-correction. It is also possible that this shift indicates a change in gaze and thus the specific addressee of the remarks.

3. It might be expected that this type of invitation to speak would invite a relational response. We have found throughout our data, however, that the form of litigant accounts bears little, if any, apparent relation to the form of the judges' invitations to speak.

CHAPTER FIVE

1. The extensive literature on judicial decision making reflects a variety of approaches (Conley and O'Barr 1988, pp. 470–75). Some studies rely on data furnished by judges themselves in response to interview questions or written questionnaires (e.g., Ungs and Baas 1972). This approach offers the advantage of directness, since the researcher can inquire specifically about the decision-making process. However, the quality of the data collected in this manner depends largely on the researcher's ability to identify and frame pertinent questions. The more a researcher tries to focus the data by narrowing the questions, the more dependent the research becomes on prior judgments about the nature of the process being investigated. In some studies, judges have been asked to describe and evaluate their decision making at some degree of removal from the actual process, creating another source of potential bias.

Other researchers focus on the results in actual cases in order to construct mathematical models which assess factors influencing decisions (e.g., Gruhl, Spohn, and Welch 1981). Such studies must deal with the problem of insuring that the different cases compared are indeed comparable on all relevant dimensions. In addition, mathematical models have inherent limitations: even the most powerful models leave some variation unexplained, and the process of statistical inference can never answer absolutely the question of what caused the result in a particular case.

A third category of research relies on experimental simulation of decision making (e.g., Van Koppen and Ten Kate 1984). Experimentation eliminates the problem of comparability by presenting all subjects with the same case, and permits the precise assessment of the impact of specific variables on the outcome. However, one can never claim with certainty to have captured in an experiment all the elements that may affect decisions in real cases, nor can one be sure that experimental subjects respond to stimuli in the same way as they would in the courtroom. It is also significant that the researcher must select for study a limited number of potential influences on the decision, while trying to hold all other factors constant. Thus, the researcher's prior judgments about how the process works are critical determinants of the practical significance of such experiments.

Seen against this background, ethnographic evidence drawn from the actual interaction of judges with litigants offers a number of advantages.

2. This generalization is based on the particular courts we studied. There are other jurisdictions in which judges inform litigants of their decisions by mail.

3. Although the pattern is generally consistent, not every judgment contains all four of the components, and the order in which some of the elements follow the notice may vary somewhat from judgment to judgment.

4. Atkinson and Drew (1979, pp. 87–91) discuss attention-getting devices in legal and oratorical contexts.

5. Vidmar (1984, pp. 518–20) has argued persuasively that in the calculation of success rates in litigation, it is important to evaluate a party's success with reference to what was sought. By this standard, a plaintiff who asks for $500, but is willing to settle for $250, and is awarded a judgment for $50 would be considered unsuccessful. We have adopted Vidmar's reasoning in considering which party is the more disadvantaged.

In a set of typical judgments from eight judges in two states, we found 61 second-person references to the parties, and 34 third-person references. Of the 61 second-party references, 57 were directed toward the party whom we deemed to be disadvantaged by the ruling being delivered. Of the 34 third-person references, 24 of these were made by "proceduralist" judges who tend to be oriented toward procedural concerns rather than substantive considerations.

6. Students of conversation have noted that while one may give a perfunctory affirmative response to a request (for example, a simple "Yes, I can come" in response to an invitation), a refusal is almost always accompanied by an explanation and other forms of attention to the needs and feelings of the requesting party (Pomerantz 1984). In deciding the case, the judge is effectively denying the request of one of the parties. In speaking directly to that party, the judge is behaving in precisely the way that studies of refusals in everyday conversations would suggest. It is interesting that under the pressure of face-to-face interaction with the litigants,

without the luxury of reflection, even legally trained judges conform to such everyday interactional principles.

7. Federal Rule of Civil Procedure 52(a) requires that "[T]he court shall find the facts specially and state separately its conclusions of law thereon. . . ."

8. The frequency of such references in her judgments suggests that such remarks are not merely empty rhetoric, but rather a significant clue about her outlook on decision making. Judge Alexander issued disclaimers in five of eleven cases we studied. For comparative purposes, we examined forty-six judgments by five other judges from Judge Alexander's state and found only five other such disclaimers.

9. We observed only two instances of open expressions of hostility toward a judge in a courtroom. In posttrial interviews, several litigants expressed dissatisfaction with judges in a manner that we considered hostile.

10. Judge Alexander does not offer advice to all litigants, and the question of which litigants she takes particular interest in is a provocative one. Although we lack adequate background information about litigants to answer this question definitively, it is our impression that she reserves her personal concern for those who are more similar to her socially and culturally. (If one is interested in how litigants perceive Judge Alexander, "our impression" is a highly relevant datum.) Conversely, her behavior in court, as well as some of her out-of-court comments about litigants, suggest a lack of interest in the personal plight of those with whom she has little in common.

11. To those familiar with the literature of legal anthropology, this judicial type will evoke similarities with the judicial procedures described in a variety of non-Western societies. For example, in *The Judicial Process among the Barotse of Northern Rhodesia (Zambia),* Gluckman (1955) writes of judges in tribal courts who take an expansive view of jurisdiction, evidence, and their remedial authority, and are prepared to wink at supposedly binding precedent in pursuit of workable solutions to interpersonal and societal problems.

12. The form of address to the parties in the judgment in Text 5.3 is consistent with the tendency of judges to address the judgment to the loser (see pp. 83–84). However, in this case where Judge Barkely expressly declines to name a loser, she speaks of both parties in the third person.

13. Another possible legal justification for the result is that the promise to make the payments was a promise to give a gift in the future. Such a promise is generally unenforceable.

14. The plaintiff showed the judge the document connected with the sale. She glanced at it briefly but did not refer to it as an exhibit or discuss its contents. We did not have an opportunity to examine it.

15. Judge Barkley shows similar activism and creativity in her approach to legal procedure. In several cases she raised the possibility of settlement while the parties were testifying, and sometimes was able to mediate an agreement. She is quick to identify a problem which, in her judgment, would benefit from a mediated solution. For example, in one case in which a homeowner allegedly dumped construc-

tion debris on his neighbor's lawn, she suggested, "Well, if I were you, I'd work awful hard on a good neighbor policy." She is equally adept at identifying the issues that stand in the way of a voluntary resolution. In the same case, she asked the defendant, "Is it possible to replant the grass . . . [and] repair what damage was done to his yard before the room addition [the source of the debris] is completed?" To avoid issuing an immediate judgment that may be both unenforceable and provocative, while still maintaining control over the dispute, she sometimes continues a case until the parties have had time to comply with the terms of the mediated solution, asking one of them to report the outcome to her.

This flexible approach to procedure conveys the same impression as Judge Barkley's handling of substantive legal questions. She seems to see herself as a problem-solver with a broad mandate to do whatever is necessary to achieve results she deems to be fair. While her language surrounds all of her actions with an aura of legalism, she treats the substance of the law and the legal process as tools rather than constraints.

16. The goals of litigants in coming to the legal system are discussed more fully in chapters 7 and 8.

17. Judge Dexter can engage in this kind of outburst with little concern about review by a higher court. Out of the more than fifty cases that were heard during the two weeks we were observing in his city, only one was appealed.

18. For example, "I don't think I really need to say anything about mailing cash and not getting, not having any way of proving it."

19. For example, "Well, I'll tell you what. When I give my judgment here and if you're not happy with it, you just keep your mouth shut and appeal it."

20. For example, "Why don't you get your contract signed in the future and there would be no questions." It should be pointed out that Judge Dexter's outbursts were directed at both plaintiffs and defendants, landlords and tenants, and business people and consumers.

21. As noted earlier in this chapter in the discussion of the linguistic structure of judgments, the announcement of impending judgment is a simple attention-getting device. Similarly, the perfunctory advice at the conclusion of the judgment can be seen as a device for getting the parties to leave the courtroom so that the next case can begin.

22. Contrast Judge Alexander, the strict adherent to the law, whose language suggests that she sees herself as personally accessible but powerless in administering the law.

23. Readers may also be interested in the decision-making styles and backgrounds of the entire set of judges. Twelve of the fourteen judges exhibited one of the five approaches clearly and consistently; we found the other two difficult to categorize because our observations of them were more limited. We identified two strict adherents. One is a white woman, the other is a black man; neither is legally trained. The one law maker we observed is a white woman without legal training. The three mediators we observed are all women. Two are white and are legally

trained; the third is black and not a lawyer. All three of the authoritative decision makers are white male lawyers, as are all three of the proceduralists. The other two judges are both white males; one of the two is a lawyer.

24. Readers familiar with the literature of conversation analysis may be inclined to interpret the differences between Judge Alexander and Judge Dexter in terms of social interactional styles. The conventions of everyday conversation demand attention to a telling of troubles and explanation or apology for the denial of a request. The law deems such things to be largely irrelevant. In his courtroom discourse, Judge Dexter seems to have lost touch with the relational aspects of everyday interaction, whereas Judge Alexander seems torn between the competing sets of conventions.

CHAPTER SIX

1. In actual practice, of course, individual litigants and judges are rarely purely rule- or relationally oriented, but most are oriented, at least in particular cases, toward one end of the continuum we have described. In this chapter, we are considering the logic of the system by examining typical encounters between litigants and judges who are oriented similarly. In chapter 7, we consider discordant patterns of interaction. We emphasize throughout that our purpose is to analyze the logic of the system rather than to attempt to account exhaustively for every specific litigant, judge, and encounter. Our goal in this chapter is an understanding of the interaction of litigants and judges who exhibit similar orientations toward rules or relationships.

2. In this respect, the judge displays a degree of relational orientation.

3. By making this analytic distinction, we do not mean to suggest that there is a clear distinction between the form and content of language.

4. The court is limited to hearing claims for $1,500 or less. The amount of overdue rent exceeds $1,500, but the landlord has reduced the claim to that amount in order to avoid having to hire a lawyer and go to a formal court. More importantly, perhaps, the judgment will be a first step for the landlord in evicting the impecunious tenant.

5. In lines 10–15, the agent appears to anticipate a relational response by Evans and attempts to preempt it. In effect, she anticipates that she may be blamed for being unsympathetic or unreasonable, and tries to head off such criticism before it develops. In their analysis of English trials, Atkinson and Drew (1979, p. 136) note a related tendency for witnesses to give "qualified answers [which] can indicate the witness's anticipation that the questions are leading to a blame allocation," and then to "give answers which contain, or are primarily, justifications/excuses—or, more generically, defences—for their actions." Both our observations on this point and theirs underscore the principle that accounts are sensitive to the context in which they are given rather than being fixed and simply factual in nature.

6. Note that he first makes a tentative, but ultimately successful, rule-oriented objection to the amount of the claim (lines 3–6).

7. Contrast this open-ended invitation to speak with the highly focused question posed by the rule-oriented judge in Text 6.1.

8. Atkinson (personal communication) has observed that English small claims judges facilitate the telling of stories by offering receipt tokens such as "yes," "right," and "I see" during the course of a witness's narrative. In transcript form, the litigant's account given in Text 6.3 has the appearance of a lengthy narrative told without any collaboration or even acknowledgement on the part of the judge. However, we observed the judge using gestures, nods, and glances to indicate her interest in the unfolding story and encourage the speaker to continue. The fact that the transcript does not reflect these important features of the discourse argues for the use of video recording in future studies.

9. As we observed in the analysis of Text 6.3, judges participate in the production of accounts nonverbally as well as verbally. The transcript of the audio tape recording in this case shows that the judge was sufficiently attentive to the discourse to discern that the husband wanted to assist his wife in telling her story and invited him to do so.

10. The written repayment agreement might have been a legally adequate defense. Most leases provide that their terms can be modified only by a written agreement signed by both parties. Thus, had Mr. Ridley and Mr. McCall signed a document that extended the time for payment of rent, the judge might have construed it as a valid modification of the payment terms contained in the lease. However, Mr. Ridley could not produce the written agreement, and Mrs. McCall denied its existence. It is common for relational litigants to refer to and rely on documents they cannot produce or did not think to bring to court. Compare Text 4.4 in which the litigant refers to a settlement agreement that he claims his lawyer negotiated on his behalf. We never observed a case in which we felt that the litigant was simply lying about the existence of such a document. In some cases, the litigant may have attributed more to a document than it actually contained. In others, the contents of the document were probably essentially as represented, but the litigant made no effort to have it in court because of a lack of appreciation for the significance that the law attaches to documents. We suspect that a combination of these factors is at work in this case.

11. The judge repeats her question because the original elicited another relational digression rather than the specific response she sought.

12. This statement is as close as the Ridleys come to a commitment to pay the money. The power of the relational concord between the Ridleys and the judge is such that a judgment is postponed for two more weeks even though the Ridleys are unable to make a firm promise that they will be able to pay as scheduled.

13. The case took another interesting turn after the agreement was concluded. Following the sequence reported in Text 6.6, Mrs. Ridley said, "We have a question," and then proceeded to complain about some faulty roof repairs. The judge told them that the law required that they give the landlord a written statement of any such complaint. She then told Mrs. McCall, "If they [the Ridleys] come in here

at a later date for nonpayment of rent, be prepared to defend on the basis of failure to make repairs." Thus, not only have the Ridleys postponed the day of reckoning, they have managed to set the agenda for a future court confrontation in the event that they fail to comply with the settlement agreement.

14. We would characterize nine of the judges we have studied as predominantly rule-oriented, three as predominantly relational, and two as difficult to categorize because of limited observations. Because a given judge may not react the same way to every interaction with a litigant, we emphasize the difficulty of making such characterizations and do not wish to overstate the precision of this count.

15. The excerpt contained in Text 5.4 contains striking examples of this tendency.

16. One instance of such concord occurs in Text 5.4, when the law-making judge decides the ownership of the former fiancé's bedroom suite. The ownership of the furniture is but one issue in the context of the breakup of the parties' relationship. The judge invents a purported legal rule to resolve the case, a result that is probably motivated by her sensitivity to the underlying relational problem.

17. The case of *Rawls v. Bennett* in chapter 4 illustrates these advantages.

CHAPTER SEVEN

1. We use the expression "come to court" to refer to the various activities of litigants associated with their approaching and using the legal system to solve problems in their lives. Used in this way, "coming to court" may or may not involve an actual trial between opposing parties as a part of the litigants' encounter with the legal system.

2. The procedural justice tradition began with the work of Thibaut and Walker (1975). More recently, procedural justice researchers have begun to isolate some of the psychological factors that influence disputants' procedural preferences. For example, Brett and Goldberg (1983) show that disputants value control of the decision-making process because they view it as a means of controlling outcome; and Tyler, Rasinski and McGraw (1985) found process control to be highly valued because of the opportunities for self-expression that it guarantees to the parties. Lind and Tyler (1988) contains a comprehensive review of procedural justice research.

3. A default judgment is one entered in favor of the plaintiff against a defendant who does not appear for trial.

4. Later in the interview, the judge noted that it is his practice to call the complete list of cases at the start of each court session and to dispose of all the defaults before hearing any contested cases.

5. Research in the conversation analysis tradition has shown that trouble tellings in everyday contexts entail certain regular features that are frequently absent in institutional contexts like courts. For example, Pomerantz (1978) has shown that trouble tellings are typically strongly influenced by the reaction of the recipient of the telling. Her findings suggest that it is common for the recipient of an account about trouble to assist in its production by asking appropriate questions that pro-

vide an environment for the account to be fully developed. Jefferson (1985) has revealed the degree to which many accounts are joint productions of the teller and the recipient such that elaborated accounts occur only as a consequence of certain actions on the recipient's part. By contrast, Atkinson (1985) has shown that institutional environments in which accounts of troubles are told may lack these ordinary and thus expected behaviors on the part of the recipients, who in the case of informal courts are the judges. Based on the insights available from the conversation analysis research tradition, it is reasonable to suspect that a significant part of the general dissatisfaction of litigants may result from the fact that the recipients of accounts in legal institutional contexts simply do not provide the types of responses and supports that are regular and thus expected features of noninstitutional behavior in our culture.

6. It is unclear whether he is in fact a cosigner. He did not put the contract into evidence, and the judge did not ask him about its contents. The defendant testified that the plaintiff was the only signer.

7. It should be noted that Mottley is not a native speaker of American English, a fact that will help to explain some of the more unusual features of his testimony. We do not believe, however, that there are any essential differences between this litigant and the large number of others whose cases we have studied.

8. The issue of responding to accusations of blame before they have been made is discussed in Atkinson and Drew (1979). Because denials are the usual, linguistically unmarked response to accusations of blame, the inversion of the response to occur before the actual accusation is unexpected, unusual, and linguistically marked. See Levinson's (1983, pp. 333–45) review of preference organization in adjacency pairs in conversation.

9. The documents from the sale might have given him that right, but they were not put into evidence. The evidence that was offered showed only an oral promise by Newell to reimburse Mottley for any payments he had to make.

10. In a study of informal justice in Maine, McEwen and Maiman (1984) demonstrate that litigants are more likely to comply with the terms of a mediated agreement than an imposed judgment.

11. One might well ask why Newell simply did not return the furniture to Mottley. Presumably, as in so many domestic cases, she reached a point where she could not discuss the matter with him and looked to the court to intercede.

12. It may be significant that the interviewer is a female law student of about the same age as Newell.

13. Throughout the research, we were struck by litigants' repeated references to "The People's Court." While we initially joked about the "Wapner factor," we ultimately concluded that the program is a significant factor in many litigants' decisions to go to informal courts and an important influence on the way they prepare their cases.

14. The attribution of economic motivation is debatable because the litigant is responding to a suggestion made by the interviewer. Although we tried to minimize

such intrusions of our ideas and suggestions in the interviews, some contamination is inevitable. We repeat in this context the position we have taken throughout this analysis: talk is a joint endeavor on the parts of speaker and addressee. Trials are less subject to contamination by the researchers, but the accounts litigants give in court are responsive to the behavior of judges and other parties to whom they are addressed.

CHAPTER EIGHT

1. Social scientists are inconsistent in their use of the term "ideology." Most usages, however, share the core element of ideology as a system of beliefs by which people interpret and impart meaning to events. Scholars from different disciplines tend to elaborate on this core in different ways, selecting from a range of additional attributes that have been discussed in a literature that is both broad and deep (Hunt 1985, p. 12).

Marxist scholarship has traditionally emphasized at least three other defining elements of ideology. First, the set of beliefs called ideology is not an attribute of the individual, but of a group or a class. In this view, ideology "expresses the essential conditions of a social class, section or group within society and in a historical situation" (Kulscar 1980, p. 61; cf. Deutsch 1983, pp. 395–96). Second, the consciousness which comprises ideology is often false, distorting the underlying and usually repressive reality (Hunt 1985, pp. 20–21). The third and related element is that by legitimating the status quo through the perpetuation of false consciousness, ideology performs a hegemonic function (Hunt 1985, p. 19; Merry 1986, p. 254). Contemporary Marxist scholarship has tended to deemphasize the issue of false consciousness and, more generally, the distinction between action and representation, and to argue instead that "the nature of the relationship between reality and its ideological representation should be seen as 'the problem', or object of analysis, without prejudgement as to the way in which the relationship can be captured or portrayed" (Hunt 1985, p. 21; cf. Bourdieu 1977, pp. 2–4).

Anthropologists have treated ideology as an aspect of culture, emphasizing its constitutive role as a system of meaning. For purposes of our analysis, we find most useful Merry's (1986, p. 253) effort "to join the anthropological view of ideology as an aspect of culture with the Marxist view of ideology as a way of maintaining relations of power and dominance." She argues that one must look simultaneously at the constitutive and hegemonic aspects of law, reasoning that "[t]hinking of ideology as culture highlights questions of harmony, integration, and consensus, while thinking of ideology in terms of power and dominance highlights questions of conflict, control, and hegemony" (1986, pp. 253–54).

2. The degree of litigant contact with clerks differs across jurisdictions. Most jurisdictions do not require lengthy, detailed interviews conducted by members of the clerk's staff. The particular case under discussion was filed in a jurisdiction where such interviews are a prerequisite to filing a complaint.

3. One might well question Higgins' statement of values as disingenuous. However, he has just spent fifteen minutes with a clerk, responding to detailed questions about his case. This interview dealt with names, dates, places, and documents, and there was no discussion of beliefs and values. In his very first statement to the first person he saw after coming out of the clerk's office, Higgins put aside the mundane content of the prior conversation and took up the abstract question of justice.

4. In their study of divorce lawyers' interviews with their clients, Sarat and Felstiner (1986) have shown how lay people's conceptions of the law and their cases are transformed by the interaction with their lawyers.

5. A delay constitutes a breach of contract only when the contract specifically provides that "time is of the essence." It is inconceivable that a court would find this delay to be of any legal significance.

6. He also noted that the judge had reduced his damages by about 20 percent. He said that his brother had prepared for him this, and told him to "hit for more, they'll come back for compromise." He was concerned again about "the average person" without access to inside information who "would have been terribly disappointed" with this result.

7. This case was studied in a city in which it was not possible to interview plaintiffs before trial. Our analysis of the case thus centers on the trial and the posttrial interview.

8. Mrs. Sutter and her sister testified prior to Mr. Sutter. Mr. and Mrs. Ross cross-examined each of them, frequently injecting statements of their own position. Mr. Sutter's testimony is responsive to issues raised both by the previous witnesses in the trial and by the Rosses in attempts to negotiate a settlement before the suit was filed.

9. The law requires plaintiffs in misrepresentation cases to prove that they reasonably relied on the defendants' misrepresentations. Courts are reluctant to find reasonable reliance where the allegedly misrepresented condition is plainly visible.

10. The judge who heard this case is one of the few we observed who regularly invited lay litigants to cross-examine their adversaries. Most litigants have difficulty framing questions and end up arguing with the other party or trying to make a statement. From a tactical standpoint, the Rosses' cross-examination of the Sutters is by far the most effective we observed.

11. Interestingly, Mrs. Sutter claims to have noticed the communication gap between the judge and herself even as it was developing: "I was so confident, you know, I had everything planned. And so I knew in my mind when I was saying this one, that it wasn't coming out like I was thinking it or wanting it to, but, on the same hand I wasn't sure how to change it."

12. Not all litigants manage dissonance in this manner. On rare occasions, a litigant may openly challenge the legitimacy of the court. In one case that we studied, a litigant accused the court of collusion with a large corporation in the oppression of poor people. The judge dismissed the litigant's grievance on technical evidentiary

grounds (the lack of supporting statistics), and the litigant dropped the argument. In the out-of-court interviews we conducted, litigants occasionally raised similar fundamental questions about the legitimacy of the system. However, these comments tended to have a quality of off-hand complaints and none of these other litigants provoked a direct confrontation in the courtroom.

13. Compare this interpretation with that of Merry (1986), who characterizes the "ideology of formal justice" as the basic working-class orientation, in contrast to the "ideology of situational justice" held by court professionals.

Chapter Nine

1. In our earlier research on speech styles, we found that court reporters routinely eliminate pauses, hesitations, and nonverbal utterances. Some reporters also told us that they attempt to "clean up" bad grammar and incorrect usages (compare Walker 1986).

2. Ronald Dworkin's *Law's Empire* (1986), perhaps the most-discussed work of legal philosophy to appear in the last ten years, illustrates the point. In the opening chapter of his 470-page book, he gives one- or two-page summaries of four actual cases that will serve as the empirical referent for his theory of law.

3. There are, of course, many instances of the law hearing and ultimately responding to the individual and collective voices of disadvantaged litigants. Witness, for example, the many landmark successes of civil rights litigants. Our point, rather, is that all litigant voices are literally transformed by a process which has an inherent capacity for bias. Our concern is with the law's lack of awareness of this process.

References

Abel, Richard
1982   *The politics of informal justice.* New York: Academic Press.
Abelson, Robert P.
1975   Does a story understander need a point of view? In *Theoretical Issues in Natural Language Processing,* ed. R. Schank and B. L. Nash-Webber. Cambridge: MIT Press.
Arno, Andrew
1985   Structural communication and control communication: An interactionist perspective on legal and customary procedures for conflict management. *American Anthropologist* 87:40–55.
Atkinson, J. Maxwell
1985   A comparative analysis of formal and informal courtroom interaction. Paper presented at Conference on Language in the Judicial Process, Georgetown University.
Atkinson, J. Maxwell, and Paul Drew
1979   *Order in court: The organization of verbal interaction in judicial settings.* Atlantic Highlands, N.J.: Humanities Press.
Atkinson, J. Maxwell, and John Heritage, eds.
1984   *Structures of Social Action.* Cambridge: Cambridge University Press.
Bauman, Richard
1977   Verbal art as performance. *American Anthropologist* 77:290–311.
1984   *Verbal art as performance.* Prospect Heights, Ill.: Waveland Press.
Bennett, W. Lance, and Martha B. Feldman
1981   *Reconstructing reality in the courtroom.* New Brunswick, N.J.: Rutgers University Press.
Bloch, Maurice, ed.
1975   *Political language and oratory in traditional society.* New York: Academic Press.
Bloomfield, Leonard
1927   Literate and illiterate speech. *American Speech* 2:432–39.
Bohannan, Paul
1957   *Justice and judgment among the Tiv.* London: Oxford University Press.
1964   Anthropology and the law. In *Horizons in Anthropology,* ed. Sol Tax. Chicago: Aldine.
1969   Ethnography and comparison in legal anthropology. In *Law in Culture and Society,* ed. Laura Nader. Chicago: Aldine.

Bourdieu, Pierre
1977   *Outline of a theory of practice.* Cambridge: Cambridge University Press.
Boyle, James
1985   The politics of reason: Critical legal theory and local social thought. *University of Pennsylvania Law Review* 133:685–780.
Brenneis, Donald
1988   Language and disputing. *Annual Review of Anthropology* 17:221–37.
Brett, J. M., and S. B. Goldberg
1983   Mediator-advisors: A new third party role. In *Negotiating in Organizations,* ed. M. Bazerman and R. Lewicki. Beverly Hills: Sage.
Briggs, Charles
1988   Disorderly dialogues in ritual impositions of order: The role of narratives and reported speech in Warao dispute mediation ceremonies. Unpublished paper presented at the American Ethnological Society Meetings, St. Louis.
Burger, Warren
1982   Isn't there a better way? *American Bar Association Journal* 68:274–77.
Carlen, Pat
1976   *Magistrates' justice.* London: Martin Robertson.
Coates, Dan, and Steven Penrod
1980–81 Social psychology and the emergence of disputes. *Law and Society Review* 15:655–80.
Comaroff, John L., and Simon Roberts
1981   *Rules and processes.* Chicago: University of Chicago Press.
Conley, John M., and William M. O'Barr
1988   Fundamentals of jurisprudence: An ethnography of judicial decision making in informal courts. *North Carolina Law Review* 66:467–507.
Conley, John M., William M. O'Barr, and E. Allan Lind
1978   The power of language: Presentational style in the courtroom. *Duke Law Journal* 78:1375–99.
Coulmas, Florian, ed.
1986   *Direct and indirect speech.* Berlin: Mouton de Gruyter.
Deutsch, Jan G.
1983   *Corporate law as the ideology of capitalism,* Review of *The politics of law* by David Kairys. New York: Pantheon, 1982. *Yale Law Journal* 93:395–408.
Dworkin, Ronald
1986   *Law's empire.* Cambridge: Harvard University Press.
Felstiner, William, Richard Abel, and Austin Sarat
1980–81 The emergence and transformation of disputes: Naming, blaming, claiming. *Law and Society Review* 15:631–54.
Fillmore, Charles
1971   Santa Cruz lectures on deixis. Bloomington: Indiana University Linguistics Club.

Fineman, Martha
1988   Dominant discourse, professional language, and legal change in child cus-
        tody decisionmaking. *Harvard Law Review* 101:727–74.
Galanter, Marc
1983   Reading the landscape of disputes: What we know and don't know (and
        think we know) about our allegedly contentious and litigious society.
        UCLA Law Review 31:4–71.
Gilligan, Carol
1982   *In a different voice: Psychological theory and women's development.* Cambridge:
        Harvard University Press.
Gluckman, Max
1955   *The judicial process among the Barotse of Northern Rhodesia (Zambia).* Man-
        chester: Manchester University Press.
Goldman, Laurence
1986   A case of "questions" and a question of "case." *Text* 6:349–92.
Grimshaw, Allan, ed.
1989   *Conflict talk.* Cambridge: Cambridge University Press.
Gruhl, John, Cassia Spohn, and Susan Welch.
1981   Women as policymakers: The case of trial judges. *American Journal of Polit-
        ical Science* 25:308–22.
Hunt, Alan
1985   The ideology of law: Advances and problems in recent applications of the
        concept of ideology to the analysis of law. *Law and Society Review* 19:11–
        37.
Hymes, Dell
1981   *"In vain I tried to tell you": Essays in Native American Ethnopoetics.* Philadel-
        phia: University of Pennsylvania Press.
Jarvella, R. J., and W. Klein
1982   *Speech, place, and action: Studies in deixis and related topics.* Chichester:
        Wiley.
Jefferson, Gail
1980   Final report to the (British) SSRC on the analysis of conversations in
        which "troubles" and "anxieties" are expressed. Mimeographed.
1985   On the interactional unpackaging of a 'gloss.' *Language in Society* 14:435–
        66.
Kennedy, Duncan
1976   Form and substance in private law adjudication. *Harvard Law Review*
        89:1685–1778.
Kulscar, Kalman
1980   Ideological changes and the legal structure: A discussion of socialist expe-
        rience. *International Journal of the Sociology of Law* 8:61–81.
Levinson, Steven C.
1983   *Pragmatics.* Cambridge: Cambridge University Press.

Lind, E. Allan, and Tom R. Tyler.
1988   *The social psychology of procedural justice.* New York: Plenum.
Llewellen, Karl, and E. Adamson Hoebel
1941   *The Cheyenne Way.* Norman: University of Oklahoma Press.
Maine, Sir Henry
1861   *Ancient law.* London: J. Murray.
Malinowski, Bronislaw
1926   *Crime and custom in savage society.* New York: Harcourt Brace.
Marcus, George E., and Michael M. J. Fischer
1986   *Anthropology as Cultural Critique.* Chicago: University of Chicago Press.
Mather, Lynn, and Barbara Yngvesson
1980–81 Language, audience, and the transformation of disputes. *Law and Society Review* 15:775–821.
McEwen, Craig A., and Richard J. Maiman
1984   Mediation in small claims court: Achieving compliance through consent. *Law and Society Review* 18:11–49.
Merry, Sally E.
1986   Everyday understanding of the law in working-class America. *American Ethnologist* 13:253–70.
Mertz, Elizabeth
1988   Consensus and dissent in U.S. legal opinions: Narrative structure and social voices. Unpublished paper presented at the American Ethnological Society Meetings, St. Louis.
Metzloff, Thomas B., and Neil Vidmar
1988   Empirical studies of medical malpractice litigation. Paper presented at Conference on Empirical Studies of Civil Procedure, Duke Law School.
Miller, Richard E., and Austin Sarat
1980–81 Grievances, claims, and disputes: Assessing the adversary culture. *Law and Society Review* 15:525–66.
Nader, Laura, ed.
1969   *Law in culture and society.* Chicago: Aldine.
1978   *The disputing process: Law in ten societies.* New York: Columbia University Press.
1979   Disputing without the force of law. *Yale Law Journal* 88:998–1021.
O'Barr, William M.
1982   *Linguistic evidence: Language, power and strategy in the courtroom.* New York: Academic Press.
O'Barr, William M., and John M. Conley
1988   Lay expectations of the civil justice system. *Law and Society Review* 22:137–61.
Ochs, Eleanor
1979   Transcription as theory. In *Developmental pragmatics,* ed. E. Ochs and B. B. Schieflein. New York: Academic Press.

Parmentier, Richard J.
1986   The political function of reported speech: A Belauan example. Unpublished manuscript.

Philips, Susan U.
1986   Reported speech as evidence in an American trial. In *1985 Georgetown University Roundtable on Languages and Linguistics,* ed. D. Tannen. Washington: Georgetown University.

Pomerantz, Anita
1978   Attributions of responsibility: blamings. *Sociology* 12:115–121.
1984   Agreeing and disagreeing with assessments: Some features of preferred/dispreferred turn shapes. In *Structures of Social Action,* ed. J. Maxwell Atkinson and John Heritage. Cambridge: Cambridge University Press.

Rosenberg, Maurice
1980–81 Civil justice research and civil justice reform. *Law and Society Review* 15:473–84.

Ruhnka, John C., and Steven Weller
1978   *Small claims courts: A national examination.* Williamsburg, Va.: National Center for State Courts.

Sarat, Austin, and William Felstiner
1986   Law and strategy in the divorce lawyer's office. *Law and Society Review* 20:93–134.

Sibley, Susan S., and Sally E. Merry
1986   Mediator settlement strategies. *Law and Policy* 8:7–31.

Steele, Eric H.
1981   The historical context of small claims court. *American Bar Foundation Research Journal* 1981:293–376.

Stocking, G. W., ed.
1983   *Observers observed.* Vol. 1 of *History of Anthropology.* Madison: University of Wisconsin Press.

Tannen, Deborah
1984   Waiting for the mouse: Constructed dialogue as involvement in conversational narrative. Paper presented at the Annual Meeting of the American Anthropological Association, Denver.

Tannen, Deborah, ed.
1981   *Spoken and written language: Exploring orality and literacy.* Norwood, N.J.: Ablex.

Thibaut, John, and Laurens Walker
1975   *Procedural justice: A psychological analysis.* Hillsdale, N.J.: Erlbaum.

Trubek, David M.
1988   Can research help us increase access to justice? Paper presented at Conference on Empirical Studies of Civil Procedure, Duke Law School.

Turton, David
1975   The relationship between oratory and the exercise of influence among the

Mursi. In *Political language and oratory in traditional society,* ed. Maurice Bloch. New York: Academic Press.

Tyler, Tom R., K. Rasinski, and K. McGraw
1985   The influence of perceived injustice on support for political authorities. *Journal of Applied Social Psychology* 15:700–725.

Unger, Roberto
1975   *Knowledge and politics.* New York: The Free Press.

Ungs, Thomas D., and Larry R. Baas
1972   Judicial perceptions: A Q-technique study of Ohio judges. *Law and Society Review* 6:343–66.

Van Koppen, Peter J., and Jan Ten Kate
1984   Individual differences in judicial behavior: Personal characteristics and private law decision-making. *Law and Society Review* 225–47.

Vidmar, Neil
1984   The small claims court: A reconceptualization of disputes and an empirical investigation. *Law and Society Review* 18:515–50.

Walker, Anne G.
1986   The verbatim record: The myth and the reality. In *Discourse and institutional authority: Medicine, education, and law,* ed. Sue Fisher and Alexandria Dundas Todd. Norwood, N.J.: Ablex.

Walker, Laurens G.
1988   Perfecting federal civil rules: A proposal for restricted field experiments. Paper presented at Conference on Empirical Studies of Civil Procedure, Duke Law School.

Weinstein, Jack
1977   The Ohio and Federal Rules of Evidence. *Capital University Law Review* 6:517–32.

West, Robin
1988   Jurisprudence and gender. *University of Chicago Law Review* 55:1–72.

Wolfson, Nessa
1982   *CHP: The conversational historical preent in American English narrative.* Dordrecht: Foris Publishers.

Yngvesson, Barbara, and Patricia Hennessey.
1974–75 Small claims, complex disputes: A review of the small claims literature. *Law and Society Review* 9:219–74.

Index

Abel, Richard, 25–26, 198 n4, 202 n14
Abelson, Robert P., 39
Account(s): credibility of, 197 n16; definition of, 197 n15; evidentiary constraints on, 36; eyewitness, 196 n7; issues associated with the study of, x, xi, 31; nonsequential, 40; relational, 58–63; rule-oriented, 58–60, 63–66; sequential, 40–41
Agency, 48, 56
Analysis: empirical, xii; unit of, 8, 9, 29
Anthropology, legal, 3–9, 166–67, 195 n2; discourse of, 167; focus of, 3; history of, 3
Arbitration, 24
Arno, Andrew, 198 n5
Atkinson, Max, 198 n19, 200 n1, 203 n1, 206 n5, 207 n8, 208 n8, 209 n5

Baumann, Richard, 40, 196 n6
Berger, Warren, 199 n12
Blame, 26, 48, 56, 176
Bohannan, Paul, 3–8, 195 n1, n2, n3
Briggs, Charles, 196 n7
Brown v. Board of Education, 197 n11

Carlin, Pat, 14
Case: as unit of analysis, 4, 29, 167; summaries of small claims trials included in this book, 186–194
Class: and critical legal studies, 11; and rule vs. relationship distribution, xiv, 80
Comparative law, 3, 195 n2
Concord: between litigant and judge, 113–25, 174; rule-rule, 113, 174; relational-relational, 114–23, 174
Conflict, between rule and relationship orientations, 149. *See also* Discord

Constraints, on witnesses, 13–14; frustration as result of, 14
Conversation analysis, 48, 203 n6
Courts: case load, 199 n12; litigants' assumptions about, 141; role in righting wrongs, 151
Courts, formal: definition, 24; characteristics, 198 n1
Courts, informal: definition, 25; characteristics, 26, 198 n1; functions, 26–27
Critical legal studies movement, 11–12
Cross-examination, as a non-sequential account, 40

Data analysis, 35. *See also* Research: methods
Data collection, 30–33
Decision making, judicial approaches to, 82, 111
Deductive approach, 47–48
Deixis (deictic markers), 200 n1
Discord: between judges and litigants, 175; between litigants and legal system, 126; management of, 150; types of, 148
Discourse: definition, 2; analysis of, 2; of legal anthropology, 167, 195 n2
Discourse, ethnography of, 3–9, 35–36; definition of, 35
Discourse, legal: everyday, 2–3, 15, 17, 35, 168; official, 1–3, 9, 12, 19, 168, 172; professional, 197 n13
Disputes, issues associated with study of, x, 26
Dissonance: ideological, 163; management of, 211 n2
Drew, Paul, 198 n9, 203 n4, 206 n5, 209 n88
Dworkin, Ronald, 11, 212 n2

219